Sir Henry Neville,
Alias William Shakespeare

Sir Henry Neville, Alias William Shakespeare

Authorship Evidence in the History Plays

MARK BRADBEER *and* JOHN CASSON

Foreword by William D. Rubinstein

McFarland & Company, Inc., Publishers
Jefferson, North Carolina

We are grateful to the Trustee of the Tudor Players (Rufford), the owners of the annotated Hall's *Chronicle*, for permission to publish photographs of the marginal annotations. The watermark on Hardwick MSS 44 in Appendix 1 is © Devonshire Collection, Chatsworth, and is reproduced by permission of the Chatsworth Settlement Trustees. Images from the Northumberland Manuscript are reproduced by permission of the Archives of the Duke of Northumberland at Alnwick Castle (DNP: MS 525). The illustrations from the Worsley Manuscripts are published with the permission of the Eighth Earl of Yarborough and Lincolnshire Archives. Images of books possibly annotated by Henry Neville are published with permission of the owners: Private Collection. The facsimile from the *Edward III* quarto in Appendix 2 is courtesy of the Thomas Fisher Rare Book Library, University of Toronto.

LIBRARY OF CONGRESS CATALOGUING-IN-PUBLICATION DATA

Bradbeer, Mark, 1956–
Sir Henry Neville, alias William Shakespeare : authorship evidence in the history plays / Mark Bradbeer and John Casson ; foreword by William D. Rubinstein.
p. cm.
Includes bibliographical references and index.

ISBN 978-0-7864-9481-1 (softcover : acid free paper) ♾
ISBN 978-1-4766-1837-1 (ebook)

1. Shakespeare, William, 1564–1616—Authorship. 2. Shakespeare, William, 1564–1616—Authorship—Neville theory. 3. Neville, Henry, Sir, 1564?-1615. I. Casson, John, 1951– II. Title.

PR2947.N48B73 2015
822.3'3—dc23 2014049702

BRITISH LIBRARY CATALOGUING DATA ARE AVAILABLE

Printed in the United States of America

McFarland & Company, Inc., Publishers
Box 611, Jefferson, North Carolina 28640
www.mcfarlandpub.com

To our long-suffering
and supportive partners,
Allen and Viviane

Acknowledgments

We are most grateful to Professor William Rubinstein for his foreword. Vian Smith's advice and practical assistance helped ensure the quality of the writing, the illustrations and the tables. We are grateful to Tony Minchin, Dave Ewald and John O'Donnell for their proof reading. Dave has also contributed to the research, for example by discovering Neville's distant relationship to King John, discussed in Chapter 1, and the Blunt-Neville connections covered in Chapter 4. John pointed out to us the significant spelling of Sonnet 121 and advised us on Neville's letter about Essex of November 15, 1600 (see Chapter 5). We are grateful to Bruce Leyland, who pointed out the Talbot-Neville connections in Chapter 6. We are grateful to the Rev. Leonard Deas for translating the fragment of Dudith's letter in Chapter 2 and help with Latin and Greek in Chapters 9 and 11. We are also indebted to David Seal, who provided the first translation of Carleton's dedication (Chapter 11). Thanks are also due to Dwight Peck for checking his research notes concerning the annotations about the Countess of Salisbury (Chapter 2) and Marcus Brutus (Chapter 9) on manuscript versions of *Leicester's Commonwealth*. We are grateful to Malcolm Moncrief-Spittle of Renaissance Books, New Zealand, for noticing the pairs of words coupled by "or" in both Neville's trial statement and *Hamlet* (see Chapter 10), which led to our further research into Neville's use of hendiadys. Images of books possibly annotated by Neville are published with permission of the owners, who wish to remain anonymous.

Table of Contents

Foreword

Sir Henry Neville and the Shakespeare Authorship Question

by William D. Rubinstein

For over 150 years, many people have questioned whether William Shakspere, the man who was born in Stratford-upon-Avon in 1564 and died there in 1616, and who was certainly an actor and a "theatre-sharer" (part owner) in London, wrote the plays and poems attributed to him. Perhaps the main reason for this is the almost incalculable gap between the magnitude of the achievement—Shakespeare is universally regarded as the greatest English-language writer, and one of the half-dozen greatest writers in history—and the meagerness of his background. He had no schooling past the age of thirteen; his two daughters were illiterate; he grew up in a small market town with few cultural resources. Moreover, William Shakspere had no documented interest in any cultural or literary matter. His will fails to mention any books or manuscripts. Although he left legacies to three of his fellow actors in London, he omitted to mention anyone connected with the English literary world. The second reason for questioning the authorship of Shakspere of Stratford is the equally complete lack of evidence for his being a writer (as opposed to an actor and theatre-sharer, as well as a wealthy businessman in Stratford-upon-Avon). The only examples of his handwriting that survive are six signatures on legal documents. (It is widely believed that the portions known as "Hand D" in the manuscript of a play by several authors, *Sir Thomas More,* were written by Shakespeare, although the evidence for this hand being his is unconvincing.) Apart from this, not a single scrap of writing by Shakspere survives. There are many other reasons for rationally questioning the identity of the real author.

The problem until now in learning the truth about what is known as the "Shakespeare authorship question" is that there has been no credible alternative authorship "candidate." The two best known alternative Shakespeare authorship candidates, Edward de Vere, the seventeenth Earl of Oxford, and Sir Francis Bacon, have glaring deficiencies and, more importantly, a complete lack of credible evidence demonstrating that they wrote Shakespeare's works. The Earl of Oxford, for example, died in 1604, while Shakespeare's plays continued to be written until 1613, requiring the proponents of the Oxford theory to invent a novel chronology for the dating of Shakespeare's works unsupported by the evidence.

Just over a decade ago, Brenda James, an independent scholar then living in Sussex, proposed a new authorship candidate: Sir Henry Neville (1562–1615).[1] Despite both his obvious qualifications and the remarkable manner in which his life and career dovetail with the accepted chronology of Shakespeare's works, no one had ever previously suggested that he was the real "Bard of Avon." When a friend introduced me to Brenda James's theory in 2003, I immediately became convinced that she had, extraordinarily, hit upon the true author. We collaborated on an account of Neville's life, *The Truth Will Out: Unmasking the Real Shakespeare* (James and Rubinstein, 2005), which received wide publicity. A number of other researchers became interested in the Neville candidacy, most notably Dr. John Casson, who has proved to be a tireless and outstanding researcher, and who has himself written two books about the case for Neville. In this present work, Dr. Casson and Mark Bradbeer, a perceptive and knowledgeable researcher in Melbourne, Australia, show how Neville's life, background, education, and career are reflected in Shakespeare's history plays, in which his own ancestors appear. His personal knowledge of politics and political life, of courtiers and kings, suggests a confidence and familiarity with these aristocratic circles that William Shakspere, from an (at best) middle-ranking provincial background, could not possibly have had. Neville, for instance, served as a member of Parliament for the whole of his adult life, with the exception of the period (1601–03) when he was incarcerated in the Tower of London for his part in Essex's rebellion, along with the Earl of Southampton, Shakespeare's alleged patron. Unlike other alternative Shakespeare candidates, much new and surprising evidence for Neville as the real Shakespeare is offered in this book, on virtually every page. Along with other new works about Sir Henry Neville, this book will hopefully reorient our most basic interpretations of our greatest writer, opening up new ways of understanding his work.

William D. Rubinstein is an adjunct professor at Monash University in Melbourne, Australia, and is the co-author (with Brenda James) of The Truth Will Out *(2005), the first book about Sir Henry Neville as Shakespeare.*

Preface

This book surveys the Shakespeare history plays to discover what evidence they contain for Henry Neville's authorship. We take each play in the order of its place in the kings' reigns and examine it to see if there is an inherent bias towards members of the Neville family. We also examine the politics of the plays and the subtle meanings that emerge from such scrutiny. We focus on the English history plays and only offer one chapter on the Roman plays. We have not looked at Shakespeare's comedies and tragedies except to consider the links between *Hamlet,* the disaster of the Essex rebellion, and Neville's own vocabulary in his letters and the statement he made at his trial in 1601. We have included a chapter on a newly discovered Latin poem that we think points to Neville's authorship and put that in the context of 1603. Our two appendices offer more detailed scholarship relevant to particular areas of our study.

This research was conducted by careful examination of each play, following up clues in the text, in previous scholarship and the examination of primary sources, extant letters, notebooks, annotated books and manuscripts as well as resources now available on the Internet. Whenever possible we have checked the accuracy of the latter by referring to the printed literature. Our co-authorship has also enabled us to check each other's discoveries. We have avoided speculating until our final chapter, when we offer some suggestions for further research. We have deliberately chosen to report facts and leave the reader to make up his or her own mind from the evidence we offer.

This research is crucial to the growing body of evidence that supports the identification of Henry Neville as the hidden author of the works of Shakespeare. While many people may doubt the value of our endeavor, we think that discovering the real identity of Shakespeare in the politician and scholar Henry Neville illuminates the greatest of writers, lighting up obscure texts and revealing half-hidden motives and meanings, enriching our understanding of the plays.

A Note on Typography

We have quoted extensively from documents written by Henry Neville, who used an italic hand when emphasizing names or writing out Latin quotations. In *Winwood's Memorials*, the printed collection of Neville's letters, these italics were retained (Sawyer, 1725). Per standard usage, we have also used italics for the names of plays and other works. We have therefore chosen not to use italics for emphasis in our own text but have used **bold** to highlight certain words and phrases. For example, similar words and phrases across different texts are in bold to draw attention to possible shared authorship.

Introduction

Beneath every history, another history.—H. Mantel, *Wolf Hall*

The Shakespeare authorship question has bedeviled scholarship. Some have denied there is any question to answer, while others have affirmed there is a problem but offered solutions that do not bear careful scrutiny. Reasonable doubts about William Shakspere's role as the writer of the plays and poems have been firmly established by researchers who have examined the question without asserting any one solution (Price, 2001; Pointon, 2011; Shahan and Waugh, 2013). When referring to the actor from Stratford, we have spelled his name "William Shakspere" to distinguish him from the writer of the plays, William Shakespeare. The Shaksperes of Stratford spelled their name thus, and William never spelled his own name with a central "e." (See Pointon, 2011, for a thorough examination of this.)

Henry Neville (1562–1615) only emerged as an authorship candidate in 2005. Since then six books presenting evidence for his authorship have been published. More evidence for his hidden identity as the bard continues to emerge, and several new books on the subject are due soon. There is now far more evidence supporting him than any other candidate including William Shakspere from Stratford (Rubinstein, 2012). This book offers further evidence for Neville.

Half hidden in the Shakespeare history plays are members of the Neville family, disguised by their titles; their true identities, the family name, thus being obscured. So often is a Neville hidden behind a title that we do not realize who has walked on stage: the Earl of Westmoreland is Ralph Neville! In fact, Henry Neville was related to all the kings and many of their senior liegemen depicted in Shakespeare's history plays (James and Rubinstein, 2005, 60). Furthermore, Shakespeare demonstrates a Neville bias, either inserting or foregrounding a member of the Neville family to bring them glory, or removing Nevilles to avoid exposing them or damaging their reputations. He also includes many minor characters that have links to the Nevilles. In this book we track the Neville connections to be found within the texts of the plays. These discoveries add to the evidence that supports Henry Neville as the hidden writer of the works of Shakespeare. Indeed, with this new perspective we have been able to explain passages, distortions and details in the Shakespeare history plays that were previously opaque, anomalous or cryptic.

James and Rubinstein (2005) first pointed out that members of the Neville family were prominent in the history plays and revealed the importance of the banned political tract *Leicester's Commonwealth* (1584) as a source for Shakespeare's history plays. Casson (2010) examined Neville's manuscript copy, Worsley MSS 47, in detail and confirmed their findings. This book builds on that research and offers evidence to show that Henry Neville had the motivation to write about his family, distorting and shaping the historical material to foreground or conceal Nevilles. William Shakspere from Stratford had no such reason to highlight or hide members of the Neville family. Indeed, because he left no personal correspondence there is no evidence extant for William Shakspere's political standpoint. He held no political or public office. Sir Henry Neville, diplomat, parliamentarian and political prisoner, offers a new perspective for understanding the history plays. His letters and notebooks still exist. Indeed, there are four books annotated by Neville that have particular relevance to Shakespeare's history plays:

1. The earliest is Neville's manuscript copy of *Leicester's Commonwealth* Worsley MSS 47, 1584–5, a possible source for Shakespeare's history plays (Casson, 2010).

2. Another is the annotated Hall's *Chronicle* (Alan and Lubbock, 1954), which James and Rubinstein (2005, 51) identified as having come from the library of Neville's son-in-law, Richard Worsley, at Appuldurcombe; Casson (2010, 75) dated the annotations to 1586–96. Hall's *Chronicle* has been identified as a source for Shakespeare's history plays.

3. Neville's notebook, annotated during his time in the Tower of London, is dated 1602–3. James and Rubinstein (2005) identified this as a possible source for the coronation ritual in *Henry VIII.*

4. A copy of Thomas Milles' *A Catalogue of Honor* was annotated by Neville from 1610 to 1612 (he referred to Prince Henry being alive, and Henry died in 1612). This book was printed by William Jaggard, who was the printer of both the False and First Folio of Shakespeare's plays. Neville's annotated

copy seems to have been a proof copy (the picture of James I was printed upside down), and Neville was carefully correcting the text and suggesting cuts. Some of his suggestions were indeed picked up by the editor, because there are printed slips of his corrections pasted into another copy of *A Catalogue of Honor* to be found in the British Library. This, then, is evidence of a possible relationship between Neville and Jaggard in 1610–12.

These books span the entire period of the writing of the history plays and contain notes for all the reigns covered by the plays. Neville thus demonstrates a consistent, lifelong interest in history, politics, kings and powerful members of the nobility. All these books also contain handwritten notes referring to members of the Neville family. With Neville as author, we can understand why there are so many hidden Nevilles in the plays and appreciate the Neville bias and other Neville links and references.

Table 1. Neville's Notebooks as Sources for Shakespeare's History Plays

Notes on the Reign of Kings	*Leicester's Commonwealth Worsley MSS 47, 1584–5*	*The Annotated Hall's Chronicle 1586–96*	*The Tower Notebook 1602–3*	*T. Milles' A Catalogue of Honor 1610–12*
John	√		√	√
Edward III	√		√	√
Richard II	√	√	√	√
Henry IV	√	√	√	√
Henry V	√	√	√	√
Henry VI	√	√	√	√
Richard III	√		√	√
Henry VIII	√			√

The history plays are largely based on the second edition of Holinshed's *Chronicles* of 1587, which was edited by the government censors, Sir Henry Killigrew (Neville's father-in-law), Thomas Randolph and John Hammond. Ralph Newbery, the publisher of this edition of Holinshed, was "a neighbor of Neville's in Berkshire, and father of a man who was ultimately to become a beneficiary under Sir Henry Neville's will" (James, 2008, 71). Books signed and annotated by Neville have been found at Merton College, Oxford University and Audley End House (where they were taken by the Braybrook-Nevilles from Neville's Billingbear library in the 19th century). Many of these contain annotations relevant to the works of Shakespeare. Neville's letters, preserved both in manuscripts and in print (in Winwood's *Memorials of State* [Sawyer, 1725], offer an opportunity to compare his vocabulary with that of

Shakespeare (see Chapters 5 and 10). These letters also provide evidence of Neville's political positions relevant to the plays.

More than any of his other plays, Shakespeare's history plays were a political act. "The writing and rewriting of national history in the 1570s and 1580s was not happening in a vacuum, still less in an atmosphere of easy tolerance, in which one person's viewpoint was considered just as deserving of hearing as another" (Wilson, 2012, 143). The motive for writing the history plays was not just to entertain or provide a dramatized history lesson: the plays were intensely political. Among other things, they were concerned with a safe, legitimate succession to the throne and the dangers of civil war. Shakespeare was fascinated "with politics.... History is above all an exploration of human political behavior, of the desire for power, of men's response to gaining it and being deprived of it.... Shakespeare's use of history consists, then, in selecting, shaping, amplifying ... chronicle material in order to intensify concentration on political issues and on their human consequences" (Smallwood, 1986, quoted by Warren, 2003, 36). Our research has enabled us to see the layering in Shakespeare's history plays. The bard was not only using history as a metaphor for contemporary political situations, exploring the problems of a disputed succession to the throne, for example, even imbuing English history with his own moral values, he was also seeing the patterns in personal and political histories so that he could explore contemporary issues that would not have been allowed in a censored theater. With Neville the life-long politician as the hidden Shakespeare, this political fascination is explained. The history plays are intensely political, exploring what happens when ambitious men make bids for power, when kings become tyrants, when rebellion, civil war, riot and anarchy break out. The plays examine the motives of men and women, especially those of the aristocracy, and are analytic essays on the personal and political. While actual historical facts and dates are bent to the playwright's purposes, this is not just for dramatic effect but to create a unified structure that examines in detail what happens to the body politic when there is disunity and dangerous rivalry for power. Shakespeare himself acknowledged this when Hamlet calls the players "the abstract and brief chronicles of our time" (2.2.520) and states that the purpose of playing was to show "the very age and body of the time his form and pressure" (3.2.19–23).

Some may say, "What's in a name? that which we call a rose, by any other name, would smell as sweet" (*Romeo and Juliet,* 2.2.43), meaning, "Does the authorship really matter?" Indeed, the Shakespeare authorship question is of little value unless it illuminates the meaning of the text. A scientific hypothesis stands or falls on its ability to explain and predict different scenarios and actions. Likewise, an authorship candidate stands or falls by his or her ability to explain the text of the Shakespeare canon. The Henry Neville candidature has this explanatory power: for example, in explaining why the role of Essex is vestigial in *King John,* or why the dramatis personae differ between the First Quarto and the First Folio of *Henry V,* or why there are anachronistic scenes and characters in *Edward III.* Just as Romeo responds to Juliet, saying, "Call me but love, and I'll be new baptized" (*Romeo and Juliet,* 2.2.50), we feel that uncovering Neville's authorship of the works of Shakespeare can make the canon more meaningful and accessible.

The history plays cover the reigns of the Plantagenet and Tudor kings up until Henry VIII. Henry II (1154–1189) was the first Plantagenet king of England, beginning a dynasty that lasted over 300 years. When Henry's eldest son, Richard I, the Lionheart (1189–1199) died, his brother John (1199–1216) took the throne. John's son succeeded as Henry III (1216–1272). His son, Edward I (1272–1307), popularly known as Longshanks, became king. Edward II (1307–1327) was deposed: his alleged homosexuality and murder was the subject of a play by Marlowe. Edward's son, Edward III, is then the subject of the next play identified, in recent years, as by Shakespeare.

After the reigns of Edward III (1327–77) and Richard II (1377–99), the dynasty divided into Lancaster and York factions.[1] The Lancastrian kings, Henry IV (1399–1413), Henry V (1413–22) and Henry VI (1422–61 and 1470–71), reigned until the latter was challenged by the York faction, leading to the short reigns of the Yorkist kings, Edward IV (1461–70 and 1471–83), Edward V (1483) and Richard III (1483–85). The Wars of the Roses ended with the defeat of Richard III and the beginning of the Tudor dynasty, starting with Henry VII (1485–1509), followed by Henry VIII (1509–47), Edward VI (1547–53), Mary (1553–1558) and finally, Elizabeth I (1558–1603), who presided over a renaissance in theater during which Shakespeare wrote ten plays about these Plantagenet kings. All of Shakespeare's history plays about Plantagenet kings were written during Elizabeth's reign. The one play about a Tudor king (*Henry VIII*) was written in 1612 during the reign of James I, which followed Elizabeth's.

We are not the first to notice the predominance of the Neville family in Shakespeare's history plays. In *Shakespeare's English Kings*, Saccio (1977, 49) observed, "The dynastic connections of the Nevilles made them one of the most powerful forces in fifteenth century politics. Over half the people mentioned in this book were the issue of or otherwise related to the first earl of Westmoreland (Ralph Neville)."

In his 1602 Tower notebook, Neville noted "Ra. E. Westmoreland."

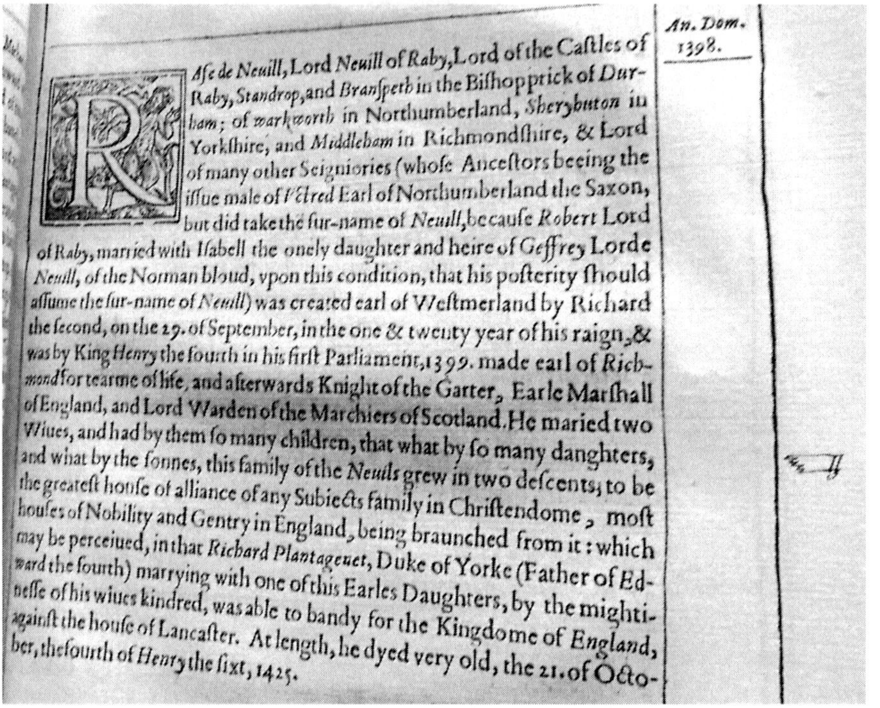

An. Dom. 1398.

Rafe de Neuill, Lord Neuill of Raby, Lord of the Castles of Raby, Standrop, and Branspeth in the Bishopprick of Durham; of warkworth in Northumberland, Sherybuton in Yorkshire, and Middleham in Richmondshire, & Lord of many other Seigniories (whose Ancestors beeing the issue male of Veltred Earl of Northumberland the Saxon, but did take the sur-name of Neuill, because Robert Lord of Raby, maried with Isabell the onely daughter and heire of Geffrey Lorde Neuill, of the Norman bloud, vpon this condition, that his posterity should assume the sur-name of Neuill) was created earl of Westmerland by Richard the second, on the 29. of September, in the one & twenty year of his raign, & was by King Henry the fourth in his first Parliament, 1399. made earl of Richmond for tearme of life, and afterwards Knight of the Garter, Earle Marshall of England, and Lord Warden of the Marchiers of Scotland. He maried two Wiues, and had by them so many children, that what by so many danghters, and what by the sonnes, this family of the Neuils grew in two descents, to be the greatest house of alliance of any Subiects family in Christendome, most houses of Nobility and Gentry in England, being braunched from it: which may be perceiued, in that Richard Plantagenet, Duke of Yorke (Father of Edward the fourth) marrying with one of this Earles Daughters, by the mightinesse of his wiues kindred, was able to bandy for the Kingdome of England, against the house of Lancaster. At length, he dyed very old, the 21. of October, the fourth of Henry the sixt, 1425.

***A Catalogue of Honor,* 1610, 991 (private collection).**

When annotating his copy of *A Catalogue of Honor,* 1610, Neville drew a hand in the margin pointing out a passage about Ralph Neville's descendants.

The text reads: "This family of the *Neuils* grew in two descents, to be the greatest house of alliance of any Subiects family in Christendome, most houses of Nobility and Gentry in England, being braunched from it."

Neville was so proud of this lineage that when his father died in 1593 he had the following inscription put on his monument at Waltham St. Lawrence:

> HERE LYETH BURYED Sr HENRY NEVILL KNIGHT. DESCENDED OF THE NEVILLS BARONS OF ABERGAVENNY WHO WERE A BRANCHE OF THE HOWSE OF WESTMORELANDE.

It might be argued that because they were key players in the history of the Plantagenet kings, any playwright dramatizing these reigns would inevitably have to bring members of the Neville family onto the stage. This book aims to show that the bard had a pro–Neville bias that led to his distorting history, not simply for dramatic effect, but to show the power and influence of the Nevilles and do so in a way that was sufficiently concealed as to suggest, rather than openly brag: only a Neville who had set out to hide his own identity would have the motive to both reveal the Nevilles' prominence and conceal their true identity. Indeed the playwright began by naming the Nevilles: in the 1594 quarto version of *Henry VI* part 2 (*The First Part of the Contention*), arguably the first play by Shakespeare, he named the "Nevils" eight times. As time went by he was more circumspect.

To ensure historical clarity we have chosen to present each play in a separate chapter in the order of the kings' reigns, not in the order the plays were written, which is generally believed to be as follows:

Henry VI parts 2, 3 and 1
Edward III
Richard III
Richard II (a sequel to *Thomas of Woodstock*)
King John (a revision of *The Troublesome Raigne of John King of England,* 1591)
Henry IV parts 1 and 2
Henry V
Henry VIII

We suggest, though, that *King John* was composed first, possibly co-written with George Peele as *The Troublesome Raigne of John King of England* and then re-written after Peele's death in 1596 (see Chapter 1). We have included a chapter on the Roman plays because we have found a Neville leitmotif running through them and they are also history plays with political themes (see Chapter 9). We have included a chapter on the echoes of *Hamlet* to be found in the vocabulary of Neville's writings from 1600 to 1601 (see Chapter 10) when Neville himself was on trial for treason and was imprisoned (Hamlet says, "Denmark's a prison": 2.2.243). Bradbeer's discovery of George Carleton's dedication to Henry Neville of his 1603 *Heroici Characteres* is given a chapter because of what it reveals (see Chapter 11).

This book adds to the growing evidence for Henry Neville's authorship of Shakespeare's works and further explains why the bard might have concealed his identity: these plays were dangerously political. We acknowledge Brenda James as the first to discover Neville's authorship and have built on her work, in effect testing her suggestions and finding them credible as more and more evidence has emerged, often surprising us. A few pieces of evidence connecting Shakespeare and Neville might be regarded as coincidence. As more evidence has emerged we can see that different pieces of evidence have differing value; some are weak and others stronger. Gradually, however, like a snowball gathering mass as it rolls downhill, the sheer weight of evidence has become compelling. This book therefore can be placed alongside the other books on Neville to show that the authorship question is now largely solved, with Sir Henry Neville emerging as the true author of the works of Shakespeare. This consequently opens up new areas of inquiry. We invite readers to examine the evidence and judge for themselves. There is now considerable evidence that for some of his plays the bard had assistance from co-authors, who hid behind the pseudonym as much, we suggest, as Neville did. Further research in this field will clarify these creative relationships.

Shakespeare is now a global phenomenon, and our co-authorship reflects this, with one of us in England searching archives and libraries for letters, manuscripts and annotated books, the other in Australia exploring the treasure trove of the Internet for information. Our co-authorship has been particularly fruitful and has led to the emergence of new evidence. We have striven to test and check evidence rather than speculate, grounding our research in texts and original manuscript documents. These primary sources give us confidence that our discoveries are real and significant. We have used the British Library, the National Archives at Kew, the Bodleian Library, and the libraries of Merton College, Oxford, Audley End House, Lancaster University, Chatsworth House, and John Rylands in Manchester, as well as the Lincoln Archives and the Salisbury Collection at Hatfield House.

We identify quotations from Shakespeare by putting the act, scene and line in parentheses after the quotation: "To be or not to be that is the question" (*Hamlet,* 3.1.56). We have generally used the Arden editions of the plays but have also used the Oxford, Cambridge and other editions. This can lead to some confusion as, for example, the above quotation is (3.1.57) in the Oxford edition. Although this is only one line different from the Arden, readers may need to search a little in their editions, if lineage is different, to find the full passage.

The year 2015 is the 400th anniversary of Henry Neville's death. We can now celebrate the true author who successfully hid his identity, thus ensuring he had the freedom to write what he wanted during a period of censorship and political uncertainty. However, he left sufficient clues in his texts to identify him, and this book confirms that Henry Neville was Shakespeare.

CHAPTER 1

King John (1199–1216)

This ... semblance hath disguised me quite.—*King John* (4.3.4)[1]

The Life and Death of King John is thought to have been written in 1595–6 and was published in the First Folio of 1623. An earlier version, *The Troublesome Raigne of John King of England*, was written in 1589–90 and printed in 1591. We will examine both and the relationship between them as we explore the hidden Neville connections in the texts.

The Historical Background

King Richard I, the Lionheart, died in 1199, leaving no legitimate heir. John, his youngest brother, took the throne, and his succession was in dispute from several quarters, including these:

1. Arthur, son of Geoffrey, John's older, deceased, brother, who had a strong claim to the throne;
2. King Phillip of France and the Dauphin, Lewis, who saw an opportunity to conquer England;
3. The papal legate, Pandulph, who disputed King John's control of the Church in England.

This disputed succession offered the play's first audiences a mirror for their own time, as the aging Queen Elizabeth I had not named her successor. The possibilities of a foreign claim on the throne and a religious dimension to the succession crisis were sources of great anxiety for government and people.

King John's reign was a period of constitutional struggle, with the nobles challenging the king and establishing limits on his power in Magna Carta. However, this is not shown in either version of the play. We do see John struggling to maintain his power. When the young Arthur died he was widely believed to have been murdered. Some English noblemen turned against King John after Arthur's death. In the play, a notable exception is the semi-fictional Bastard Philip Faulconbridge.[2] Ironically, the Bastard may also be seen as a threat to King John, when he is revealed as a son, although illegitimate, of Richard I, as well as being the avenger of that king's murder. However, he remains loyal to King John, and this makes sense when we put Henry Neville into the picture. He was illegitimate, born before his mother and father were legally married (James and Rubinstein, 2005, 64). He was a loyal subject who sought to serve the crown and preserve the realm, as his father and grandfather had done.

This reign also saw religious dissension, as King John contested the pope's choice of candidate for archbishop of Canterbury, deplored the selling of indulgences by the Roman Catholic Church and expropriated the Church's wealth to support his military campaigns. King John was excommunicated and so made vulnerable to Catholic assassins. In the play John eventually makes peace with Rome and the excommunication is revoked, but the papal legate struggles to get King Philip to agree to a peace treaty. Only after the English noblemen unite, Philip's reinforcements are drowned at sea, and John is poisoned by a disgruntled monk is the papal legate able to orchestrate a peace. At the end the Bastard Faulconbridge advises the future King Henry III and has the last word with a patriotic speech. As we shall see, the name Faulconbridge has a Neville connection. *King John* (*KJ*) and its early version, *The Troublesome Raigne of John, King of England* (*TR*), offer possible insights into the playwright's motivations and further clues to his identity.

The Political Context of the Play

Within this play, there are obvious resonances with contemporary Elizabethan history. Elizabeth I was excommunicated by Pope Pius V in 1570 and by Sixtus V in 1588. There were numerous Catholic plots to assassinate her, such as the Babington Plot of 1586, which led to the execution of Mary, Queen of Scots. The play is history as metaphor for the present. Indeed, when King Philip says "a whole armado of connected sail is scatter'd and disjoin'd from fellowship" (*KJ* 3.3.2), he is clearly referring to the destruction and dispersal of the Spanish Armada in 1588.

Some scenes in the play are at a siege of Angiers, a strong fortress in the province of Anjou, France. King John was involved in battles over Angiers for much of his reign, in an effort to lay claim to his French inheritance. During King John's time there were no cannon, whereas in the play *King John* we hear the kings of France and England threaten the poor town with their cannon. In this play Shakespeare refers to cannon more than in any other work:

The thunder of my cannon shall be heard [1.1.26].
our cannon shall be bent Against the brows of
this resisting town [2.1.37].
The cannons have their bowels full of wrath [2.1.210].
bullets wrapped in fire [2.1.227].
our cannons' malice shall be vainly spent [2.1.251].
their battering cannon charged to the mouths [2.1.382].
turn thou the mouth of thy artillery [2.1.403].
shall rain their drift of bullets on this town [2.1.412].
what cannoneer begot this lusty blood [2.1.461].
he speaks plain cannon fire, and smoke and bounce [2.1.462].

This contrasts with *The Troublesome Raigne*, in which there is only one reference to cannon (and that is a metaphor, not an actual weapon) and none to bullets or artillery. In 1585 Angiers was under siege and cannon were used (Davila, 1678, 290). This siege involved the Huguenots and other French Protestant forces, pitted against the Catholic League. Henry Neville had a cannon foundry, inherited from his great uncle, Thomas Gresham (James, 2008, 71, 84, 214). He owned this from 1578 till 1598 (in other words until after *King John* had been written), and he would have been alert to reports of their use.

The opening scene includes two characters that are not in *Chronicles*.

Chatillon

In the first scene of *King John,* the French ambassador is named "Chatillon."[3] However, "there is no historical authority for Chatillon's embassage" (Boswell-Stone, 1907, 47; Forker, 2011, 107). Where, then, does this name come from? Elizabethan England was sympathetic to the Huguenots, and English agents tried to give them support. These agents included the English ambassadors to France, Sir Francis Walsingham and Sir Nicholas Throckmorton, and the diplomat Sir Henry Killigrew, all of whom were strongly Protestant.

Walsingham and Killigrew, Henry Neville's father-in-law, witnessed the massacre of Huguenots on St. Bartholomew's Day in 1572. Killigrew's second marriage was to a Huguenot refugee, Jael de Peigne (James and Rubinstein, 2005, 85), and he visited France regularly up until 1591 (the date that the early version of *The Troublesome Raigne* was published). Killigrew knew the Huguenot leaders, Admiral Coligny and his brother Cardinal Chatillon.[4] Chatillon visited England in 1568, and England granted him asylum at the royal palace of Hampton Court in 1572. Unfortunately, it was a poor refuge; he was poisoned by a Catholic servant, just as King John is poisoned. Copying out *Leicester's Commonwealth*, Neville wrote (c. 1585):

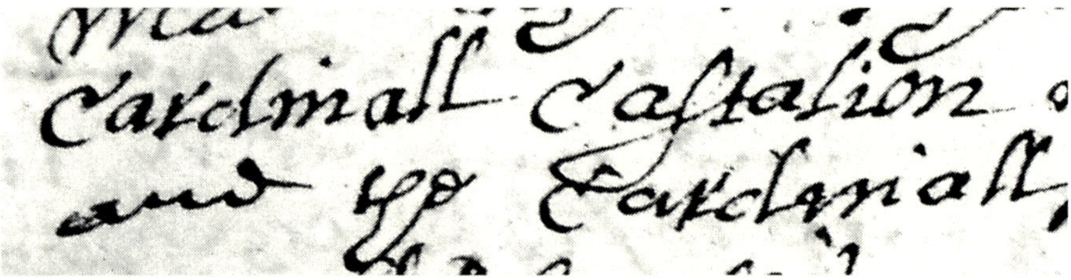

"Cardinall Castalion," Worsley MSS 47, 9V (by permission of the Eighth Earl of Yarborough and Lincolnshire Archives).

At this point the text of *Leicester's Commonwealth* tells how Cardinal Chatillon was "soon after punished (as is thought) by this man with poison" (Peck, 80/57[5]). This proves that Neville was well aware of the Huguenot cardinal prior to the writing of the play *King John,* or indeed prior to the earlier version, *The Troublesome Raigne.* When Henry Neville was himself ambassador to France (1599–1600), he referred in his letters to the St. Bartholomew's Day Massacre in Paris. The similarities between Shakespeare's French envoy, Chatillon, who appears in the English court of *King John* (but not in the historical source), and the French envoy, Chatillon, who appeared in the English royal courts seventeen years before the first performance of *The Troublesome Raigne*, are surely more than coincidence. Men named Chatillon also occur in *Edward III* and *Henry V.* On the other hand, perhaps it is only coincidence that in 1604 Sir Francis Chatillion was appointed as the deputy officer of Newbury Manor, replacing Henry Neville, who had been steward of Newbury since his father's death.

The Bastard Philip of Faulconbridge

Following the opening encounter with Chatillon in the play, King John adjudicates Philip Faulconbridge's dispute with his brother, Robert, the legitimate son of Sir Robert and Lady Faulconbridge, for his inheritance. The king resolves the dispute and knights Philip as Sir Richard Plantagenet, because it is revealed that his real father was King Richard I. In Holinshed's *Chronicles* we find this reference:

> Philip, bastard sonne to king Richard, to whome his father had given the castell and honor of Coinacke, killed the viscount of Limoges, in revenge of his father's death, who was slaine in besieging the castell of Chalus Cheuerall [Holinshed, 1587, vol. 6, 160].

In the play, the bastard Philip Faulconbridge kills Lymoges, the Duke of Austria. Other aspects of Philip's story appear to be drawn from other bastard sons in history. Boswell-Stone (1907) suggested that the dramatic scene in which Philip is given the choice between inheriting titles (i.e., being a knight) or property is based on the story of Jean de Dunois, Bastard of Orleans, the Count of Longueville, who is mentioned in *Henry VI* part 1. A Longueville also appears in *Love's Labour's Lost.* James (2008, 215) noted that the Nevilles were related to the Longuevilles. Neville's father, grandfather and father-in-law had all been to France, so they might have known this story. Philip is not surnamed Faulconbridge in Holinshed, so this name is the invention of the playwrights of *TR* and *KJ.*

The name "Faulconbridge" conceals a Neville connection: Thomas Neville (1429–71), Bastard of Falconbridge, was an illegitimate son of William Neville, Lord Falconbridge and Earl of Kent (James, 2008, 215). Alternative spellings of Faulconbridge were Faulconberg or Fauconberg. The Faulconbridges in the *King John* subplot highlight the issues of the transmission of property, power and legitimacy from generation to generation, an issue especially close to Henry Neville as he was born illegitimate. This secret shame may indeed be one of the factors behind his decision to remain a hidden author. Not only is Faulconbridge an invention of the author, he "is Shakespeare's first character who speaks with a voice entirely his own" (Bloom, 1999, xiv). Indeed the bastard Faulconbridge can be seen as an alter ego for Neville: "The character is changed from a witty, detached, even self-interested commentator into an increasingly thoughtful participant in, and eventually a major director of, the political action" (Bruanmuller, 1989, 72). Furthermore, by knighting the bastard as Sir Richard Plantagenet, the playwright also hints at the fact that his family, the Faulconbridge/Nevilles, were of royal blood.

In *Henry VI* part 3, "Stern Falconbridge commands the narrow seas" (1.1.239) is a clear reference to Thomas, Bastard of Falconbridge (son of William Neville), a sailor who received the freedom of the City of London in 1454 for his part in removing pirates from the North Sea and the English

Channel. He was made Vice-Admiral of the Fleet by his cousin Richard Neville, the Earl of Warwick, of whom he was a zealous supporter. The Falconbridge name is used in *Henry VI* part 1 (4.7.67) where it is used as a title—"thrice victorious Lord of Falconbridge"—awarded to the heroic Talbot. A Jacques Falconbridge is mentioned in *Love's Labour's Lost* (2.1.42). In *The Merchant of Venice* (1.2.66) Falconbridge is a young English baron who is a hapless suitor for Portia's hand. Fauconbridge (or Faulconbridge) occurs twice in *Henry V* (3.5.44 and 4.8.100), where he is listed as one of the French lords before the battle of Agincourt and then as one of the dead afterwards. Thus from 1590 to 1599 Shakespeare was unaccountably using the name of an illegitimate member of the Neville family in his plays.

After King John has been excommunicated by the papal legate in act 3, scene 1, the king appoints the Bastard Faulconbridge to force the clergy in England to give their money to fund his military campaign in France:

> Cousin, away for England! Haste before;
> And, ere our coming, see thou shake the bags
> Of hoarding abbots; imprisoned angels
> Set at liberty: the fat ribs of peace
> Must by the hungry now be fed upon:
> Use our commission in his utmost force [3.3.6–11].

Although there is no 13th century character called the Bastard of Faulconbridge in the Holinshed *Chronicles,* there is a Hugh Neville. The text tells how King John "gaue commandement vnto **Hugh Neuill high iustice of his forrests**, that he should award his precepts vnto all forresters within the realme, to **giue warning to all the white monks**, that before the quindene of S. Michaell they should remoue out of his forrests all their horses of Haraz, and other cattell, vnder the penaltie to forfeit so manie of them, as after that day chanced to be found within the same forrests. The cause that moued the king to deale so hardlie with them was, for that **they refused to helpe him with monie**, when before his last going ouer into Normandie, he demanded it of them towards **the paiment of the thirtie thousand pounds** which he had couenanted to pay the French king, to liue in rest and peace, which he coueted to haue done **for reliefe of his people**, and his owne suertie, knowing what enimies he had that laie in wait to destroie him, and againe, what discommodities had chanced to his father and brethren, by the often and continuall wars" (our emphasis: Holinshed, 1587, vol. 6, 161).[6]

No other figure in Holinshed was commissioned by King John to raise money from the churches. Furthermore, according to Holinshed, Hugh Neville was one of the last lords to remain with the king. He needed to be threatened with war by the confederacy of barons before he joined their league, which eventually forced King John to sign Magna Carta (Holinshed, 1587, vol. 6, 185).[7] Thus Hugh Neville may be a model for the Bastard of Faulconbridge. Like Hugh, Henry Neville was a custodian of the royal forest at Windsor, as his father had been. The two Holinshed models for the Bastard of Falconbridge, Philip and Hugh, occur within a page of each other.

Just as the Bastard was commissioned to raise funds from English monasteries, members of the Neville family had benefited from the disposal of religious property during the Reformation, and Henry Neville himself lived for a time in the palace at Mayfield, an old monastic property that had housed Cardinal Wolsey and Archbishop Cranmer (see Chapter 8 and Casson, 2009, 165, 177), and also at Blackfriars. This property was later to become the Blackfriars Theatre.

Annotating his Tower notebook in 1602, Neville wrote "de fawconbridge" in the margin (Worsley MSS 40 in the Lincoln Archives). In the first quarto of *Henry VI* part 3 (published anonymously as *The True Tragedie of Richard Duke of Yorke* in 1595), the spelling is identical to that in the Tower notebook: "Sterne Fawconbridge commands the narrow seas."

Casson (2010) has shown that the play *Look About You,* a comic history of Henry II in which Richard (the young Lionheart) attempts to seduce Lady Faukenbridge, is an early play by Neville, dated circa 1585–7. It must therefore have been written before *TR*.

Table 2 clarifies the relationship between the Faulconbridges and the Nevilles and shows how many of these closely related men appear as key figures in Shakespeare's plays.

William "Long-Sword," the Earl of Salisbury

Another prominent character of the play is the Earl of Salisbury, who comments about the heroic Bastard:

> That misbegotten devil, Faulconbridge,
> In spite of spite, alone upholds the day [5.4.4].

Salisbury is William de Longespée, third Earl of Salisbury, c. 1170–1226, who was acknowledged by Henry II as his illegitimate son. Therefore Salisbury himself was "misbegotten." His mother was unknown for many years, until the discovery of a charter of William mentioning "*Comitissa Ida, mater mea.*" This Ida was further identified as the wife of Roger Bigod, second Earl of

Table 2. Faulconbridge and Other Relatives of Henry Neville

Westmoreland appears in:
***Henry IV* part 1**
***Henry IV* part 2**
Henry V

Salisbury in:
***Henry V* Quarto**
***Henry VI* part 1**
***Henry VI* part 2**

Warwick in:
Edward III
***Henry V* Quarto**
***Henry VI* part 2**
***Henry VI* part 3**
Richard III

Faulconbridge in:
King John
***Henry VI* part 1**
***Henry VI* part 3**
Henry V
Merchant of Venice
Love's Labour's Lost

Abergavenny (2)[8] in:
Henry VIII

Ralph Neville m. Joan Beaufort
Earl of Westmoreland
c. 1364–1425

Richard Neville Earl of Salisbury 1400–1460	William Neville Lord Faulconbridge 1405–1463	Edward Neville Lord Abergavenny (1) 1414–1476
Richard Neville Earl of Warwick 1428–1471	Thomas Neville Bastard of Faulconbridge 1429–1471	George Neville Lord Abergavenny (2) 1440–1492
		Edward Neville 1471–1538
		Henry Neville c. 1520–1593
		Henry Neville 1562–1615

Norfolk (Forker, 2011, 111, note). It is therefore interesting that this stepfather, Lord Bigot (or Bigod), defends his stepson, Salisbury, during a confrontation in act 4, scene 3. The authors of the *TR* and *KJ* therefore show special knowledge of the family. In the opening scene of the play, Salisbury is a silent witness as his half brother, King John, and Queen Eleanor pass judgment on Philip the Bastard when he chooses the honor of his natural father, Richard Plantagenet, over the Faulconbridge inheritance. William de Longespée, the Earl of Salisbury, himself gained his title when he married Ela, Countess of Salisbury. By her, he had four sons and four daughters, including Ela, who married Thomas de Beaumont, sixth Earl of Warwick, and Ida, who first married Ralph de Somery, and then William de Beauchamp. Sir Henry Neville was related to the earls of Warwick and Salisbury, and to the Beauchamps.[9]

The writers of *TR* misidentify this Earl of Salisbury: he introduces himself as "I, **Thomas Plantagenet**, Earle of Salisbury" (Part 2.3.221). Who then might this be? The earldom of Salisbury was granted in 1337 by Edward III to William de Montacute (1301–1344), in whose family it remained till 1400, when John, third earl of this line, was attainted and his titles forfeited. His son **Thomas** (1388–1428) was restored in blood in 1421 and married twice: his second wife being Alice Chaucer, granddaughter of Geoffrey Chaucer the poet. Thomas' daughter (of the first marriage) and heiress, Alice, married Sir Richard Neville (1400–1460), who was a younger son of Ralph Neville, first Earl of Westmoreland and a grandson of John of Gaunt. Richard sat in parliament in right of his wife as the Earl of Salisbury (Casson, 2009, 22).

Eleanor, Constance and Lady Fauconbridge

There are three mothers in the play—Eleanor, Constance and Lady Faulconbridge, each advocating for their sons. Eleanor supports King John's kingship. Constance supports Arthur's claim to the throne. Lady Faulconbridge, while supporting her son Robert, eventually admits that the father of her other son, Philip, was King Richard I. It is Eleanor who has the insight and wisdom to determine Philip's heritage, having herself had an unfaithful husband, Henry II, who sired their illegitimate son, Salisbury. Forker (2011, 68) mused, "It can be hardly accidental that three of the four female characters are mothers and widows." Henry Neville's father had three wives, two of whom were mothers to young Henry. When his natural mother, Elizabeth Neville, née Gresham, died, Elizabeth Bacon became his stepmother. The nature of their relationship may be reflected in the furious legal dispute between them after his father's death in 1593 (see Chapter 4). This may be reflected in *The Troublesome Raigne,* when John says to the Bastard about his mother, Lady Faulconbridge:

> A Mother though she were unnatural
> Is better than the kindest stepdame is [Part 2. 2.140].

In *KJ* Constance, confronting Queen Eleanor, calls John "Thy usurping son" (2.1.121). This is the fourth use of this word "usurp/er/ing" in four lines. In his copy of *Leicester's Commonwealth* (which predates the play) Neville made a note, "Knige John an **vsurper**," whereas in the printed text is "King Iohn a Tyraunt." The words "usurp," "usurpation" and "usurper" are to be found in *TR,* the last being spoken by King John himself.

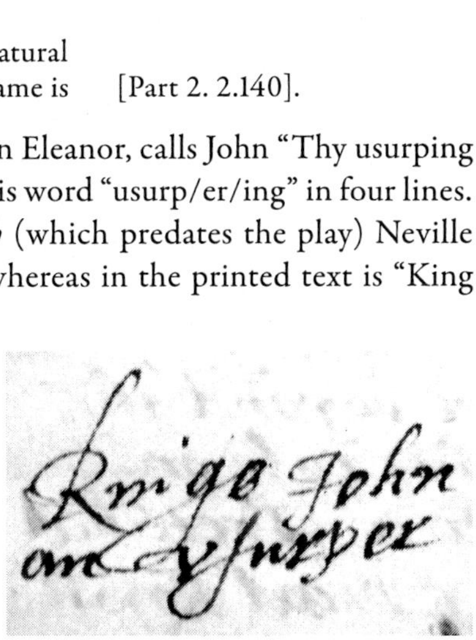

Worsley MSS 47, 48V (by permission of the Eighth Earl of Yarborough and Lincolnshire Archives).

The Earl of Essex

As he set off for France, King John left "the **rule of the realm** unto Geoffrey FitzPeter" (Holinshed, 1587, vol. 6, 181), who was the Earl of Essex. In *TR,* John declares, "Essex, thou shalt be **ruler of my realm**" (1.1.311). The similarity in the wording suggests the writer had referred to Holinshed for this detail. This, however, is omitted from *King John.* Thus it can be seen that the First Folio version of *King John* censored the Earl of Essex's valid historic role. Essex is present through much of the first scene of *KJ,* albeit in a minor role. However, this first scene is his only appearance in the play, and he has only one insignificant sentence to say. His presence is a vestige of a much larger role in *TR.* As Forker (2011, 106) stated, spectators of *TR* would almost certainly have associated this title with that of Robert Devereux, the second Earl of Essex, whereas the role of Essex is effectively invisible in *KJ.* Devereux was seen by some as a potential future king and so this statement in *TR:* "Essex, thou shalt be ruler of my realm," would have had a contemporary political significance. In contrast to *TR,* Essex is not named on stage in *KJ,* and he is only mentioned once in a stage direction. His parts in the play appear to have been parceled out to a variety of characters. Essex's interrogation of Lady Faulconbridge in *TR* is given to the Bastard of Faulconbridge himself in *KJ;* the appeal for the release of Arthur is transferred to Pembroke in *KJ;* it is Salisbury in *KJ,* not Essex, who draws his sword to threaten Hubert, the supposed killer of Arthur; it is Hubert and the Bastard who take Arthur for burial in *KJ,* not Essex. Thus, a major rewriting of the play was required. Most important of all, the 286 lines of part 2, scene 3 of *TR* are left out altogether in *King John.* This scene details Essex's conspiracy to meet secretly with other noblemen at Bury St. Edmunds and plan their rebellion. *KJ* was not printed until 1623. After Devereux's uprising in 1601, it would have been inappropriate to give a heroic, rebellious role to an Earl of Essex, albeit during King John's reign. Henry Neville spent two years in the Tower and nearly lost his head, due to being caught up in the Essex rebellion. He would have been under no illusion as to the need to tone down references to the Earl of Essex. It is therefore possible that the final version of *KJ* (1623) represents a censored or an authorial revision, post–1601.

King John *and* The Troublesome Raigne

With this perspective on *King John,* we have an opportunity for a new appreciation of its controversial predecessor, *The Troublesome Raigne of John*

King of England. Structurally, *KJ* and *TR* are very similar plays with largely the same plot and dramatis personae. *The Troublesome Raigne* was published in 1591 and must have been written in 1589–90 (Forker, 2011, 31). *King John* has been dated to 1596. This date is partly because Francis Meres listed Shakespeare's play *King John* in his book *Palladis Tamia: Wit's Treasury* in 1598. Meres could have been referring to *TR*, as the old play was attributed to Shakespeare in 1611. Furthermore, we have suggested above that *KJ* was revised again after the Essex rebellion of 1601. *King John* was never officially registered as a new play but appears to have been accepted as a revision of the earlier *TR*.

TR is particularly Protestant in tone. Philip, the Bastard, offers Christian ministry to the dying King John, but it is specifically anti–Catholic, and he calls the assassination of John "the fruit of popery" (part 2, 8.114). Thomas Orwin, who printed *TR,* was established as the propaganda mouthpiece of the archbishop of Canterbury, John Whitgift, and such a printer would welcome an anti–Catholic play. The anti–Catholic sentiment in both *TR* and *KJ* has confounded scholars advocating a "Shakespeare" who might have covertly supported the Roman Catholic religion (such as the Earl of Oxford or possibly William Shakspere from Stratford-upon-Avon).

Many of the differences between *TR,* printed in 1591, and *KJ,* published in 1623, can be attributed to the changing political climate. This period saw not just the transition from Queen Elizabeth I to King James I, but also the passing of powerbrokers such as Sir Francis Walsingham, the Earl of Essex, Archbishop Whitgift and William Cecil. *TR* was performed by the Queen's Men, a company established in 1583 by Walsingham, the queen's spymaster, for political purposes: "The Queen's Men were a deliberately political company in origin, and their repertory appears to have followed the path no doubt pointed out for them by Sir Francis Walsingham." In the plays they acted, "one finds no conflict or disturbance that is not settled in the interests of Tudor conservatism"[10] (McMillin, 1987, 59). However, it is possible to detect other political currents in the plays when we consider that Henry Neville owned copies of the banned tract *Leicester's Commonwealth* (*LC*; see Casson, 2010). Until his death in 1588 the Earl of Leicester had been Elizabeth I's favorite, and *LC* was a defamatory attack on his power and ambition. This tract, being published in 1584, predates the plays. Reference to King John is to be found in *LC:* "Arthur ... was declared by King Richard his uncle ... lawful heir apparent to the crown of England ... albeit after King Richard's death his other uncle John most tyrannously took both his kingdom and his life" (Peck, 160/*107*).

TR and *KJ* are about the dangers and damage done to the country when the wrong person inherits or usurps the crown: they therefore dramatize the forbidden topic of the succession, a core concern of *LC.* While fighting for John's right to succeed his brother, Richard I, Eleanor (the queen mother) reveals she has a will that expresses Richard's wishes for the succession. In both versions Arthur's mother Constance repudiates this testament, suggesting it is a forgery by Eleanor and not valid. We find just such an argument over Henry VIII's will in *LC.* One of the signatories of that disputed testament was none other than Sir Henry Neville (Neville's father). In his copy of *LC* Neville inserted a unique marginal annotation, "K: H: 8th s testam^{te}."

This reference to Henry VIII's will is in a discussion about foreign birth being one **bar** to succession. In *KJ* Eleanor says the will "**barres** the title of" Arthur (First Folio spelling, 2.1.192). In *TR* Elinor says the will "**barres** the way" (1.2.99). In *LC* the writers use the word "**bars**" in discussing the impediments to the succession of the Queen of Scots and her son, of which Henry VIII's will was one (Peck, 2006, 154/*103*) and in his own handwritten copy Neville spells the word with a double consonant: "**barrs**" (see above).

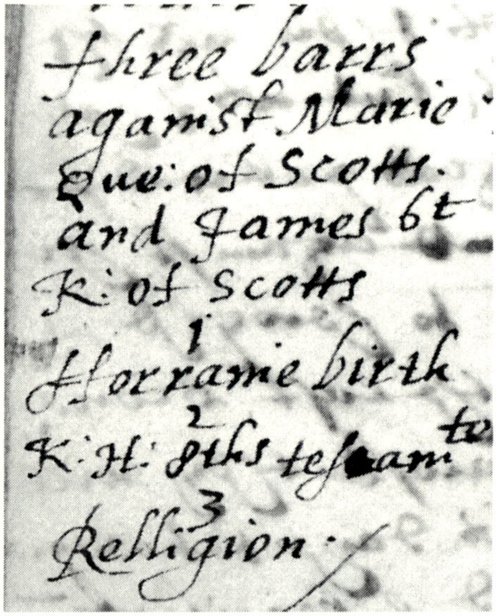
three barrs
against Marie
Que: of Scotts.
and James 6t
K: of Scotts
1
fforrame birth
2
K: H: 8ths testam^{te}
3
Religion.

Worsley MSS 47, 45V (by permission of the Eighth Earl of Yarborough and Lincolnshire Archives).

If history is being used as metaphor for the present in *TR,* John might stand in for Leicester and Arthur for young James of Scotland, whose "foreign birth" was a topic discussed in *LC.* Arthur's life is threatened by the tyrannical King John. In *LC* the threat to James' life is made explicit: "I think the youth of Scotland be of much more importance for their purpose to be made away, both for that he may have issue and is like in time to be of more ability for defense of his own inheritance, as also for that he being once dispatched his mother should soon ensue by one sleight or other" (Peck, 2006, 178/*118*).

Here, in 1584, the author of *LC* linked Arthur and James of Scotland and suggests Mary, Queen of Scots might also be eliminated. Sir Ralph Sadler and Sir Henry Neville (Neville's father) were given custody of Mary, Queen of Scots in 1584–5, the very period when *Leicester's Commonwealth* appeared. From April 1585 Sir Amias Paulet was appointed keeper of Mary, Queen of Scots. He refused Elizabeth's suggestion that he kill Mary. Such a monarch's request to a servant, to assassinate a rival claimant to the throne, troubles the consciences of Hubert[11] in *TR* and *KJ*. Paulet had sufficient conscience to refuse to gratify his sovereign. Only someone in Neville's position could have known about such a secret request from the queen to eliminate her rival (Casson, 2010, 131). As the threat of Leicester's usurping the throne ceased after his death in 1588, *TR* may have been written as early as 1587–8 (Casson, 2010, 20).

The Authorship of TR*: George Peele and Henry Neville as Co-Authors*

Some scholars have suggested that *TR* was authored by William Shakespeare. Charles Forker (2011) recently provided evidence that George Peele was the author. In his writings Peele showed he was vehemently anti–Catholic. Peele was a supporter of Essex from at least 1589, when he wrote a poem welcoming Essex back from Portugal (Vickers, 2004, 172). Not long before he died in 1596 Peele sent a presentation copy of *The Tale of Troy* to William Cecil, Lord Burghley, inviting his patronage (ODNB, 2004, s.v. "Barbour"). This suggests he had previously worked for the government. Indeed, Peele had written plays for Walsingham's theater company, the Queen's Men.

We have several reasons to suggest *TR* was in fact co-written by Peele and Neville, rather than by George Peele alone. Both men were at Oxford University 1577–78, so they may have met then. Both were supporters of the Earl of Essex, who was son-in-law to Walsingham. Neville had known Essex since 1583, when he had accompanied a party led by Walsingham to visit Scotland (James and Rubinstein, 2005, 234–5). In his poem *The Honour of the Garter* (1593) Peele wrote:

> Hail Windsore, where I sometimes tooke delight
> To hawke and hunt... [Vickers, 2004, 171].

Neville's estate at Billingbear was near Windsor and his father was the royal Windsor forester, a keen falconer, and he taught the queen to hunt deer (James and Rubinstein, 2005, 124). It is therefore possible that Peele was referring to a visit to the Windsor forest of which the Nevilles were guardians.

It was normal for one playwright to compose a plot structure and others to write the text. It is therefore possible that much of the plot of *TR,* including the invention of the Faulconbridge family, was Neville's creation. Sams stated that Shakespeare was a "master of structure before he was a master of language" (Forker, 2011, 7; Sams, 1995, 146). In confirmation of this hypothesis, Forker (2011, 8–9) noted two points:

1. Sampley (1936) implied "that Peele's loose or even incompetent habits in play construction would deny him authorship of a play such as *TR*."
2. Wells (1940, 222) asserted that Peele "was a dramatist of little distinction" who could hardly "have written so ... well constructed a play" as *TR*.

That Peele and Shakespeare co-wrote has been confirmed by their joint authorship of *Titus Andronicus* (Vickers, 2004, 148). This play was on stage in 1594 and so must have been written during 1589–93, most likely after *TR*. Shakespeare this time wrote most of the play. The date of Peele's reference to visiting Windsor (1593) would put him in Neville's neighborhood about the time of the composition of *Titus Andronicus.* It is possible that Neville served a playwriting apprenticeship with Peele and then out-grew him. If Peele had been the dominant partner in *TR* their roles were reversed in *Titus Andronicus.* Their co-authorship of *TR* would explain the attribution of the play to Shakespeare by Francis Meres in his list of plays in 1598, to "W. Sh." when it was printed in 1611 and "W. Shakespeare" in the 1622 quarto, all before *King John* finally appeared in the First Folio (1623). Perhaps the bard rewrote *TR* as *KJ* because he was freed by Peele's death, in 1596, to rewrite their early co-authored play to his own satisfaction.

The final version of *KJ* is a 17th century version of *TR,* possibly revised under pressure from the monarchy. Evidence for this can be seen in *King John:*

> But that your royal pleasure must be done,
> The act is **an ancient tale new told**,
> And in the last repeating **troublesome** [4.2.17].

King John is the "**ancient tale**" of *The **Troublesome** Reign,* "**new told**."

In both versions of the play, the fictional character Philip Faulconbridge plays a central and heroic part. In the *TR* scene about Philip's parentage, the brothers are brought before King John, by the Earl of Salisbury, the bastard son of Henry II. Perhaps only Neville, the bastard writer with a family connection to the Earldom of Salisbury, could enjoy the secret irony of a bastard introducing a bastard to the king (Casson, 2010, 139). This bastard theme is further underlined with a classical reference. When Philip begs his mother to tell him his natural father's identity, he refers to Phaeton, a figure from Greek mythology. Philip describes himself as, "Phaeton, Mistrusting silly Merop for his sire" (part 1, 1.342). Thus, doubting Sir Robert Fauconbridge was his father, Philip is suggesting that he is to Richard the Lionheart what Phaeton was to the Sun-god. In his other works, George Peele never referred to Phaeton or Merop. This unusual motif about illegitimate birth is mentioned in *The Two Gentlemen of Verona* when the Duke says, "Phaeton, for thou art Merops' son" (3.1.153). Shakespeare mentioned Phaeton five times in canonical works, all in the early period (1590–96). This thematic preoccupation, and associated myth, may therefore be considered a signature motif of the bard. The Phaeton sonnet, published the same year as *TR* in John Florio's *Second Fruits,* can be seen as pointing to Neville's identity as the bard. Casson (2009, 15–45) suggested that Phaeton was the nom de plume he chose before he decided on the pseudonym William Shakespeare.

The Vocabulary in the Plays, Leicester's Commonwealth *and Neville's Notes and Letters*

In *TR,* Lady Fauconbridge pleads with Philip:

> Upbraid me rather with the Roman Dame
> That shed her blood to wash away her shame [part 1, 1.406].

This is a reference to the Ovid/Livy story of Lucrece, who was raped by a son of the ruling royal Tarquin family in Rome, and Lucrece's subsequent suicide, which led to a revolution and the founding of the Roman republic. In *Leicester's Commonwealth* there is an implicit reference to the aftermath of the rape of Lucrece. In complaining about Leicester's intolerable sexual appetite "upon men's wives" the writers refer back to how in previous times, "offences ... were extremely punished in princes themselves, and that not only in the person delinquent alone, but also by **extirpation of the whole family** for his sake, as appeareth in the example **of the Tarquinians** among the Romans" (Peck, 87/*61*[12]). In *TR* Essex plans "to **roote** and **cleane**[13] **extirpate** tirant John" (2.3.42). The underlying political meaning of Shakespeare's poem *The Rape of Lucrece* is revealed in the final section of the opening argument:

> They all vowed to **root out the whole** hated **family** of **the Tarquins**; and bearing the dead body to Rome, Brutus acquainted the people with the doer and manner of the vile deed, with a bitter invective against the tyranny of the king: wherewith the people were so moved, that with one consent and a general acclamation the Tarquins were all exiled, and the state government changed from kings to consuls.

In a letter dated November 19, 1599, Neville wrote the words, "**cutt off the Roote** and Foundation of all true Friendship" (Sawyer, 1725, vol. 1, 130). Neville, a forester, knew about trees. Casson (2010) has shown how Neville's notes and vocabulary in his annotated copy of *Leicester's Commonwealth,* and his letters, match the vocabulary of *KJ* and *TR*. When he later revised *TR* as *KJ* Shakespeare cut this reference to Lucrece but simultaneously revealed the political significance of the story by having the King of France accuse King John of committing "a rape upon the maiden virtue of the crown" (2.1.97). (See Chapter 9 for further exploration of the Lucrece theme and hidden Neville connections.)

While both Peele and Neville supported Essex, it is undoubtedly Neville who was closest to the earl and paid a very high price for his political involvement. During his subsequent imprisonment, Neville made notes on historical documents kept in the Tower of London. In his 1602 Tower notebook, now preserved as Worsley MSS 40 in the Lincoln archives, he noted, "Knig Joh. magnacart" (folio 210 verso). In Neville's copy of the 1610 *A Catalogue of Honor,* the first annotation in the book is about the location of King John's tomb. These notes show Neville continued to be interested in this king's reign.

The Bastard's Commodity Speech

King John is renowned for the 38-line Bastard's speech about "commodity" at the end of act 2 (2.1.561–598). There are many possible meanings to Shakespeare's repeated use of the word "commodity," and no doubt many were intended by the bard, as suggested by this:

> This bawd, this broker, this all-changing word,
> Clapp'd on the outward eye of fickle **France** [2.1.582].

Neville as the English ambassador to France wrote to the secretary of state, Robert Cecil, referring to commodities in a letter dated June 21, 1599, from Paris:

> In the mean tyme, beseeching your Honor I may be informed what *Customes* and *Impositions* have bin raised upon *Forreigne Marchants* in *England;* and namely upon the *Frenche,* since in the Yeare 1572: Or what Restraints have bin made for bringing thither **the Commodities** of *this Countrey,* which will be materiall for me to know, when I shall Treat with the Counsail heere [italics in the original; additional emphasis ours; Sawyer, 1725, vol. 1, 51].

In September the same year Neville wrote further about "*Greevances* and *Impositions* raised upon our **Commodities**" (italics in the original; additional emphasis ours; Sawyer, 1725, vol. 1, 112). Like other contemporary authors, Shakespeare used the word "commodity" in the sense of "advantage," "expediency" and "profit," and antithetical to virtue as suggested in Richard Edwards' *Damon and Pithias* (1571)—"For virtue's sake only, they would honor friendship and not for commodity" (Edwards and Farmer, 1906, 18; Johnson and Stevens, 1788, 37). But historians have also indicated that the moral problems relating to personal "commodity" during Elizabethan times, as exemplified by the allusions to prostitution in the Bastard's speech, were being challenged by a more positive view of capitalist ideology, later expounded upon by early Jacobean writers (Wrightson, 1986). This conflict is suggested in the Bastard's speech, when he says:

> Well, whiles I am a beggar, I will rail
> And say there is no sin but to be rich;
> And being rich, my virtue then shall be
> To say there is no vice but beggary [*KJ*, 2.1.593].

The Commodity speech does not feature in the early version of the play (*TR*). Rather, it is only in the First Folio version of *King John.* This might again suggest the play was further revised after the Essex uprising; i.e., after 1601. Henry Neville further raised concerns over commodity trading with France, in another letter to Cecil dated February 19, 1601 (Casson, 2010, 265). Henry Neville's personal wealth and status, which enabled him to make informed commentary, were due less to his noble Neville name and more to his extremely wealthy Gresham inheritance from his mother's family, who were involved in the trading of English-French commodities, including cannon, which feature so much in *King John.* Henry Neville may also have been aware that when his great-grandfather, Sir Richard Gresham, died in 1549, an anonymous poet published a poem denouncing this banker/usurer for selling his honor for profit (Childs, 2006).

As shown in this play about the early Plantagenet period of King John's reign, the Bastard had the choice of either the noble title of Richard Plantagenet or the wealth arising from land ownership. But rather anachronistically, he also seems to acknowledge the third way to power, i.e., the emerging capitalist class of Elizabethan times, who acquired "advantage, this vile-drawing bias," from commodities. Neville thus highlighted his ambivalence about his own legacy of both Plantagenet royalty on his paternal Neville side (although as a bastard), and the nouveau riche mercantile class (albeit "vile") on his maternal Gresham side. Goddard suggested, "I cannot escape the conviction that those words (about Commodity) come as directly from Shakespeare's own heart, as from the Bastard's" (Goddard, 1951, vol. 1, 143).

The Blot Image Cluster

A number of scholars have identified a blot image cluster in expressing shame in Shakespeare's works. This image cluster places the word "**blot**" in relation to "heaven/sky," "night," "moon," "constancy/inconstant," "disguise," "winter/coldness/frost," "sovereign," "eye," "sun" and "cheeks" (face/complexion) (Muir, 1960, 22). The words "**stain**," "**spot**" and "**blemish**" are also used with these images. The imagery contrasts the wish to hide the shame of a blot/stain/disgrace (by disguise, darkness, night or cloud) and the revealing of a shamed face to the eye of day (= sun = sovereign); the resulting blush is also seen as sunburn (Casson, 2010, 142; 2009, 198). Professor Kenneth Muir, in *Shakespeare as Collaborator* (1960), remarked: "The presence of image clusters is one of the strongest arguments for Shakespeare's authorship." Furthermore, "as no two poets employ the same image clusters, therefore work of doubtful provenance can be assigned to a poet with certainty if it contains clusters, or exhibits principles of cluster formation, characteristic of writings known to be authentic" (Armstrong, 1979, 203, 198).

Elements of this cluster are to be found in both *TR* and *KJ* specifically connected with questions of illegitimacy (and therefore shame). When, in *TR,* the Bastard Philip confronts his mother about his paternity, he says, "The son that **blotteth** you with wedlock's breach" (1.1.356). Within the same speech he uses the words "face" and "heaven's"; in this scene we also have "shame," "concealing," "blush," "shroud," and two references to the sun's charioteer, Phaeton. Later Constance, talking to Arthur about his birthright, refers to the "sky" before "black-spotted," "heavens" and "the colour flies thy face." Philip Fauconbridge, speaking of the shame, "the ignominious scandal" of John's retreat in battle, uses the words "night," "shadowed," "sable curtains," "eye." In three adjacent lines we find "shadow," "sovereign" and "stain," referring to Arthur's legitimate succession. John at his second coronation uses the words "stain," "heavens," "sunshine," "storm," "constancy," and "king." Later he refers to the "welkin" (= sky), "cloud," "heaven," "sun" and "moon." While some of these might be considered commonplaces, it is their occurrence together in a cascade of references that suggest the blot cluster is already emerging in the poet's vocabulary. It also confirms our assertion that *TR* was at least partly by the bard.

In *KJ* there are more birth blots:

> ELEANOR: There's a good mother, boy, that **blots** thy father.
> CONSTANCE: There's a good grandam, boy, that would **blot** thee [2.1.132].

Both King Philip and Constance use the words "blots" and "stains," in relation to paternity (2.1.114; 2.2.43). Constance (whose very name echoes the constancy/inconstant of the cluster) says:

> Now **shame** upon you, whether she does or no!
> His grandam's wrongs, and not his mother's **shames**,
> Draws those **heaven**-moving pearls from his poor **eyes**,
> Which **heaven** shall take in nature of a fee [2.1.167].

Later (2.2.45 onwards) Constance, talking with Arthur about his legitimate claim to the throne, uses the words "blots," "stains," "eye-offending marks," "swart," "foul moles," and "sovereignty."

Following the shameful death of Arthur, John asks a pale messenger:

> A fearful **eye** thou hast: where is that blood
> That I have seen inhabit in those **cheeks**?
> So foul a **sky** clears not without a **storm** [4.2.106].

He remonstrates with Hubert for not questioning his suggestion that Arthur be killed:

> Hadst thou but shook thy head or made a pause
> When I spake **darkly** what I purposed,
> Or turn'd an **eye** of doubt upon my **face**,
> As bid me tell my tale in express words,
> Deep **shame** had struck me dumb, made me break off [4.2.231].

In the discussion between Philip and his mother about his paternity we find "heaven," "light," "night": these are fewer elements than are found in the equivalent scene in *TR*, but in *KJ* the scene is much shorter. The word "shame" occurs more often in *KJ* than any other Shakespeare play (eighteen times, three more than in *TR*), and many of these refer to illegitimacy. This makes sense when we realize that the illegitimate Neville was the writer.

Elements of this cluster are to be found in two of Neville's letters written in 1602 when, deeply shamed, he wrote to Cecil from his prison in the Tower. On May 11, 1602, Neville wrote:

> My state is wholly decayed and my health of late much impaired. There is little left but my life, which if it please God and her Majesty I am willing to preserve, chiefly in hope to **wipe** and **wear out** this **blemish** and **blot** that lies now upon me in **her eye**" [Salisbury, 1906, 151].

Here we have "blemish," "blot," and the queen's "eye." "Blemish," "blot" and "wipe" occur together in *The Rape of Lucrece.* In *King John* we find "wear out" (3.1.36) and "wipe" (5.2.45). Two months later on July 31, 1602, Neville also wrote:

> And yf there be no other means to **wipe away** this **blot** wherewith I am **soiled** yet yt is possible, that yf I were at liberty, I might shed so much of my bloud in som place where she hath occasion to use men as might serve for a laver for the crime which hath made me so ugly in **her eye**. [Salisbury, 1906, 268].

Here again we have "blot" and the queen's "eye." In two plays of this period the word "soil'd" appears. In *Hamlet* (written 1600–1601) Polonius uses the words "soil'd" and "crimes" within three lines (2.1.41–44). Furthermore, Hamlet says, "I'll **wipe away** all trivial fond records." The words "liberty," "occasion," "serve," "ugly" and "crimes" are also in the play. In *Troilus and Cressida,* which dates from 1602, the very year of these letters, the words "soil'd," "occasion," "serve" and "ugly" are used. Having searched these words in the Manchester University Library LION (Literature Online) and EEBO (Early English Books Online) databases, we can confirm that while a number of writers during the period 1599–1604 associate "blot" with shame, none use the words "blot" or "blemish" in association with the queen's eye. As Neville was born illegitimate himself, this image cluster takes on a powerful resonance.

Conclusion

The contemporary political context of the play, along with an Earl of Essex being edited out of scenes; the protestant themes as exemplified by the two unhistorical characters in the first scene, Philip the Bastard Faulconbridge and the Huguenot, Chatillon; the myth of Phaeton; and the blot image cluster are all pointers to Henry Neville's authorship. In addition, Henry Neville had early access to the central source document of the play, the second edition of Holinshed's *Chronicles,* released in 1587, edited by his father-in-law. In particular, the aughor invented "Shakespeare's first truly 'natural' character" (Bloom 1999, 52), who speaks "directly from Shakespeare's heart" (Goddard 1951, 143), and called him the Bastard of Faulconbridge. He is an amalgam of the 13th century Hugh Neville, the 15th century Thomas Neville, also called the Bastard of Faulconbridge, and Philip, the bastard son of Richard the Lionheart. The author is thus revealed as the 16th century bastard, Sir Henry Neville. Furthermore, Neville was distantly related to King John through his grandmother, Eleanor Windsor.[14] A list of plays made in 1669 attributed Shakespeare's *King John* to Thomas Killigrew, a relative of Henry Neville (Braunmuller, 1989, 81).

Chapter 2

Edward III
(1327–1377)

Truth hath pulled the vizard from his face.—*Edward III* (1.1.77)

The Play

First published anonymously as *The Raigne*[1] *of King Edward the Third*, in 1596, the play had been entered the previous December on the Stationers' Register. It was written during the years 1589 to 1594. A reference to Turkey may be to a war that broke out in June 1593; references to the stories of Hero and Leander (Marlowe died in 1593) and Lucrece (the poem was published in 1594) suggest a date after 1593 for the finished text (Prior, 1993, 259, 260). Scholars have noted an uneven quality to the two halves of *Edward III*, so it may have been written over this whole period of time. As it was not included in the First Folio, it languished for centuries outside the canon, finally being accepted as being wholly or mostly by Shakespeare in the 1990s. Publication may have been impossible in the reign of James I because of its anti–Scottish humor. The play falls into the period of the late 1580s to early 1590s, when the first works by the bard were printed anonymously: the earliest plays to be acknowledged on their title pages as by Shakespeare were not published until 1598.

Given that the play was anonymous for so many years, it is of special interest that it contains a couplet spoken by Warwick (who, as we shall see below, has Neville connections) referring to a poet and a spear[2]:

> The poets write that great Achilles' spear
> Could heal the wound it made [2.1.393].

The fact that a fictional figure, with hidden connections to the Neville family, speaks of a poet and a spear is suggestive of a link between the writer Shakespeare and a hidden Neville.

Neville and Edward III

Edward III does have Neville connections: Henry Neville was descended from John of Gaunt, son of Edward III. Edward III was Neville's great, great, great, great, great, great-grandfather (James, 2008, 352). In his copy of *Leicester's Commonwealth,* dated circa 1585, Neville made a particular note of "John of Gaunt Duke of Lanc" and "the yssue of K: Edw 3" and made a list of the sons of Edward III (Worsley MSS 47; Casson, 2010, 214–5). Just such a list is in *Henry VI* part 2 (see Chapter 6).

In act 5, scene 1, of *Edward III,* Copland presents the captured Scottish King David to Edward. David had been defeated at the battle of **Neville's Cross** in 1346 (Melchiori, 1998, 58). Neville traveled through Northumberland in 1583 on the way to Scotland and so would have known the landscape where the rough Scottish invaders of act 1, scene 2, raided castles and threatened the inhabitants. Richard Eedes reported meeting Neville in Durham in his *Iter Boreale* (James and Rubinstein, 2005, 83). The battlefield was immediately to the west of the city. Neville could therefore have seen the cross that commemorated the battle. He would also have had opportunity to observe the Scots and catch their ways of speaking, as parodied in the play.

Three characters in the play, Salisbury, Montague and Warwick, have titles that the Neville family eventually held. In the play the Earl of Warwick is made warden of the north (2.2.201). This is not historically accurate. The real title holder was Ralph Neville,[3] who set up the cross to commemorate the victory over the Scots (Melchiori, 1998, 58, 104, 138). In the play Henry Percy reports to the king in Calais, "From her highness, and the lord vicegerent, I bring this happy tidings of success" (4.2.38–9). As Melchiori (1998, 58; 138) noted, the vicegerent was Ralph Neville (Froissart and Berners, 1910, 5).[4]

History as Metaphor: Henry Carey, First Baron Hunsdon, the Lord Chamberlain and His Family

Prior (1993, 261) provided detailed evidence showing that *Edward III* was based on the copy of Froissart's *Chronicle* personally annotated by Henry Carey, the Lord Chamberlain. In the play the dramatist reminded Carey of "his military experience on the Scottish border, his part in the Armada year, his pride in his sons, and his love of Froissart" (one of the main sources for the play). This evidence offers further proof that the play was not merely a history but had contemporary meanings, and was "a vehicle for topical reference" (Prior, 1993, 253). By praising Carey's achievements, the playwright was perhaps sheltering his play, with its multilayered messages, under the Lord Chamberlain's protection.

Henry Neville shared some deeply personal characteristics with the Lord Chamberlain. Both had family members beheaded by Henry VIII: Neville's grandfather Edward Neville and Edward's sister and nephew were beheaded; the Lord Chamberlain lost two aunts and an uncle. They both also lived with the secret stigma of illegitimacy. In Carey's own lifetime there were rumors he had been born as a result of his mother, Mary Boleyn, being Henry VIII's mistress. Neville was born before his father was married to his mother. Carey and Neville were related by marriage.[5] Henry Carey as Lord Chamberlain was patron of the theater company the Lord Chamberlain's Men, who performed Shakespeare's plays during 1594–96, the very years when *Edward III* was written and published. Furthermore, there is evidence that Neville's father knew Henry Carey, because he wrote to Lord Burghley to be his friend in a contest with the Lord Chamberlain on December 31, 1590.[6]

Henry Neville's family home was at Billingbear, Berkshire. Ten miles from Billingbear is Bisham Abbey. This was the residence of Neville's wife's aunt, Elizabeth Hoby, née Cooke (1527–1609: see Chapter 4). Elizabeth's husband, Sir Thomas Hoby, was the translator of Castiglione's *Courtier,* a book which influenced Shakespeare. In his diary account of his Marian exile in Italy in 1554, Sir Thomas Hoby recorded—"*we arrived in Padua the 23rd of the month of August, where we met with Sir Thomas Wroth, Sir John Cheke, Sir Henry Neville* [father of Henry Neville (1562–1615)], ... *and diverse others. And shortly after here arrived Sir Anthony Cooke* [future father-in-law to Thomas Hoby and grandfather to the wife of Henry Neville (1562–1615)]" (Powell, 1902, 116[7]).

Thomas Hoby's first son, Edward, married Margaret Carey (1567–1605), daughter of the Lord Chamberlain, Henry Carey. Their first daughter, Elizabeth (born 1562), may have been named after her godmother, Elizabeth Gresham, who was pregnant at about the same time with her son, Henry Neville (1562–1615). The godmother of their second daughter, Anne, born in 1564, was Henry Neville's mother-in-law, Catherine Cooke (c.1530–83) (Powell, 1902, 128–130). These relationships are proof that Neville knew the Hobys and would therefore have been a visitor to Bisham.

The Bisham Abbey Tombs

At Bisham there were the tombs of Richard Neville, the sixteenth Earl of Warwick (1428–71) and his brother, John Neville, the first Marquess of Montague (1431–71). The first Earl and Countess of Salisbury, William Montague, 1301–44, and Catherine Montague, née Grandison, 1304–49, were also buried there. This earl and his countess appear in *Edward III.* Furthermore, Edward III himself lived at Bisham briefly during his infancy and later laid the foundation stone for William Montague's priory there (Mortimer, 2008, 26, 213, 286).[8]

The Hidden Neville Behind the Countess of Salisbury

In the play, the Countess of Salisbury is a powerful character who resists the Scottish siege of her castle of Roxburgh and also the "unnatural siege" (2.1.413) of King Edward III's forceful amorous advances. She speaks of a cousin named Montague, and he calls her aunt. In the play Sir William Montague is the captain of Roxburgh castle, which was besieged by the Scots. He escaped to seek Edward III's help in lifting the siege (1.1.123). His uncle, the countess's husband, also called William Montacute[9] (1301–1344), was away campaigning in France. He had accompanied Edward III in repelling an earlier Scottish invasion in 1327. He was created Earl of Salisbury in 1337 (Melchiori, 1998, 57). An annotation in *A Catalogue of Honor* proves Neville was aware of this man:

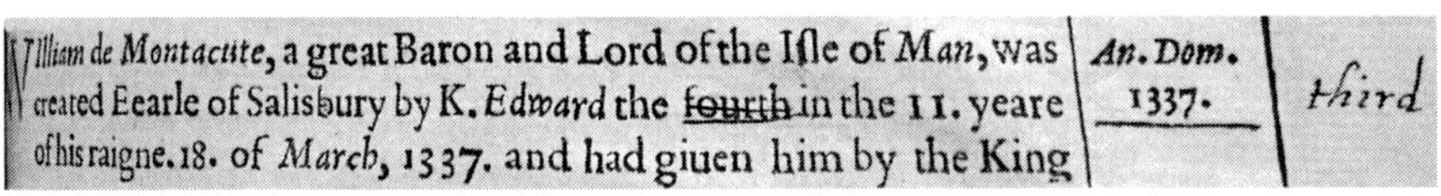
William de *Montacute*, a great Baron and Lord of the Isle of *Man*, was created Earle of Salisbury by K. *Edward* the ~~fourth~~ in the 11. yeare of his raigne. 18. of *March*, 1337. and had giuen him by the King | *An. Dom.* 1337. | third

***A Catalogue of Honor*, 1610 (private collection).**

Neville corrected page 1041, identifying Edward III (not Edward IV as in the text) as the king who honored William de Montacute as the Earl of Salisbury. William married Catherine, daughter of William first Baron Grandisson. Legend holds that Edward III was in love with her, and the Order of the Garter derives its name from an incident when the king picked up her dropped garter. The original source for the Countess of Salisbury story was Jean Le Bel's *Vrayes Chroniques*, which accused Edward of the violent rape of the countess (Melchiori, 1998, 23, 186). In act 2 of the play, Edward III threatens to rape the countess (2.1.343–4, 413, 2.2.128–132). In the play her husband, the Earl of Salisbury, narrowly escapes being executed by the French king. In the final scene, he reports to the English king and queen the dishonorable behavior of the French king, in the longest speech in the play (5.1.109). Edward III might well be relieved when he realizes that the earl is unaware of his attempted seduction. The personal life of the monarch was a national and an international issue. In 1600 Neville, as ambassador, reported on the French king's love life in his diplomatic dispatches.

The earldom of Salisbury only became a Neville title in 1429, when Richard Neville married Alice Montague, daughter of Thomas Montague the fourth Earl and granddaughter of Geoffrey Chaucer. The eldest son of Alice Montague and Richard Neville was the famous Richard Neville the Kingmaker, better known as the Earl of Warwick. The earldom of Warwick became a Neville title when Anne Beauchamp, daughter and heiress of Richard Beauchamp, married Richard Neville.[10] Their daughter was Anne Neville, who appears on stage in *Richard III.* Shakespeare, then, had chosen a story of a countess who had links to Lord Hunsdon, the Earl of Southampton (through the Montagues[11]) and the Nevilles.

Melchiori (1998, 184) noted, "The Italian Matteo Bandello invented a father for her (the Countess) and gave him an important role in the story. He called him 'Ricciardo conte di Varuccio'"; this refers to the historical Richard Neville, Earl of Warwick, although the translator, William Painter, and playwright, William Shakespeare, disguised his identity by dropping his first name." This character features in *Henry VI* parts 2 and 3 and *Richard III.* Salisbury's long speech in act 5 of *Edward III* describes Prince Edward at the battle of Poitiers "as like a bear fast chained unto a stake" (5.1.143). This was the heraldic symbol of Richard Neville, Earl of Warwick (*Henry VI* part 2, 5.1.203).[12]

Edward III was written at the same time or just after Shakespeare wrote *The Rape of Lucrece.* James (2011, 85) revealed that Edward IV attempted to rape Anne Neville, the daughter of the Earl of Warwick, Richard Neville, and this may have motivated Neville's interest in the politics of rape (see Chapters 6 and 9). This would also explain Neville's interest in the countess: she was a woman who, unlike Lucrece, was able to say "No!" to a tyrant and survive. The king makes an explicit reference to Lucrece that clearly refers to poets writing her story:

> Arise, true English Lady, whom our Isle
> May better boast of than ever Roman might
> Of her, whose ransacked treasury hath taskt
> The vain endeavour of so many pens [2.2.193].

When we consider history as metaphor we can see that Shakespeare had chosen the story of the countess for a complex of political and family reasons, as is evident in the images and historical precedents that have Neville connections.

Anne Neville's sister, Isabelle Neville, married George, Duke of Clarence.[13] Isabelle's daughter, Margaret Pole, née Plantagenet (1473–1541), lived into Tudor times. Cecily Neville was her paternal grandmother. She was a widow for the last thirty-six years of her life but was one of the few women to carry the title of Countess of Salisbury in her own right. Just as her grandfather Richard Neville was the sixteenth Earl of Warwick, so also her brother became the seventeenth Earl of Warwick. Her son, Henry Pole, was Lord Montague/Montacute. Margaret appears in *Richard III* as a "girl" (2.2.63: see Chapter 7). The countess, her son Henry Pole, his wife, Jane, née Neville, their son Henry and Jane's brother Edward Neville, were all beheaded in a purge of people who disapproved of King Henry VIII's behavior towards his wives and children. The king was particularly incensed by the public condemnation from the countess's other son, Cardinal Reginald Pole. However, the assassination squads sent to the continent where Reginald lived failed. Reginald Pole's family was eliminated as revenge.

In his copy of *Leicester's Commonwealth* Neville made a special note of these executions:

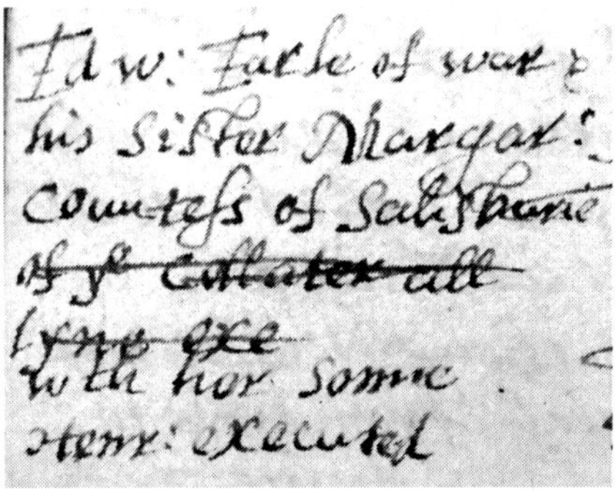

Worsley MSS 47, 57V (by permission of the Eighth Earl of Yarborough and Lincolnshire Archives).

The unique[14] marginal annotation states: "Edw: Earle of war his sister Margar: countess of Salisburie of ye collaterall lyne exe[15] with her sonne Henr: executed." Earlier in this document Neville had also made other unique annotations drawing attention to the countess (shown on next page).

The text of the marginal annotation reads: "The yssue of the Du. of Clarence. Ed: Ea: of Warrwick & Marga: countess of Sallisburie the yssue of Mar: Count: of Salisb: Cardin: Poole & Henr: Poole." Dwight Peck, who made a major study of *Leicester's Commonwealth,* found no substantial annotations or interpolations concerning the Countess of Salisbury in any of the fifty-eight other manuscript versions of *Leicester's Commonwealth.* Neville continued to be interested

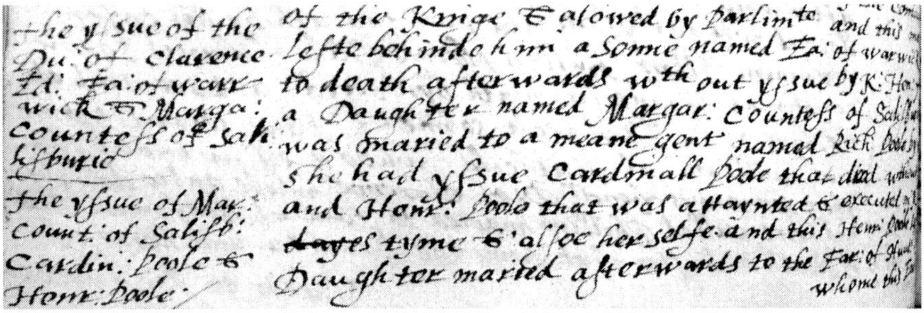
the yssue of the Du: of clarence Ed: Ea: of warwick & Marga: Countess of Salisburie
the yssue of Mar: count. of Salisb: Cardin: Poole & Hen: Poole
of the Kinge & alowed by Parlimt and this
lefte behinde him a Sonne named Ed: of warw
to death afterwards wth out yssue by K. Hen
a Daughter named Margar: Countess of Sal
was maried to a meane gent named Rich Poole
she had yssue Cardinall Poole that died
and Hen: Poole that was attaynted & executed
dayes tyme & alsoe her selfe and this Hen: Poole
Daughter maried afterwards to the Ea: of Hunt
whome this

Worsley MSS 47, 43V (by permission of the Eighth Earl of Yarborough and Lincolnshire Archives).

in the countess, as his corrections to *A Catalogue of Honor,* 1610, demonstrate:

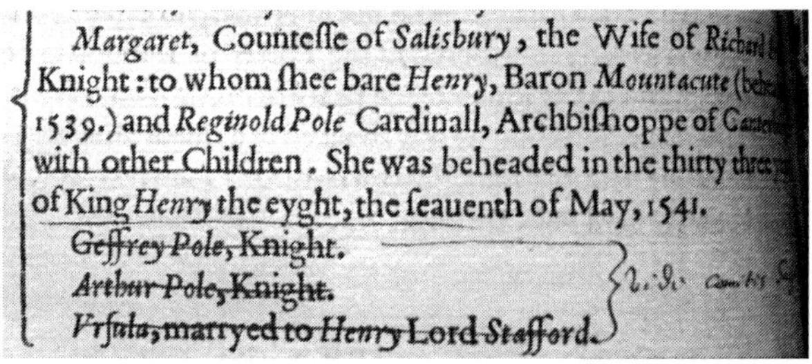
Margaret, Counteſſe of *Salisbury*, the Wife of Richard
Knight: to whom ſhee bare *Henry*, Baron *Mountacute* (behe
1539.) and *Reginold Pole* Cardinall, Archbiſhoppe of Cant
with other Children. She was beheaded in the thirty three
of King *Henry* the eyght, the ſeauenth of May, 1541.
~~Geffrey Pole, Knight.~~
~~Arthur Pole, Knight.~~
~~Vrſula, marryed to Henry Lord Stafford.~~

***A Catalogue of Honor* 1610, 340 (private collection).**

As the Countess of Salisbury, Margaret Pole (1473–1541), was beheaded for treason, she was given no burial place, but "the Mansion House at Bisham had been the residence of Margaret, Countess of Salisbury, whose arms, impaled with those of her husband Sir Richard Pole, are still to be seen there in the council-chamber window" (Powell, 1902, 12). It is unsurprising that Henry Neville, living near Bisham, would identify this 16th century Countess of Salisbury with the 14th century Countess of Salisbury of the play.

Henry Hastings, great-grandson of this 16th century Countess of Salisbury, had a claim to the throne, which was being urged by Robert Dudley, Earl of Leicester, according to *Leicester's Commonwealth.* In the same passage Neville's father is depicted having a conversation with Sir Thomas Leighton about what office Sir Henry Neville might expect if Leicester and Hastings gained power on the queen's demise (Peck, 2006, *86*). The Neville family's involvement in covert high politics illuminates the meanings inherent in the play *Edward III.* The above annotations show that before and after *Edward III* was written, Henry Neville was aware of and interested in this countess (see Casson, 2010, 215, 225).

Further Evidence for Margaret Pole as the Model for the Countess

The Countess of Salisbury, Margaret Pole,[16] was esteemed by King Henry VIII in 1515 as "the saintliest woman of England," and he was "greatly delighted to honor" her. This he did in 1522, by appointing her the governess of his only legitimate child, Princess Mary. (This was the same year the king took Mary Carey, née Boleyn, as a mistress.) The countess's son, Reginald Pole, was a man of great learning, whose friends included Thomas More, Desiderius Erasmus and Ludovicus Vives. Henry VIII and his Queen Catherine (of Aragon) appointed Ludovicus Vives as Princess Mary's tutor in 1524. Ludovicus had already dedicated his book *Commentaries on St Augustine's Civitas Dei* to Henry VIII in 1522.

Ludovicus bears a strong resemblance to Edward III's secretary, Lodowick, in the play. As described in the play, he is "well-read in poetry" and he could "turn his ink into gold." In 1524, his first year in England, Ludovicus Vives published his *Introduction to Wisdom, The Soul's Escort,* and *The Education of a Christian Woman.* The last two were dedicated to Princess Mary and Queen Catherine, respectively. His *Education of a Christian Woman* was radical for its time in recommending an extensive education and reading list for women. But most notable for us is that Ludovicus "expresses his utter revulsion to the maiden's reading of romances, and singing of vulgar songs, literature which trespassed too often beyond the bounds of modesty" (Watson, 1912, 23). In the play Lodowick is ironically commissioned by the king to compose "love-lays" (2.1.97), but Edward is disappointed to discover his secretary is a dismal failure. In 1528, Ludovicus was imprisoned in the Tower for six weeks for representing Princess Mary's interests. Henry VIII was starting proceedings to divorce his wife and make Princess Mary a bastard child. Ludovicus was then expelled from England.

The association of this countess with both Warwick and Lodowick strongly suggests that acts 1 and 2 were inspired by Margaret Pole as Countess of Salisbury and Henry VIII as Edward III. While it is not suggested that Henry necessarily attempted to seduce Margaret Pole, it is likely that she represented a virtuous ideal who would have used the strategy suggested in act 2 to resist such a lustful, cruel and corrupt king, whereas other women had been forced to accommodate his desires. The identification of Edward III with Henry VIII is further suggested by the countess's statement that her body is her soul's abbey (2.1.235). Henry VIII desecrated many abbeys. (For further insights into the hidden use of the history of *Edward III* as a metaphor for contemporary and recent history in relation to Henry Carey and his mother, Mary Bullen, see Appendix B.)

While Henry Neville would have heard his father's account of his grandfather's troubles with King Henry VIII, and of his execution, it is also known that he stayed with the Protestant cleric Andreas Dudith in Hungary, during his Grand Tour from 1578 to 1582. In 1581 Dudith wrote a letter in which he praised Henry Neville and Robert Sidney as "nobiles & doctrina ac moribus praestantes adolescents" (Feingold, 1984, 127) which translates as "fine, exceptionally well taught and well mannered young men." This visit to Dudith predated the writing of the play. Dudith had been secretary to Reginald Pole when he was archbishop of Canterbury, and he wrote a biography of Reginald Pole. It is possible that they talked about the purge that wiped out most of Pole's family, as well as Henry Neville's grandfather, Edward Neville. Edward "became close to Henry Pole, Lord Montagu (his brother-in-law) and was accused of helping Reginald Pole." Before Edward was executed, he was "defended by [Reginald] Pole" (Mayer and Walters, 2008, 382).

Cannon and Other Imagery

The first scene of act 3 describes a naval cannonade. Edward III did develop the use of cannon on land (Mortimer, 2008, 238, 287), but the earliest use of cannon on warships was during King Henry VIII's reign in the 16th century, not in the 14th century. There were no such "iron-hearted navies" (3.1.144) in Edward III's reign. The description in act 3 of the naval battle of Sluys is anachronistic. The reference to the warship *The Nonpareille*, which fought the Spanish Armada, and use of the word "armado" date the creation of this play to after 1588. The sound of "echoing cannon shot" (3.1.123) is further described:

> the hideous noise was such,
> As each to other seemed deaf and dumb [3.1.159].

The word "deafening" was coined by Shakespeare (McQuain and Malless, 1998, 42). The plays in which "deafening" occurs (*Pericles* and *A Winter's Tale*) were written after Neville complained of deafness in 1600. "Deafing" occurs in *Henry IV* part 2 and *The Two Noble Kinsmen*. At the time *Edward III* was written, Neville was a manufacturer of cannon and so would have known about the roar of cannon and may also have been deafened by it.

The supply of cannon and gunpowder was overseen by the Ordnance[17]

Office at the Tower of London. William Painter (1525–1594) became clerk of ordnance in 1561. In 1593–1594 (the very years *Edward III* was written) Painter was accused of fraudulent accounting at the Tower of London.[18] He was more than just a clerk. He translated many Italian novellas into English, providing the source for several of Shakespeare's plays, such as *Romeo and Juliet, Timon of Athens* and *All's Well That Ends Well*, and the poem *The Rape of Lucrece.* Painter's translation of Bandello's *Countess of Salisbury* is also a source for acts 1 and 2 of *Edward III.* As a manufacturer of cannon Neville had dealings with the Ordnance Office from 1583, so he was in a position to have known Painter.

The play contains imagery of falconry, forestry and the law: Neville's father was a keen falconer and a forester: indeed Neville took over his role as royal forester. From 1583 Neville had been a justice of the peace involved in legal cases. There are also examples of the blot cluster in the play, elements of which Neville used in two letters during his imprisonment in 1602 (see Chapter 1).

Neville and the Sources for Edward III

There are three major sources for the play: Holinshed, Painter and Froissart. We have already seen that there are possible Neville connections with all three of these (see Chapter 1 for Holinshed). Among the books from Neville's Billingbear library is a copy of Froissart in Latin, and there is one marginal annotation on page 45 in the section on Edward III, showing it had been read. We also noted above that Neville listed Edward III's descendants in his copy of *Leicester's Commonwealth.* Furthermore, in that document he specifically made an annotation concerning the Salic Law, which blocked inheritance through the female line in France, and this is obliquely referred to in the opening scene of the play (Worsley MSS 47, 39; Casson, 2010, 37). This law is also referred to by the annotator of a volume of pamphlets about French politics dated 1592, which has been identified as a possible source for *Edward III* (*The Contre-Guyse* 13V, Bodleian Library, Oxford, 4° L. 90. Art; Casson, 2010, 181). A passage about the Salic Law was also underlined in the annotated Hall's *Chronicles*, which James and Rubinstein (2005, 233) showed was once part of a library that can be traced to Neville's daughter (see Chapter 5).

The king, inviting Lodovick to compose seductive love poetry, says:

> if thou be a poet move thou so
> And be enriched by the sovereign's love

For if the touch of sweet concordant strings
Could force attendance in the ears of hell [2.1.425].

The ears of hell may either be Pluto or Cerberus, a three-headed dog, both of whom Orpheus lulled to sleep. In *The Rape of Lucrece* (written about the same time as *Edward III*), "moody Pluto winks while Orpheus plays" (stanza 79, line 553); in *Titus Andronicus,* written during 1588–1593, Marcus states:

he heard the heavenly harmony
Which that sweet tongue hath made,
He would have dropp'd his knife, and fell asleep
As **Cerberus** at the Thracian[19] poet's feet [2.3.48].

Ovid calls Cerberus a "tergeminumque canis." In *Love's Labour's Lost* Holofernes introduces "**Cerberus**, that three-headed canus" (5.2.583). The play is dated 1595–6.

Amongst the books that survive from Neville's Billingbear library is a 1518 volume of Ovid that contains the *Ars Amatoria* with a commentary in Latin. The *Ars Amatoria* was a source for *Venus and Adonis* (Bate, 2001, 24, 50). An annotator has highlighted text about Orpheus, the archetypal poet.

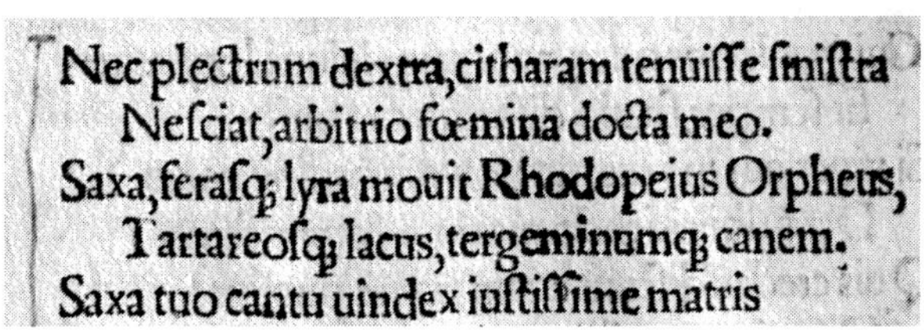
Nec plectrum dextra,citharam tenuiſſe ſiniſtra
Neſciat,arbitrio fœmina docta meo.
Saxa,feraſq; lyra mouit Rhodopeius Orpheus,
Tartareoſq; lacus,tergeminumq; canem.
Saxa tuo cantu uindex iuſtiſſime matris

Ars Amatoria: **30 verso (private collection).**

No woman trained according to my will should fail to know
How to hold her lyre in her left hand, a plectrum in her right.
Rhodopeian[20] Orpheus, with his lyre, moved stones and wild beasts,
And Tartarus's lake and Cerberus, the triple-headed dog.

We suggest this annotator was Neville and the passage a source for *Edward III.* Furthermore, we noted above that one reference to Turkey in *Edward III* may be to a war that broke out in June 1593. Also in the collection of Neville's books there is a volume, dated 1594, *Historia della Guerra Fra Turchi et Persiani* (*The History of the War Between the Turks and the Persians*). This book was published just when *Edward III* was being written. There is thus clear evidence that Neville had access to books that were sources for *Edward III.*

Rare Vocabulary in Edward III *and Neville's Letters*

An examination of some of the rare vocabulary to be found in the play provides further evidence for Neville's authorship. The countess says:

That power of loue, that I have power to giue,
Thou hast with all deuout obedience;
Inploy me how thou wilt [2.1.219].

Later King Edward uses this word: "I haue bin other wise **imployd**" (3.3.92). We have retained the spelling of the first printed version of *Edward III.* Neville used "imployed," "imploy," and "imployment" in his letter dated May 26, 1599 (Sawyer, 1725, vol. 1, 34). The uncertainty of the spelling in the quarto of *Edward III* ("in" or "im") is easily explained when one reads Neville's handwriting, where the distinction between "n" and "m" is often uncertain.

In *Edward III* the French ambassador uses the word "indirectly" (1.1.37). *Edward III* was published in 1596, the very date of the Northumberland Manuscript (NHMS) on which the word "indirectly," written upside down, appears (Dawkins, 2004, 302). Just below are the words "for profit." These also occur in *Edward III* (4.3.11). On the NHMS, just below "indirectly" and "for profit" is the word "places" (3.1.95), which also occurs in *Edward III.* The NHMS was owned by Henry Neville, whose surname appears at the top left of the front page.

Melchiori (1998, 175) suggested that one reason to suspect Shakespeare's hand is the survival in the first quarto of the play of the use of capital instead of lower case C for "Cannot" at 2.2.148. This may reflect the author's habit, noted in the three pages in Hand D in the manuscript of *The Booke of Sir Thomas Moore,* of nearly always capitalizing initial C in nouns, adjectives and verbs such as "Cannot," "Cry," "City," "Chid," "Country" and "Command" (Casson, 2010, 174). Melchiori also suggested that this use of capital C was a feature absent from "any other manuscript of the time." Neville shows this habit. In Neville's 1601 letter the words "Commodities," "Content," "Clothiers," "Complement" and "Coullour" are capitalized (Casson, 2010, 265). In the First Quarto of *Edward III* the spelling "coullours" is used (Sams, 1996, 194). This habit of using capital Cs continued in the Quartos of *Titus Andronicus* and *The Rape of Lucrece,* and can be seen in the First Folio *Henry V.*

Not only is the use of the capital C mid-sentence found in both Neville and Shakespeare, the style of writing is almost identical when we compare the initial three letters of "Com" in both Hand D and Neville's letter (which are dated 1603/4 and 1601, respectively). There are also numerous capital Cs in Henry Neville's manuscript copy of *Leicester's Commonwealth* (Worsley MSS 47) dated circa 1585, including "**Comaund**ent," spelled the same way as in *Sir Thomas More.*

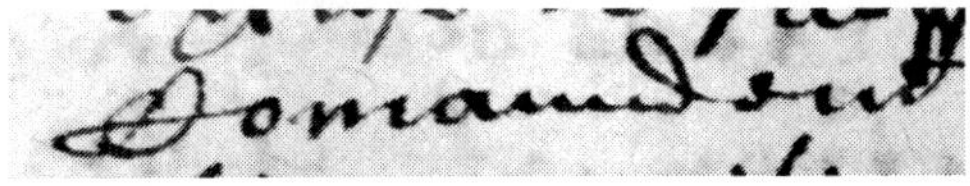

"Comaundent" in Worsley MSS 47, 18V (by permission of the Eighth Earl of Yarborough and Lincolnshire Archives).

Although the NHMS dates from Shakespeare's anonymous period (1596–1597), it was the first document to identify "William Shakespeare" as a playwright. It also includes several midsentence capital Cs. For example, there is a quotation from *The Rape of Lucrece*:

Revealing day through every Crany peeps and

The word "cranny" occurs in the Quarto of *Edward III* (Sams, 1996, line 1212; Melchiori in his 2011 edition of the play changed this to "crannied" [3.1.164]), as well as the poem *The Rape of Lucrece* (line 1086, stanza 156, where it is spelled "crannie"), both dating from the 1593/4 period. Neither play nor poem has a capital C for "cranny." The play also compares the Countess of Salisbury with Lucrece (2.2.193–5).

Sams (1996, 214) also suggested that the first edition of *Edward III* was printed from the author's own manuscript and offered a number of possible idiosyncrasies that might identify the writer.

The word "FINIS" is added at the end of the play in large letters. At the end of his manuscript copy of *Leicester's Commonwealth*, Neville added "ffinis" (shown to the right). Latin citations in the text of *Edward III* are italicized, just as Neville does several times in his copy of *Leicester's Commonwealth*, where the rest of the text is in secretary script.

***Above, right:* "ffinis" in Worsley MSS 47, 66. *Bottom: "Hic proiectus est indomitae et rabide libius catulus"* in Worsley MSS 47, 14 (by permission of the Eighth Earl of Yarborough and Lincolnshire Archives).**

Sams also found the use of double consonants at the end of words such as "sett." In Neville's copy of *Leicester's Commonwealth* we find this spelling (Worsley MSS 47, 3). The following spellings occur in the First Quarto of the play and in Worsley MSS 47: "pitifull," "fatall," "Royall," "faithfull," "severall" (see below). The letter "y" is used for "i" as in "yf" and "yt." There are numerous examples of this in Neville's letters. Sams identified variant spellings that we find in Neville's handwritten letters and manuscripts; for example, the letters "au" for "a" as in "Fraunce" and "command" (see "comaundent" in Worsley MSS 47, 18V, above). There are numerous examples of this in Neville's letters: "straunge," "commaundment" in a letter dated May 15, 1599; "straungers," September 1, 1599; "daunger," August 7, 1599 (Sawyer, 1725, vol. 1, 21, 86, 98). In a letter to Sir T. Edmonde, July 16, 1613, Neville wrote the word "commaund" (Stowe, 174, f.116, British Library). In the First Quarto of *Titus Andronicus* (1594) there are "commaund," "demaund" and "raunsome." This "au" spelling may be due to the French influence on English. Neville could speak French and had been to France.

Another habit was the use of the letters "ou" for "o" as in "coullours" (see above). Neville spelled "behould" and "bloud" with "ou" in documents dating from 1585 and 1602 (the first in Worsley MSS 47; the latter in the Salisbury Collection, Hatfield House). Furthermore in the Quarto of *Edward III* the letters "v" and "u" are interchanged, as in "Nauy," "Rauens," "Muscouites," "Reuolted," "**seueral**," "prouide," "**vppon**," "vntimely," "vnbridled," "vpshot," "**vs**," and "vp"; and this habit is to be found in Neville's copy of *Leicester's Commonwealth*, which predates the writing of the play:

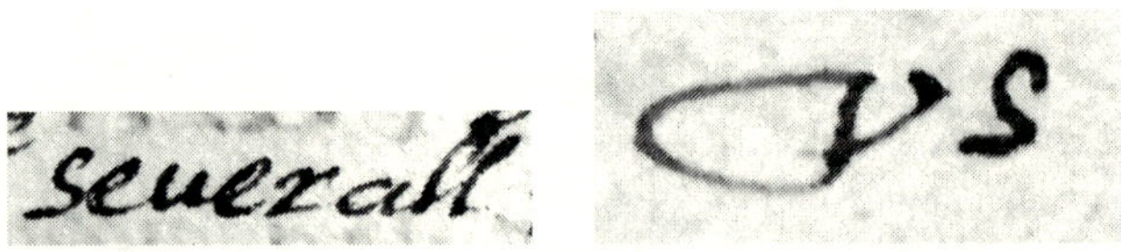

"u" for "v" in "seuerall" and "v" for "u" in "vs" in Worsley MSS 47, 52; 65V (by permission of the Eighth Earl of Yarborough and Lincolnshire Archives).

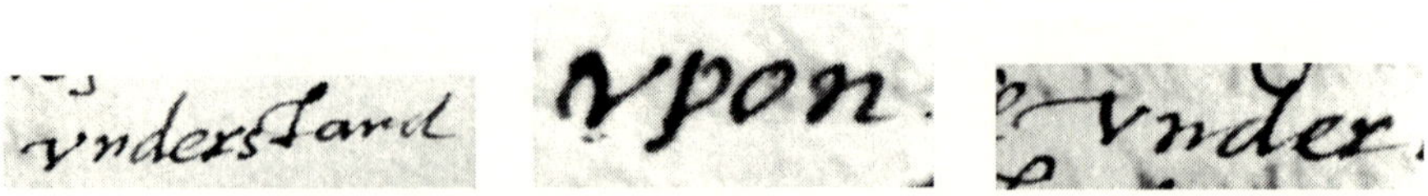

"v" for "u" in "vnderstand," "vpon" and "vnder" in Worsley MSS 47, 50 (by permission of the Eighth Earl of Yarborough and Lincolnshire Archives).

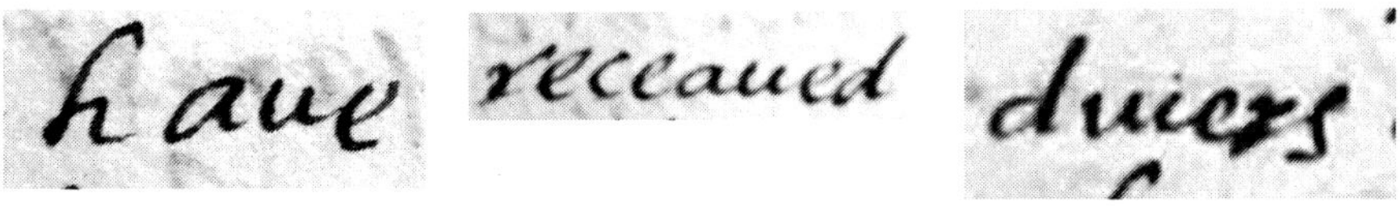

"u" for "v" in "haue," "receaued" and "diuers" in Worsley MSS 47, 50 (by permission of the Eighth Earl of Yarborough and Lincolnshire Archives).

Conclusion

The hidden Neville identities of the countess and her father; Neville's interest in the Countess of Salisbury evident in his annotations of documents dated 1584 and 1610; the Neville associations with the Warwick, Salisbury and Montague titles; the victory at Neville's Cross; Neville's characteristic vocabulary and spellings, and his use of capital C, all point to Neville's authorship. At the time the play was written, Neville had dealings with the ordnance office and so could have had contact with Painter, the translator of Bandello's story about the Countess of Salisbury, a source for *Edward III.* Neville's association with the Carey family, via the Hobys, may have been fruitful, not just in the development of Shakespeare's play, *Edward III,* but also in the patronage by Henry Carey (and his son, George Carey) of Shakespeare's theater company, the Chamberlain's Men.

Before the play was accepted as by Shakespeare, Professor Tillyard (1944, 121–1, quoted by Sams, 1996, 165) stated the author was "an intellectual, probably young, a University man, in the Southampton circle." This neatly describes Neville. His interest in the reign of Edward III is evident before and after Shakespeare wrote the play. In 1585 Neville made notes concerning Edward III in his manuscript copy of *Leicester's Commonwealth.* In 1602, in his Tower notebook, he made notes about Edward III. In the reign of James I, Henry Neville presented a document in Parliament emphasizing the importance of the monarch's virtuous family life in providing public confidence in the monarch on the national and international stage (James, 2011). This perspective is also reflected in *Edward III* (3.3.53 and 3.3.155).

The countess was identified as Alice by Le Bel and Joan by Painter, but most modern scholars believe her to be Catherine Grandison. There is confusion whether Catherine or Joan was the woman whose garter inspired Edward III to establish the Order of the Garter (Mortimer, 2008, 197, 267). Another possible confusion arises because the name Montague was also spelled Montacute (Melchiori, 1998, 57). The story of the rape of the countess is examined by Mortimer (2008, 191), who spells the name Montagu.

Table 3. The Identity of the Countess of Salisbury (1)

Edward Montague m. Alice Brotherton
1324–1351, beat his wife to death.

William Montague m. Catherine Grandison
First Earl of Salisbury Countess of Salisbury
1301–1344 1304–1349 (raped ? by) Edward III m. Phillipa Hainault

(From 1361, when he was 49, Edward III had a young mistress, Alice Perres, aged 15)

William Montague ← m. (2) Joan Woodstock m. (1) → Thomas Holland
Second Earl of Salisbury 1341 Countess of Kent 1340
1328–1397 1328–1385
(subject of marital dispute)

m. (3) → Prince Edward
c. 1361 1330–1376

Table 4. The Identity of the Countess of Salisbury (2)

Richard m. Cecily Neville
Duke of York

Richard Neville m. Alice Montague
Countess of Salisbury

Richard Neville m. Anne Beauchamp
Earl of Warwick

Prince George m. Isabelle Neville
Duke of Clarence

Anne Neville betrothed to Prince Edward
m. Richard III
(1465? raped by Edward IV)

Prince Edward

\+ Margaret m. Richard Pole
Countess of Salisbury
1473–1541

George Neville

\+ Edward Neville

\+ Jane Neville m. + Henry Pole
Lord Montague

Reginald Pole
Cardinal Archbishop
of Canterbury

Henry Neville (c. 1520–1593)

\+ Henry Pole

Henry Neville (1562–1615)

(+ Beheaded in the Pole purge)

Chapter 3

Richard II (1377–1399)

... by the glorious worth of my descent...—*Richard II* (1.1.107)

Richard II*: A Political Play*

Richard II is both a tragedy of character and a highly political play. It asks, "What is the nature and source of political authority and under what circumstances is it legitimate to resist or even to overthrow that authority?" (Dawson and Yachnin, 2011, 21). Clegg (1997) showed that "the deposition scene gives prominence to an issue that was contentious in the 1590s, namely the competing roles of Parliament and the monarchy" (Dawson and Yachnin, 2011, 14). During the 1590s Henry Neville was a member of Parliament. Act 4 begins with the stage direction, "Enter as to the Parliament" and is entirely set at Westminster. This was an environment all too familiar to Henry Neville, M.P.

Richard II was written about 1595 and first published anonymously in 1597. The following year it was published as by "William Shake-speare," one of the first plays to be identified as by this writer.

Sometime between February and April of 1598 Robert Cecil left England to negotiate with the French king, Henry IV. In his absence Robert Devereux, the Earl of Essex, was appointed acting secretary of state (Lacey, 1971, 207–8). It was during this time that Essex persuaded a very reluctant Henry Neville to accept Elizabeth's commission to be ambassador to France (James, 2008, 52). Neville was a rising star and needed a pseudonym to hide his authorship of this dangerously political play.

The second and third quartos of *Richard II* were republications of the first, and all of them lack the most politically sensitive scenes of the deposition. In contrast, quartos 4 (1608) and 5 (1615), and the First Folio (1623) include the scene in parliament when Henry Bolingbroke ascends the throne and Richard is deposed (4.1.155–318). The uncensored version may have been that performed just prior to the Essex rebellion in 1601. These performances were especially commissioned by the Essex faction to elicit support from the London populace. At this time Essex was involved in a power struggle with Robert Cecil and concerned about the succession to the throne. Queen Elizabeth herself recognized the political nature of the play. In a conversation with William Lambard, court archivist, she was reported by him as saying, "I am Richard II, know ye not that? ... This tragedy was played forty times in open streets and houses" (Dawson and Yachnin, 2011, 4). This conversation took place in August 1601, and both referred obliquely to Essex. In February 1601 Henry Neville was discovered to have had some notice of Essex's plans and consequently served two years in the Tower for failing to inform the government of what he knew. William Shakspere, the actor and supposed author, was not even questioned. By the time of the queen's conversation, Neville was in the Tower. While there, he researched historical documents (a list of manuscripts held in the Tower was presented to the queen by Lambard and prompted their conversation). Neville's research notes are preserved in his Tower notebook, dated 1602.[1] In this he recorded numerous matters concerning Richard II's reign, beginning with a major section on his coronation rituals. He made a note: "R.2. was **deposed** for his misgovernment[2]: the **articles** therof recorded & those chosen for to make known to the k. the minds of all sorts of subiects." This recalls the deposition scene in the play when Northumberland asks Richard to read

> These accusations and these grievous crimes
> Committed by your person and your followers
> Against the state and profit of this land,
> That by confessing them, the souls of men
> May deem that you are worthily **deposed** [4.1.222].
> My lord, dispatch; read o'er these **articles** [4.1.243].

In the annotated Hall's *Chronicle,* which may have been kept in Neville's daughter's library at Appuldurcombe on the Isle of Wight, where Neville visited (James and Rubinstein, 2005, 51) there are two adjacent annotations:

> **[A]rticles** declaryd [in] parliament against [K]inge Richard
> Kinge Richarde consented to be **deposyd**
> [Transcription by Alan and Lubbock, 1954, 128].

Having independently researched the original volume, Casson (2010, 75) dated the annotations to 1594–8. Richard II was written c. 1595. According to the LION[3] and EEBO databases, the words "deposed" and "articles" were only used in close proximity from 1595 to 1602 by Shakespeare, the Hall annotator and Henry Neville. We suggest that these three are the same person.

Henry Neville's Ancestors in Richard II

Henry Neville was related to Richard II through John of Gaunt's descendants. *Richard II* opens with the king talking to "Old John of Gaunt, time honoured Lancaster." John was one of the sons of Edward III, a younger brother of the Black Prince, and uncle of Richard II. His legitimate male heirs included kings Henry IV, Henry V and Henry VI. Gaunt married his mistress Katherine Roet, Lady Swynford, in 1396. On page 327 of his copy of *A Catalogue of Honor* Neville noted that Katherine's children were legitimated[4] by "authoritie" of Parliament. These previously illegitimate descendants, the Beauforts, later married into the House of Tudor, which ascended to the throne in the person of Henry VII. Katherine Swynford's daughter, Joan Beaufort, married the first Earl of Westmoreland, Ralph Neville. Westmoreland's mother was Maud Percy, wife of John, third Baron Neville of Raby, giving Neville a Percy ancestry. John was a follower and confidante of John of Gaunt and a Knight of the Garter. Katherine Swynford's third child, Thomas Beaufort, 1377–1427, married Margaret Neville.[5] Henry Neville therefore had reason to look back at John of Gaunt through rose-tinted spectacles.

The identification of Neville as the bard explains why Shakespeare distorted history and the character of Gaunt to make him such a positive figure, when in fact Gaunt was deeply unpopular during his lifetime (Mortimer, 2008, 353, 375). The playwright gives Gaunt a long and patriotic speech in act 2, scene 1, following which he confronts the king, fearlessly criticizing his reign. Shakespeare places Gaunt in a line of figures who speak truth to power that includes the Bastard Falconbridge in *King John,* the Countess of Salisbury in *Edward III* and Thomas of Woodstock (we shall examine the latter below). We have previously seen that these figures have hidden Neville connections (see Chapter 1 and 2; Casson, 2009). Furthermore Neville spoke truth to power in the person of James I: indeed the king invited Neville to do so, preferring his plain speaking to Francis Bacon's "extravagant stile" (James, 2008, 369, note 209; see Sawyer, 1725, vol. 3, 235).

In his copy of *Leicester's Commonwealth*[6] Neville annotated the text:

"John Duke of Somerset the 2 Sonnes of **John of Gaunte** The **pedigree** of K. Henr: 7th."

Worsley MSS 47, 43 (by permission of the Eighth Earl of Yarborough and Lincolnshire Archives).

This is echoed in two Shakespeare plays: "he from **John of Gaunt** doth bring his **pedigree**" in *Henry VI* part 1 (2.5.76) and "**John of Gaunt** ... a **pedigree**" in *Henry VI* part 3 (3.3.81–92). Furthermore, in the copy of Hall's *Chronicles* annotated by Neville, there is a marginal note "**John of Gaunt**" against a passage referring to Gaunt's death, Bollingbroke's exile and the seizure of his lands by Richard, all of which is dramatized in the play (Alan and Lubbock, 1954, 127).

In Worsley MSS 47, Neville added to an annotation in the printed text, "the yssue of K: Edw 3 **Rich 2**" (Casson, 2010, 215).

These annotations prove that up to ten years before the play *Richard II* was written, Henry Neville was taking a political interest in Richard II.

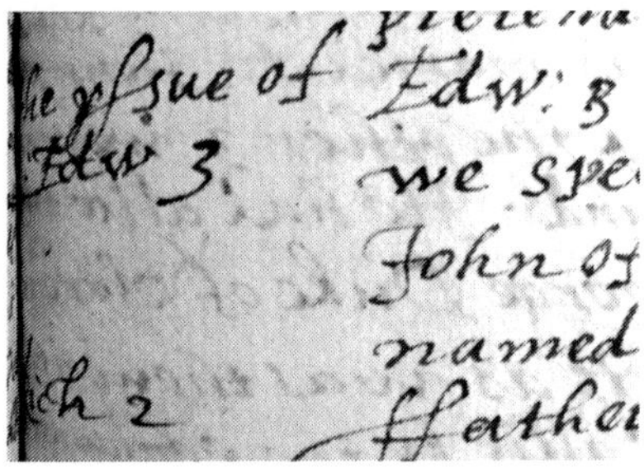

Worsley MSS 47, 43 (by permission of the Eighth Earl of Yarborough and Lincolnshire Archives).

There is further documentary evidence of a link between Neville and this play: it is listed as *Rychard the second* on the front page of the Northumberland Manuscript (NHMS). This important document was owned by Neville (Burgoyne, 1904, xvi; James and Rubinstein, 2005, 43, 237–243). Just beneath *Rychard the second* someone had repeatedly written the name "William Shakespeare" (spelled thus). The NHMS has been dated to 1596–1597. This is fifteen years before the first of the Stratford William's own signatures appeared: the earliest being "Willm Shackp" on the Belott-vs.-Mountjoy deposition of 1612. *Richard II* was first printed in 1597 without any author being named. Thus Neville knew *Richard II* was by "Shakespeare" before anyone else. He also spelled the name thus, which the Stratford Shakspere never did.

During 1610–12[7] Neville made notes on a copy of Thomas Willes' *A Catalogue of Honor* and added to a section on Edmund of Langley the comment that his uncle, Richard II, had made him Duke of York:

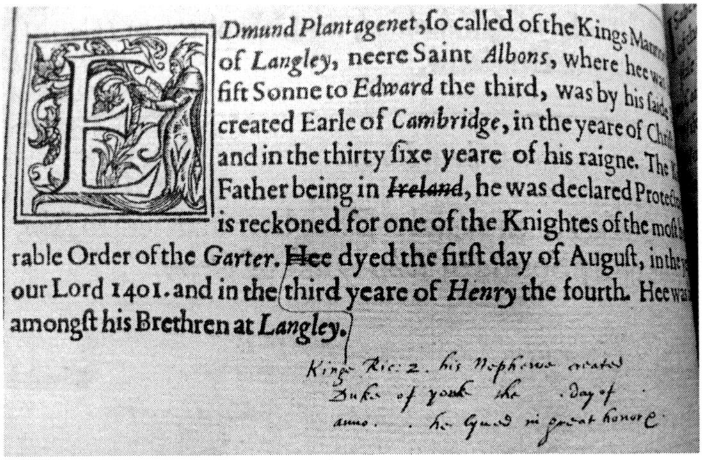

E Dmund *Plantagenet*, ſo called of the Kings Man
of *Langley*, neere Saint *Albons*, where hee wa
fift Sonne to *Edward* the third, was by his fa
created Earle of *Cambridge*, in the yeare of Chr
and in the thirty ſixe yeare of his raigne. The
Father being in *Ireland*, he was declared Protec
is reckoned for one of the Knightes of the moſt
rable Order of the *Garter*. Hee dyed the firſt day of Auguſt, in the y
our Lord 1401. and in the third yeare of *Henry* the fourth. Hee wa
amongſt his Brethren at *Langley*.

A Catalogue of Honor **(private collection).**

Edmund of Langley, who plays a prominent role in the play, was also a Neville ancestor. Several generations later Richard III's queen, Anne Neville, was descended from Edmund of Langley's daughter Constance. Thus before the play was written, before it was printed and after it was performed during the Essex rebellion, indeed until 1612, Neville was making notes about Richard II.

John Montacute,[8] the third Earl of Salisbury, appears in the play. His granddaughter, Alice, married Richard Neville, so bringing the Salisbury earldom to the Nevilles. Their son was Richard, the Earl of Warwick, the Kingmaker, who appears in the *Henry VI* trilogy.

Henry Percy, the Earl of Northumberland, married Margaret Neville, daughter of Ralph second Baron Neville of Raby, so their son, Harry Hotspur, who also appears in the play, had Neville blood in his veins. Thus we see that several major characters in the play were Neville ancestors.

Traces of Neville's European Travels, 1578–82

Thomas Mowbray, the Duke of Norfolk, when banished, speaks of "the frozen ridges of the Alps" (1.1.64). Neville had crossed the Alps as he traveled to and from Italy. Bolingbroke also speaks of his banishment as "a long apprenticehood to foreign passages" (1.3.271). Neville was away from home from the age of sixteen to twenty: a long apprenticeship indeed. Mowbray is later reported to have died in Venice (4.1.98); Neville had been there and noted this detail in the annotated Hall's *Chronicles.* The annotation reads: "duke of Norfolk [dy]ed at venice" (Alan and Lubbock, 1954, 127). This information is not in Hall's text and indicates that the annotator had independent knowledge.

The Earliest Recorded Performance

Sir Edward Hoby wrote to Sir Robert Cecil on December 7, 1595, inviting him to supper and to see "*K. Richard*," possibly a private performance of Shakespeare's *Richard II* (Halliday, 1964, 229). Edward Hoby was Neville's Berkshire neighbor and his wife's cousin.[9] James (2008, 68, 115–6) has shown there are numerous connections between the Hobys, Neville and Shakespeare.

Thomas of Woodstock*: The Other Richard II Play*

Another play about Richard II is *Thomas of Woodstock,* of which a sole manuscript copy has survived in the British Library (MS Egerton 1994). It was anonymous and written circa 1592–3, before *Richard II.* Thomas of Woodstock, Duke of Gloucester, was the uncle of Richard II, and in the play he is lord protector of England during Richard's minority. A number of scholars have seen it as part one of a two-part play, of which Shakespeare's *Richard II* is the second part. The quarrel in the opening scene of *Richard II* is explained by the events in *Thomas of Woodstock.* Thomas Mowbray, who is confronted by Bolingbroke at the start of *Richard II,* was governor of Calais at the time of Woodstock's murder there. Bolingbroke asserts, "he did plot the Duke of Gloucester's death" (1.1.100). Thomas of Woodstock's widow appears in *Richard II.* The two plays fit together: indeed *Woodstock* follows *Edward III,* so completing the entire sequence of the bard's history plays spanning the period 1327–1485. Over the last one hundred years several scholars have made the case for its attribution to Shakespeare; others have denied it. In 2006 Michael Egan published a major study of the play, showing that it was undoubtedly by Shakespeare. In 2009 Casson revealed new evidence for Neville's authorship in his book *Enter Pursued by a Bear.*

In his 1602 Tower notebook, under the heading "The Coronation of King Richard II," Neville twice noted in the margin, "Tho: de Wodstok" and "Tho: Wodstok." In the annotated Hall's *Chronicle* there is an annotation:

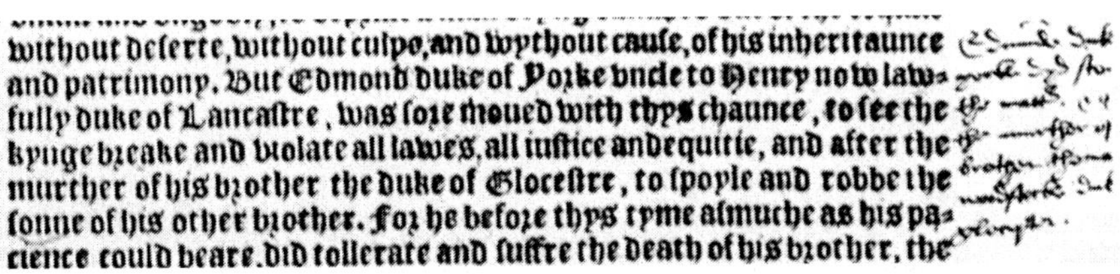
without deserte, without culpe, and wythout cause, of his inheritaunce and patrimony. But Edmond duke of Yorke uncle to Henry now lawfully duke of Lancastre, was sore moued with thys chaunce, to see the kynge breake and violate all lawes, all iustice and equitie, and after the murther of his brother the duke of Glocestre, to spoyle and robbe the sonne of his other brother. For he before thys tyme asmuche as his pacience could beare, did tollerate and suffre the death of his brother, the

"Edmund duke [of] yorke dyd sto[mack] the matt[r] & a[fter] the murther of [his] brother Thomas [of] woodstocke duk[e] [of] glocester" (transcription by Alan and Lubbock, 1954, 128; by permission of the Trustee of the Tudor Players [Rufford], the owners of the annotated Hall's *Chronicle*).

Thomas of Woodstock is not named in Hall's text, so this annotation indicates special knowledge. Neville was related to Thomas of Woodstock through his brother, John of Gaunt's descendants.

Thomas of Woodstock may well have been too politically sensitive even in 1623 to be safely included in the First Folio. Casson (2009) has shown that Neville's political thinking runs through this play. The play begins and ends with assassinations. It is about political power, right governance, law, oppression and corruption. Neville was a politician, a member of Parliament, and a son, son-in-law and grandson to political figures. He thought deeply about the governance of England. Egan (2006, vol. 1, 168) observed that one of the sources used by the author of *Thomas of Woodstock* was Parliamentary records: as an M.P. Neville would have had privileged access to these.[10] The play explores fundamental issues of statecraft, "defines the criteria of good government ... the responsibilities of Kingship, the proper administration of the law, the appropriate role of the King's council and the destructive attractions of pride and will" (Corbin and Sedge, 2002, 9–10, 14). The playwright "plainly recommends some form of constitutional monarchy as best for England.... The proposal is ... politically progressive" (Egan, 2006, vol. 1, 477). Later, Henry Neville was to attempt to negotiate such a balance between James I and Parliament; "Neville's efforts in this direction formed the basic ideas of Constitutional Monarchy" (James, 2008, 53).

Scholars have noted the unorthodox political thinking behind the play, calling it "the boldest and most subversive of all Elizabethan historical plays" (Corbin and Sedge, 2002, 37). Neville, as politician and political thinker, was such a writer and became involved in the Essex rebellion (see James, 2008, 60). The Earl of Essex was a descendant of Thomas of Woodstock and Henry Bolingbroke. Neville was a supporter of Essex. Both plays use historical examples to sanction "loyal rebellion" and suggest that the such a rebellion, because "its leadership might be supplied by a small group of nobles critical of the

Crown, could hardly fail to attract attention and stir powerful emotions. Here was the Essex uprising in embryo" (Egan, 2006, vol. 1, 130).

One dramatic incident at the heart of *Thomas of Woodstock* is when Thomas is arrested by the king and courtiers disguised as masquers. This incident is not based on historical fact but is an invention of the playwright. Corbin and Sedge (2002, 45, note 76) noticed that the masque in *Thomas of Woodstock* resembled that in Shakespeare's *Henry VIII* (see Chapter 8). The origin of both masques can be found in a Neville family story.

Henry Neville's grandfather, Sir Edward Neville, was a close friend of the king. At a banquet given by Cardinal Wolsey in 1527 he appeared disguised in a masque, and Wolsey mistook Neville for the king. Edward Neville physically resembled Henry VIII, so Wolsey's misidentification is understandable (see Chapter 8). The masque in *Thomas of Woodstock* echoes this incident when a king is disguised in a masque but was written long before *Henry VIII.* It is perhaps significant that this masque leads to the death of the protagonist. If the incident in the play is based on the family story of Sir Edward Neville at the Wolsey banquet masque, then it would be coupled with the knowledge of Edward's eventual execution. Egan (2006, vol. 1, 399) made a comparison between the masque scenes in *Thomas of Woodstock* and *Henry VIII*, finding many parallels between them. These can be summarized as follows:

1. Both share rural themes (hunters in *Woodstock;* shepherds in *Henry VIII*).
2. Both troupes of masquers arrive suddenly and unexpectedly.
3. The masquers are welcomed in similar ways: a banquet is prepared.
4. The moon is mentioned, with symbolism that points to Elizabeth I.
5. Kings are present, disguised as masquers.
6. There is whispering between the masquers.
7. A powerful figure in his home at night is solicited by masquers, among whom his sovereign is disguised. Woodstock and Wolsey both guess the identity of this disguised king. In both cases they fall from grace and ultimately die after this scene.

Thomas of Woodstock, the Nevilles and Their Enemies

Thomas of Woodstock was murdered in Calais: this much is accurate. The play, however, casts "Lapoole" as the governor of Calais: indeed Edmund, the brother of Michael de la Pole, the first Earl of Suffolk, was governor of Calais early in Richard's reign (Corbin and Sedge, 2002, 50). At the time of the murder the governor was actually Thomas Mowbray, and in *Richard II* Shakespeare corrects this historical error. When Shakespeare distorts history we look for possible explanations and have found a hidden Neville too frequently for it to be coincidence. Sir Edward Neville, Neville's grandfather, was related to the Pole and Courtenay families and became entangled in the Pole/Courtenay conspiracy. It was Sir Geoffrey Pole who, under torture in 1538, had accused Edward Neville of high treason. Neville was executed; Pole was pardoned. Thus the writer is further identifying these two men: Sir Edward Neville and Thomas of Woodstock, both of whom are betrayed by a member of the de la Pole family. The historical Thomas of Woodstock is known to have been an enemy of Michael de la Pole, the first Earl of Suffolk, forcing Richard II to dismiss him as chancellor in 1386. He was impeached and imprisoned. Richard soon released and reinstated him, but when the baronial opposition again demanded his arrest, de la Pole fled to France. This identification is further strengthened by recalling that William de la Pole, Duke of Suffolk, grandson of Michael de la Pole, is the Nevilles' adversary in *Henry VI* part 2 and arranges the murder of Humphrey, Duke of Gloucester, who, like Woodstock, was lord protector of the realm. (For further evidence of Neville's authorship of *Thomas of Woodstock* see Casson, 2009.)

Conclusion

There is both internal and external evidence linking *Richard II* with Henry Neville. These associations further strengthen the case for Shakespeare's authorship of *Thomas of Woodstock.* The radical political nature of the plays *Richard II* and *Thomas of Woodstock* provides a compelling motive for Henry Neville to keep his authorship secret. The fact that the actor William Shakspere was neither arrested, questioned nor punished for their content at a time when the Crown brooked no criticism, or discussion of the succession, implies that it was known he was not the author.

CHAPTER 4

Henry IV
(1399–1413)

KING: (to Warwick) You, cousin Nevil, as I may remember
Did speak these words.
—*Henry IV* part 2 (3.1.66)

We will treat both parts of Shakespeare's *Henry IV* as one work. The plays were written during 1596–8.

The Nevilles in Henry IV

In this two-part play, members of the Neville family and their relatives appear on stage. In part 1 Ralph Neville (1354–1425), sixth Baron of Raby and first Earl of Westmoreland, is identified only as the Earl of Westmoreland, and the king calls him "my cousin Westmoreland" (5.5.35). Ralph married Joan Beaufort, daughter of John of Gaunt, Duke of Lancaster. Ralph was grandfather of Edward IV and Richard III and was the father of Cecily Neville (wife of the Duke of York, mother of Richard III).[1] While Ralph Neville had previously been close to Richard II, "he was quick to join Bolingbroke when he landed in England to overthrow Richard in 1399."[2] In one of his annotated library books, Henry Neville added a reference to "Rafe Neuill first Earle" by inserting "of Westmoreland" in the margin (see top of next page). The Earl of Westmoreland is a key figure in *Henry IV.*

"Henry extended Richard II's policy of bolstering the strength of the Nevilles as a check to the troublesome Percys, and the family gained from the weakening of Percy power after the failure of the revolt of Henry 'Hotspur'

An. Dom. 1461.

1 of Westmorland

WIlliam Neuill, Knight, in the right of his wife was Lord *Falconberg*, being younger sonne of *Rafe Neuill* first Earle, by his second wife, Daughter vnto *Iohn* of Gaunt D. of *Lancaster*, and *Katherine Swinford* (Brother German vnto *Richard Neuil* Earle of *Salisbury*) was created Earle of *Kent* by *Edward* the fourth.

***A Catalogue of Honor,* 1610 (private collection).**

Percy in 1403."[3] Indeed the rivalry between the Nevilles and Percys in the North would explain why Shakespeare made Prince Hal's triumph over Hotspur a central plot element in the play. In the first part of *Henry IV* Hotspur's wife is called Kate, when in fact she was Elizabeth Mortimer, though she was called Elianor in the Holinshed *Chronicles.* Lady Percy delivers two long speeches (30 and 33 lines respectively), one in each of parts 1 and 2 of *Henry IV* (*Henry IV* part 1, 2.3.36–65; *Henry IV* part 2, 2.3.9–44). Each speech is in sympathy with the monarchy and against the rebellion of her husband or father-in-law. Her appeals fall on deaf ears, and she is powerless to change the men's plans. Her role may be significant in other ways.

Shakespeare's contemporary Lady Percy was Catherine (which may be shortened to Kate), who was the eldest daughter of John Neville, Lord Latimer. She married Henry Percy, the eighth Earl of Northumberland. Two of her sons, Charles and Joscelyne, were amongst the followers of Essex who arranged for the Lord Chamberlain's men to perform *Richard II* on the eve of the Essex rebellion (Scoufos, 1979, 112). Her husband had remained loyal to the crown when his brother had participated in the 1569 Rising of the North and took his title when Thomas was executed in 1572. However, in the 1580s Henry became increasingly involved with plots to free Mary, Queen of Scots. In 1583 he had met Charles Paget to discuss freeing Mary. (Henry Neville had met Paget in Scotland the same year and was to meet him again in 1599 in France.) Henry Percy was arrested and imprisoned in the Tower of London and found dead, probably murdered by a gun shot, in 1585. Lady Catherine Percy had reasons to plead with her husband and son to be loyal to the crown.

In the first scene of the play, a retainer of the Earl of Northumberland called Morton appears to give him news of the battle of Shrewsbury (1403) and the death of Hotspur. The 1569 Northern rebellion was precipitated by the rumors from a man called Morton. While the Morton in the play is a fictional character, Nicholas Morton of 1569 brought a message from Rome of the excommunication of Queen Elizabeth I and a call for revolt (Holinshed, 1587, vol. 3, 1361–2; Scoufos, 1979, 121–5). Morton was executed in 1588, less than ten years prior to this play's publication. More particularly, the allusion to contemporary times may be due to the death of Lady Catherine Percy, who died in 1596. She was the last of the powerful Nevilles of the North. The Earl of Westmoreland, Charles Neville (1542–1601), leader of the 1569 Northern rebellion, died in exile and poverty. His family were attainted and lost all their titles. This play seems to be an attempt to redeem the honor of the Westmoreland branch of Nevilles.

In *Henry IV* part 2 the Earl of Warwick is incorrectly identified as a Neville. In truth he was Richard de Beauchamp, the thirteenth Earl of Warwick. In the play, the king, addressing the Earl of Warwick, says:

> You, cousin Nevil, as I remember ... [*Henry IV* part 2, 3.1.66].

Richard's daughter, Anne, married Richard Neville, who then became the sixteenth Earl of Warwick and was subsequently called "the King Maker." He appears as such in the *Henry VI* trilogy. In this slip, then, we suggest the playwright reveals a Neville bias.

A similar bias may be evident in the unhistorical sleight-of-hand that removes responsibility for a treacherous trick from a Neville, displacing it onto Prince John of Lancaster (Scoufos, 1979, 129). At the battle of Gaultree it was Ralph Neville who deceived Archbishop Scrope and the other rebel leaders into surrendering and then arrested them, whereas Shakespeare gives this Machiavellian role to Prince John, who promises to redress the rebels' grievances and so persuades them to discharge their army, enabling Neville to arrest them (*Henry IV* part 2, 4.2.59). Stow and Holinshed both stated that it was Westmoreland (Ralph Neville) who conducted this negotiation. Their testimony is reinforced by the fact that Prince John was only sixteen at the time (Humfreys, 1966, 129, footnote) and so would have been an unlikely negotiator.

Minor Characters and Their Neville Connections

The bard's apparent Neville bias is further confirmed by the fact that some minor characters also have Neville family connections. The stage direction at the beginning of act 1, scene 3, of the 1600 quarto version of *Henry IV* part 2 states:

> *Enter th'Archbishop, Thomas Mowbray (Earle Marshall) the Lord Hastings, Fauconbridge, and Bardolphe.*[4]

As indicated in Chapter 1, Fauconbridge is a Neville name, although at the time of this scene (c. 1405), this character appears to have been the father-in-law of William Neville and grandfather of the Bastard of Falconbridge, Thomas Neville. In *Henry IV* part 2 he is a ghost character who has no role in the play. Although the quarto, dating from 1600, is believed to have been set from an authorial manuscript (Melchiori, 2007, 214), and Fauconbridge's presence is based on the Holinshed *Chronicles* (Holinshed, 1587, 529), this character does not appear in the First Folio. Shakespeare, as we have seen in Chapter 1, put a Falconbridge into several plays in the 1590s: perhaps this one was deemed one too many.

Sir John Umfrevile is mentioned in the 1600 Quarto b and First Folio of *Henry IV* part 2 (1.1.34). He has been identified as Lord Robert Umfrevile, who was one of the king's supporters at Gaultree (Melchiori, 1984, 203). Sir Robert de Umfraville was vice admiral during Henry IV's reign. Annotating Hall's *Chronicles*, Neville noted "Sr Robert Vinefrevile" in the section on Henry IV (Alan and Lubbock, 1954, 132).

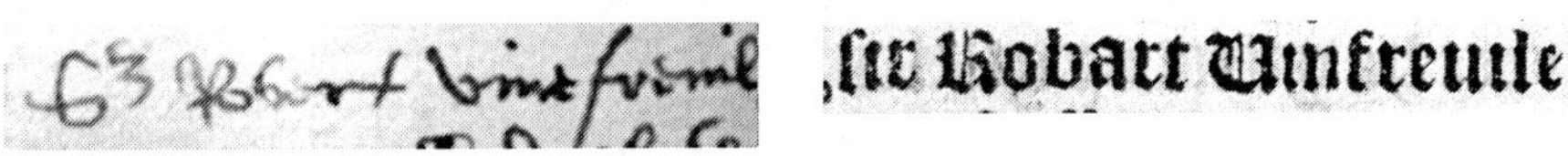

Folio xxvi of *King Henry IV* (by permission of the Trustee of the Tudor Players [Rufford], the owners of the annotated Hall's *Chronicle*).

This man is called "Sir Robart Vinfrevil" in the text and identified as vice admiral. Vinefrevil may be a misreading of the original handwriting of the scribe ("V" being used as "U" and "m" being misread as "in"). Sir Robert's nephew was Sir Gilbert de Umfreville, who married Anne Neville, daughter of Ralph Neville, the first Earl of Westmoreland.[5] On page 993 of his copy of *The Catalogue of Honor* Neville inserted the word "Lord" after "*Sir Gilbert Vmfreuile.*" The Umfrevilles, like the Nevilles, arrived in England with William the Conqueror. Neville may also have been attracted to the similar ending of their names, ville/vile, and the fact that they were both descended from Ralph Neville.

Some editors of the play change Umfrevile to Lord Bardolph (Weis, 2008, 122, footnote). In the play there are two Bardolphs: a braggart soldier and a lord. In the Tower notebook of 1602 Neville noted a "W. Bardolf" in a marginal list of those doing homage at the coronation of Richard II (the list includes a "Wm Nevill"). In his copy of *A Catalogue of Honor,* 1610, Neville noted the pedigree of the Barons Bardolph:

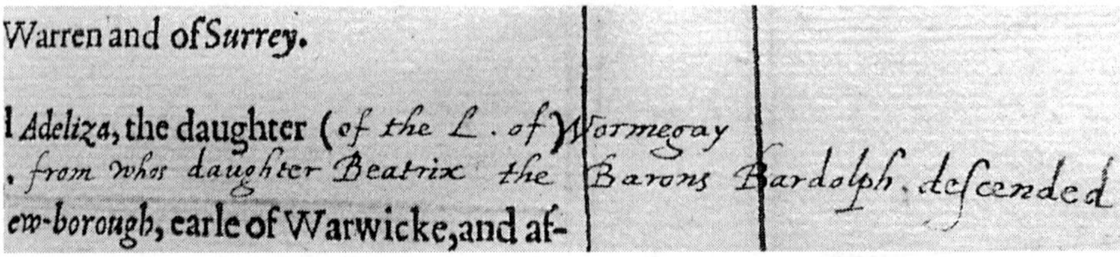
Warren and of *Surrey*.
1 *Adeliza*, the daughter (of the L. of Wormegay
. from whos daughter Beatrix the Barons Bardolph. descended.
ew-borough, earle of Warwicke, and af-

"from whos daughter Beatrix the Barons Bardolph descended," ***A Catalogue of Honor,*** **1610 (private collection).**

Thomas, the fifth Baron Bardolph, a rebel against Henry IV, was defeated by Ralph Neville.

Sir Walter Blunt is portrayed in part 1 as a noble and courageous man, described by the king as "a dear, a true industrious friend," "good Blunt" and "A gallant knight" (part 1, 1.1.63; 3.2.162; 5.3.20). He is a loyal supporter of Henry IV and gives his life for him by disguising himself as the king in battle. He was Henry Neville's great, great, great, great, great-grandfather.

Table 5. The Blount-Neville Descent

Sir Walter Blount (*Henry IV* part I)
↓
Sir John Blount + Thomas Blount (brothers)[6]
↓
Walter Blount, First Baron Mountjoy
↓
William Blount
↓
Elizabeth Blount Windsor
↓
Eleanor Windsor Neville
↓
Sir Henry Neville
↓
Sir Henry Neville (1562–1615)

Sir John Blunt was an important person to Neville because he was to inherit the Blunt fortune as Thomas's older brother. In part 2 of *Henry IV* Sir John Blunt appears several times. He is first mistakenly reported as having been killed with his father in the battle of Shrewsbury (1.1.16).[7] He is named in a stage direction as entering with Warwick and Surrey in 3.1.32 in Quarto b of 1600. He also enters with the newly crowned King Henry V (5.2.41) in Qb. This quarto followed the incomplete Qa, which was printed shortly after the play was registered in late August 1600. This imprint appears to have some connections to the Essex rebellion and the playing of *Richard II* on February

7, 1601, the night before the ill-fated rebellion. The first scene in act 3 is missing from Qa and was subsequently added to the Qb imprint. In this scene Sir John Blunt makes his silent entrance immediately after the king ends his soliloquy about his lack of sleep with the words "uneasy lies the head that wears a crown" (3.1.31). The king refers to his usurpation of the crown from Richard II and the betrayal of Northumberland. It is in this scene that Warwick is called "Nevil" and he muses:

> A man may prophesy,
> With a near aim, of the main chance of things
> As yet to come to life, who in their seeds
> And weak beginnings lie entreasured [3.1.81].

This prophetic vein perhaps intuitively anticipated the betrayals of the Essex rebellion, which cost Henry Neville his liberty. Essex was descended from Henry IV, and in 1599 John Hayward dedicated *The First Part of the Life and Raigne of King Henrie IV* to Essex. However, this resulted in Hayward's "being thrown in the Tower and the burning of all unsold copies" (Mortimer, 2008, 167). Elizabeth I was furious about the possible contemporary political implications and asked Francis Bacon to see whether the author could be accused of treason (Jardine and Stewart, 1998, 211). The book was cited during Essex's trial. The plays had been written before this, but clearly the reign of Henry IV was being seen as analogous to the political dilemmas of the time.[8] William Shakspere, however, was never arrested or questioned about the plays. Sir Christopher Blount was involved in the Essex debacle and Neville had certainly met him (Duncan, 1974, 165). Blount was Essex's stepfather and was executed for his part in the rebellion. An Edward Blount was one of the publishers of the First Folio.

In *Henry IV* part 2, Prince John orders Sir John Blunt to guard Falstaff's captive, Coleville of the Dale, who is taken away for execution (*Henry IV* part 2, 4.3.72). James (2011, 150) suggested that Neville selected this minor character, Sir John Coleville, from Holinshed, because he was suspicious of a man called John Colville who was an intelligence agent in France. Colville had been previously employed by Walsingham as a spy (Scoufos, 1979, 131). "By the time Neville used his services in Paris, Colville was already under suspicion of being a double agent.... Sir Henry Neville wrote to Winwood: I distrust Colvel every day more and more; I will quit myself of him" (James, 2011, 153; Sawyer, 1725, vol. 1, 229). This letter was dated July 17, 1600. In another letter dated August 28, 1600 Neville stated that he would not pay Colville until he had performed some real service rather than just offering empty promises. *Henry IV* part 2 was registered on August 23, 1600, when Neville had arrived back in London. The First Quarto was printed in 1600 and included the Coleville scene.

Another Sir Thomas Blunt is executed by Bolingbroke in *Richard II* (5.6.8). He was loyal to Richard II and conspired to restore the king. In *Richard III* there is Sir James Blunt, whom Richmond (later to become Henry VII) calls "good Captain Blunt" and "Sweet Blunt." Why members of this family are featured in minor, mainly positive roles in Shakespeare's plays is a mystery explained when we realize they are honorable ancestors of Henry Neville. In the notebook that Neville annotated when in the Tower of London in 1602, there are notes that refer to a Blunt in the reign of Henry IV, and to Charles Blunt as Mountjoy, with a further note that he was "creat cond: devon 1 K. James 1603" (created Earl of Devonshire in the first year of King James, 1603).

Two other names briefly appear in the First Quarto edition of *Henry IV* part 1 and thereafter are replaced by other names. Listing the robbers on Gadshill, Poins names "Falstalffe, Haruey, Rossill" (1.2.153). The latter two become Peto and Bardolph in later editions. Who were Harvey and Russel?

Bevington (part 1, 2008, 5) suggested that the name "Haruey" in the list of robbers referred to William Hervey, Baron of Kidbrooke and Ross. Hervey published a poem in 1594 in which he referred to *The Rape of Lucrece,* published that same year. Hervey married Mary, daughter of Anthony Browne, First Viscount Montagu and the widow of Henry Wriothesley, the second Earl of Southampton and of Thomas Heneage. Mary was therefore the mother of the Henry Wriothesley, the third Earl of Southampton, to whom *The Rape of Lucrece* had been dedicated. Bevington suggested that this satirical naming of Hervey as a thief, in *Henry IV* part 1, was due to Southampton's unhappiness with his stepfather. Henry Wriothesley was opposed to his mother's remarriage to Hervey and Robert Devereux, the Earl of Essex, tried to dissuade Hervey from the match (Scoufos, 1979, 233). Shakespeare would therefore have a motive for lampooning Hervey if he was a supporter of Essex and Wriothesley, which Neville indeed was. After Mary died, Hervey married Cordella, daughter of Brian Annesley, in 1608. Due to her struggle with her sisters over their senile father, 1603–4, Cordella has been seen as a model for Cordelia (*King Lear* was written in this period, the earliest recorded performance being in 1606). Neville was "in an excellent position to know of the Annesley case" (James and Rubinstein, 2005, 175).

A stage direction announcing the entry of "sir Iohn Russel" also appears in the First Quarto of *Henry IV* part 2 (2.2.0). The contemporary John Russell married Elizabeth Hoby (née Cooke). Neville's mother-in-law, Catherine, was Elizabeth's sister. Lady Elizabeth Russell's London house was within the Blackfriars precincts, and she tried to prevent the use of the premises by theater companies (Scoufos, 1979, 239). Neville had lived at Blackfriars when a boy; indeed, he was baptized there. John Russell lived at Bisham, just ten miles from the Neville mansion at Billingbear. Henry Neville's mother was godmother of Elizabeth's daughter from her first marriage. Russell's father, Francis, was the second Earl of Bedford and an exile during the reign of Mary Tudor along with Anthony Cooke and Henry Neville's father. John, Duke of Bedford (brother of Henry V), appears in *Henry V* and *Henry VI* and is highly regarded by the bard, being called "valiant," "courageous," and "noble" (*Henry VI* part 1, 3.2.87, 93, 132). This may be another example of Neville using the names of people he knew and wanted to include in minor roles.

Falstaff

The dominant character in both plays is not the king or his son Hal but the mountainous figure of Falstaff. While he is a comic creation rather than a truly historical figure (despite two men, Sir John Oldcastle and Sir John Fastolf, being possible models), James and Rubinstein (2005, 54) did find links between Falstaff and Henry Neville. The original name for the character was Oldcastle, which can be seen as an opposite to New Town: Ne-ville.[9] Scoufos (1979) in a major study of the identity of Oldcastle and the implicit topical satire behind Falstaff showed that the material was based on an antipathy to the Cobham family (the original Oldcastle being a Lord Cobham). It is inconceivable that Shakspere, a lowly player, would dare to satirize a nobleman, and in any case he would not have had access to the state secrets implicit in the satire. The Gads Hill robbery, for example, is based on an actual robbery, in 1562, of the Spanish ambassador's courier, ordered by William Cecil and conducted by Lord Cobham's brothers disguised as highwaymen (Scoufos, 1979, 87). William Brooke, the tenth Baron Cobham, first married Dorothy, daughter of George Neville, fifth Baron Bergavenny (who appears on stage in Shakespeare's *Henry VIII*; see Chapter 8). Cobham was a double agent who endangered Catholic noblemen including Lord Montague (grandfather of Henry Wriothesley, the third Earl of Southampton) and the Earl of Pembroke. Many courtiers had reason to be distrustful of Cobham. He was involved in trying to free Mary, Queen of Scots. There was another theft of diplomatic letters from a courier at Gads Hill in 1569 by Cobham's men but, just as in the case of Falstaff, the stolen property was seized and returned to the victim (Scoufos, 1979, 93). Neville's father was in an excellent position to know of these machinations and to warn his son about Cobham. In 1569–70 Henry Neville senior was custodian at the Tower of London of one of the arrested Catholic noblemen, the Duke of Norfolk. Shallow tells us that Falstaff had been a page of the Duke of Norfolk (*Henry IV* part 2, 3.2.22). There is no historical evidence for Oldcastle (Falstaff) being a page in the Norfolk household (Scoufos, 1979, 103). Shakespeare is thus pointing to links between Norfolk and Cobham: indeed Cobham supported Norfolk as a possible husband for Mary, Queen of Scots. Norfolk lost his head following the Ridolfi plot of 1571 but, despite his involvement, Cobham survived. Cobham continued to be duplicitous, and Cecil knew of Cobham's betrayals. However, Cecil protected his untrustworthy friend and suppressed information implicating him in treasonous conspiracies so that Cobham became his informer (Scoufos, 1979, 103, 106). Cobham was also an enemy of Essex (Duncan, 1974, 84). Neville positioned himself between the Cecil and Essex factions at court, overtly allied to Cecil by kinship, but secretly drawn to Essex, as subsequent events showed.

In 1596 Cobham became lord chamberlain and so was in charge of the theaters. That a rising playwright should dare to satirize Cobham as the corrupt chamberlain at the inn in *Henry IV* part 1, act 2, scene 1, was a breathtakingly dangerous act. Unlike Thomas Nashe and Ben Jonson, William Shakspere was not arrested for such topical satire. The playwright simply stated, "Oldcastle died a martyr and this is not the man" (*Henry IV* part 2, epilogue). Changing the character's name was protection enough. Likewise, Neville's pseudonym protected him.

The comic figure of Falstaff can be seen as an alter-ego for the ambassador-to-be: Neville was obliged to give up an enjoyable life for a serious diplomatic role (James and Rubinstein, 2005, 120). Indeed the play has much to do with growing up, Prince Hal being an irresponsible adolescent whom we see grow into a responsible adult. The father-and-son themes are strong. It may be significant that Neville's father died in 1593.[10] The king's deathbed scene in the play is particularly moving.

There are other elements that suggest links between Neville and Falstaff. Neville shared physical characteristics with Falstaff. He was portly, jovial and suffered increasingly from gout. In signing his name in two books, one at Merton College, Oxford (21.DD.6), the other in a private collection, Neville described himself as "Militis": a soldier or knight. Neville's father had been deputy lieutenant and so responsible for mustering men, arming and training them (Duncan, 1974, 21). He had also been a sheriff, so Neville would have grown up in a household where military and legal processes were discussed.

In 1595, following his father's death, Neville became sheriff of Berkshire. In 1596 he was made deputy lieutenant (Duncan, 1974, 78–79). Neville, like Falstaff, was responsible for mustering men for the county. In 1597 he was on parliamentary committees dealing with the reformation of sundry abuses committed by soldiers and the cost of armor and weapons (Duncan, 1974, 84–5) and the "irksome and outmodish recruitment of soldiers" (James, 2008, 340). Act 3, scene 2 in *Henry IV* part 2 shows Falstaff recruiting soldiers from a muster arranged by the old justices Shallow and Silence in a scene that dramatically mocks the ridiculous abuses of this system of recruitment, with which Neville would have been all too familiar.

Henry IV was written circa 1596–8. Neville himself became a justice of the peace in 1583. The bard's touching portrait of the ancient judges Silence and Shallow shows he had observed older judges closely, as Neville surely had. The portrait was accurate enough to prompt Sir Charles Percy to write in a letter from Gloucestershire (circa 1600), "I am so pestered with Country business that I cannot come to London. If I stay here long, you will find me so dull, that I shall be taken as a Justice Silence or a Justice Shallow."[11] Charles' mother was Lady Catherine Neville, daughter of John Neville, fourth Baron Latimer. He was one of the group who commissioned the performance of *Richard II* on the eve of the Essex rebellion and was executed for his part in the debacle.

There are also links between the use of language in the play and in Henry Neville's letters around the same time. For example, on November 1, 1599, Neville used the words "unlooked for" in a letter (Sawyer, 1725, vol. 1, 126). Falstaff says "honour comes unlooked for" in *Henry IV* part 1 (5.3.60). Richard Neville, the Earl of Warwick, uses the words "unlook'd for friends" in *Henry VI* part 3 (5.1.14; Casson, 2010, 150).

Conclusion

There are many connections between the text of the two parts of *Henry IV* and Henry Neville's life and family. Neville's experience, knowledge and family history explain much that is otherwise unexplained about the text. We maintain that it would be unreasonable to dismiss all these as coincidental. These links between Shakespeare and the Neville family continued after Henry Neville's death. *Henry IV* was performed in 1660 by Thomas Killigrew's King's Company (Bevington, part 1, 2008, 70; part 2, 2008, 59). Thomas was Neville's wife's nephew's son. He was a playwright who, with William Davenant, was given a royal warrant to perform Shakespeare's plays (Casson, 2010, 34).

Chapter 5

Henry V
(1413–1422)

> King Henry: My cousin Westmoreland? No my fair cousin—
> *Henry V* (4.3.19)

As we saw in the previous chapter, Ralph Neville (1354–1425), sixth Baron of Raby and first Earl of Westmoreland, is an important figure in *Henry IV*, and the king calls him "my cousin Westmoreland" (part 1, 5.5.35). He appears again in *Henry V* in a way that appears to confirm a Neville bias.

Henry Neville, Ambassador to France, 1599–1601

At the end of *Henry IV* part 2, Prince John says:

> Ere this year expire,
> We bear our civil swords and native fire
> As far as France. I heard a bird so sing[1] [5.5.103].

It had been rumored through 1598 that Neville was going to France as ambassador. His appointment was confirmed in November 1598, and he was in France by May 8, 1599. Written in 1599, *Henry V* includes scenes in France (and in French) and the triumphal victory at Agincourt. Neville's time in France was not so successful but perhaps, setting out, he had high hopes. The play was registered on August 14, 1600, just after Neville had arrived back in London on August 6. James and Rubinstein (2005, 137, 118–122) have already explored the connections between Neville's life and *Henry V*.

The Neville Bias at Agincourt

In other plays we have found that the bard has a tendency to emphasize, or disguise, the roles played by members of the Neville family, or those closely related to them. *Henry V* offers further examples of this, especially in the battle of Agincourt. Furthermore, there are significant differences between the First Quarto (1600) and the First Folio (1623) versions in this regard, which revealing the hidden Neville connections helps to explain.

Warwick and Salisbury in the First Quarto (1600)

In the Saint Crispin's Day speech in act 4, scene 3, of the First Quarto the king declares:

> We few, we happy few, we band of brothers,
> For he today that sheds his blood by mine
> Shall be my brother; be he ne'er so base,
> This day shall gentle his condition [4.3.60].

At first sight this speech promotes a general patriotism, by inviting any "base" foot-soldier to share, on an equal basis with the king, the glory of their victory. However, the visual effect of the play might be somewhat different. According to the stage directions, the cast of characters on stage during this generous invitation by the king to be his "blood brothers" is quite restricted. Gloucester and Clarence were already blood brothers to the king, while Exeter was the king's uncle. In this respect, the playwright has been faithful to the historical record in the Holinshed *Chronicles,* according to which, Gloucester, Clarence and Exeter were with Henry V at Agincourt. That leaves two other characters on stage according to the First Quarto: Salisbury and Warwick, who have had, up to this point, no role in the play. The addition of Salisbury and Warwick appears to be a reflex addition by the author of parts 1, 2 and 3 of *Henry VI,* in which these earls were prominent. In fact, Holinshed's *Chronicles* does not record Warwick at Agincourt at all. Which leads us to ask why the bard might include the earls of Salisbury and Warwick in this patriotic scene of an English victory?

Warwick and Salisbury in the First Folio (1623)

The First Quarto of *Henry V* was published in 1600. By the time of the revision and publication of the First Folio in 1623, the author seems to have realized that Warwick was not at Agincourt or that he was Richard Beauchamp (1382–1439) and not a member of the Neville family. In the First Folio, Warwick has been largely deleted from the scene of the St. Crispin's Day speech as recorded in the Quarto, although he is still incongruously mentioned (4.3.54) and included in the stage directions at the start of act 1, scene 2. Two of Richard Beauchamp's daughters married Nevilles: Elizabeth married George Neville, first Baron Latimer (son of Ralph Neville, Earl of Westmoreland); Anne married Richard Neville (son of Richard Neville, the Earl of Salisbury and grandson of Ralph), in 1471, and so he became the sixteenth Earl of Warwick.

In contrast to Warwick and Westmoreland, the Earl of Salisbury really was at the Siege of Harfleur and Battle of Agincourt. He was Thomas Montacute.[2] According to Hall, his daughter Alice married Richard Neville, who was Westmoreland's son (Craik, 1995, 286, note). Salisbury is mentioned in the St. Crispin's Day speech in the First Folio and he has a significant speaking role in the scene (4.3.5, 68), before and after the speech. He is listed as a hero of the battle:

> Then shall our names,
> Familiar in his mouth as household words,
> Harry the king, Bedford and Exeter,
> Warwick and Talbot, Salisbury and Gloucester,
> Be in their flowing cups freshly remember'd [4.3.51].

The historically inaccurate presence of Warwick is not corrected in this heroes list. While not a Neville, Warwick was Henry Neville's ancestor, so may have been left in the list for that reason.

Westmoreland in the First Folio (1623)

So, in the First Folio, who has replaced the role performed by Warwick in the Quarto? The dramatist introduced a new character, Westmoreland, who was not present in the First Quarto. Westmoreland was Ralph Neville, who was father to Richard Neville (1400–1460), the Earl of Salisbury, and grandfather to Richard Neville (1428–1471), the Earl of Warwick and Salisbury. He stars in parts 1 and 2 of *Henry IV.* The difficulty with this alteration is that in Hall and Holinshed, Henry V had specifically assigned Westmoreland to guard the Scottish border during this period, and this placed him in England, not at Agincourt (Craik, 1995, 285, note). In the First Folio, the king directly addresses Ralph Neville, the Earl of Westmoreland, and refers to him as "cousin" (Ralph Neville married the half sister of Henry V's father). Although not mentioned in the above heroes list, his name is mentioned twice and he is called "kind kinsman" (4.3.10) and "cousin" or "coz" three times:

> My cousin Westmoreland? No my fair cousin...
> No, faith, my coz, wish not a man from England:
> God's peace! I would not lose so great an honour
> As one man more, methinks, would share from me,
> For the best hope I have. O! do not wish one more:
> Rather proclaim it, Westmoreland, through my host,
> That he which hath no stomach to this fight,
> Let him depart... [4.3.19, 30–36].

In the First Quarto this speech was addressed to Warwick. The curious change to Westmoreland in the First Folio may be explained if both the playwright and Westmoreland were Nevilles.

Thomas Beaufort, Duke of Exeter

In the play Exeter is present at the Battle of Agincourt. This is not historically accurate, though Holinshed mistakenly reported that he was there and commanded the rearguard (Craik, 1995, 231, note). He was not a brother of Henry V, but his step-uncle. Henry IV and Exeter were stepbrothers, who shared the same father, John the Gaunt, Duke of Lancaster, but had different mothers. Exeter married Margaret Neville.

Faulconbridge and Chatillon

Among the French nobles listed in the play who fought and died at Agincourt are Chatillon (3.5.43 and 4.8.95) and Faulconbridge (3.5.44 and 4.8.101). These are in Shakespeare's *King John* (and *The Troublesome Raigne of King John*); in Chapter 1 we traced their association with the Nevilles. According to the Holinshed *Chronicles,* these nobles did indeed die at Agincourt, but the playwright has modified the chronicled name Fauconberg to Fauconbridge/Faulconbridge. It is notable that out of the long list of French casualties in the chronicles, Shakespeare chose these two names. He was in effect acknowledging that the Falconbridge name originated from France. Honigmann (2006, xxiv) pointed out, "The Faulconbridge title came to England with Belasius, Lord Faulconbridge, in 1066. In Shakespeare's day the Belasyse family of Yorks (for which the title of Fauconberg was revived in the 17th century) would be *the* Faulconbridges." The Nevilles had extensive property in Yorkshire and had themselves arrived with William the Conqueror. Gilbert de Neville was William's admiral.

Princess Katherine: The French Connection

In one of several scenes in which French is used, the French princess, Katherine of Valois,[3] is learning English prior to her marriage to Henry (3.4). Neville was a fluent French speaker and writer: letters by him in French are preserved in Winwood's *Memorials* dated June 6, 1599 (Sawyer, 1725), around the time *Henry V* was written. To be able to write playfully in French suggests an easy familiarity with the language, which Neville had. He was to teach French to Richard Carew's son, who accompanied him to France (James, 2008, 341). In addition, in early April 1600, the secretary of state, Robert Cecil, asked Neville to help a young man learn more fluent French:

> I must conclude my Letter with a Request. This Bearer is a yong Gentleman whose Name is Townshend: he hath been well bredd, and by his owne industrie attayned to a good superficiall Knowledge in the *French* and *Italian* Tongues, and would be able with a little exercise to fair Hands.[4] My end is (at his Return) to have him attend upon my Boye, in which respect I can be content to be at some moderate Charge with him. Now Sir, I shall take it for a very great Favour, if you will please to cause some of your People to place him in *la Chambre garnie* in *Paris,* and to agree to all Charges incident. For I know from Experience, that if those yong Men that goe over, were severed from Company of English, that their Language would increase in much shorter tyme: And I am purposed he shall not stay long, and doe desire his Tongue may be pure. To this I must adde only this Request, that you would be pleased (ever for my poore Boyes sake, your wive's cosen) that Mr *Wynwood* or some of yours, may hearken whether he use any riottous Life or Disorder, and certifie me, to the Intent that I may gesse whether he be fitt to be neere my Sonne [Sawyer, 1725, vol. 1, 167].

The protective father and head of the English government may have blanched at the English-French lesson given in *Henry V* with "mots de son mauvais, corruptible, gros, et impudique, et non pour les dames d'honneur d'use" (3.4.53–56). When the Princess Katherine's tutor translates the French words for "le pied" and "la robe," to "the foot" and "the coun (gown?)," the princess only hears the French words for "fuck" (*foutre*) and "cunt" (*con*). Foul-mouthed Pistol uses the word "foutre" twice in *Henry IV* part 2 (5.3.97 and 114). With a tutor like this, the lessons for the secretary of state's son would hardly be "pure"!

Furthermore, Cecil's letter, requesting that Neville ask others to spy on

Townsend's behavior in Paris to discover "whether he use any riottous Life or Disorder," appears to be a model for Polonius who, in *Hamlet,* suggests to Reynaldo that he spy on his son in Paris in act 2 scene 1. *Hamlet* was written between 1599 and 1601, i.e., just at the time of this letter or soon after. The word "riotous" occurs in the play (4.5.101). Polonius's sententious advice to his son Laertes has been thought to be modelled on William Cecil, Lord Burghley's precepts to his son.[5] Some evidence for this can be found in the name given to Polonius in the First Quarto: Corambis. W. Cecil's motto was "Cor unum, via una" (one heart, one way), and "Corambis" is wordplay meaning "double-hearted." Having been to Burghley's school when he was a boy, Neville had reason to remember the old man's wise words to his pupils. (For further evidence linking *Hamlet* and Neville, see Chapter 10.) Thus father and son, William and Robert Cecil, had provided Neville with the model for Polonius.

In *Henry V* the Duke of Burgundy makes an intriguing analogy for "handling a French maid," comparing the situation to "blind" (lustful) "flies at Bartholomew-tide" (5.2.305). This reference would certainly have aroused memories of the St. Bartholomew's Day Massacre in Paris in 1572, in which thousands of Protestants were killed. Both Essex and Neville may have heard firsthand reports of this day from their fathers-in-law, Walsingham and Killigrew, respectively, who were both diplomats in Paris at the time. Memories of St. Bartholomew's Day were still fresh when Neville wrote to Cecil from Paris and mentioned the massacre in a letter dated May 26, 1599 (Sawyer, 1725, vol. 1, 34).

Rouen is mentioned twice in the play (3.5.54, 64). At the English siege of Rouen in 1591, the Earl of Essex was accompanied by Sir Henry Killigrew, Neville's father-in-law (Archer, Adams and Bernard, 2003, 264). Neville travelled through Rouen on his way to Paris, mentioning this in a letter dated June 6, 1599 (Sawyer, 1725, vol. 1, 38).

Three Welshmen

The Welsh soldier Fluellen may be based on Dafydd ap Llewelyn ap Hywel. Fluellen is an anglicization of the Welsh Llewelyn. He was commonly known as Dafydd (Davy) Gam. Henry V knew Dafydd personally. He died heroically protecting the king at Agincourt. He is mentioned in the list of the dead in the play (4.8.106). Dafydd's daughter Gwladys married Sir William ap Thomas (after her first husband, Sir Roger Vaughan, was killed at Agincourt).

After William's death his brother Philip was supported by Sir Edward Neville, third Baron of Abergavenny. William and Gwladys's son, William Herbert, first Earl of Pembroke, was the great, great-grandfather of William Herbert, third Earl of Pembroke and patron of the First Folio. Henry Neville was supported in the Privy Council by this Herbert in James I's reign.

Another soldier in *Henry V* is called Williams. The name Williams may have recalled a contemporary figure. An Elizabethan Welshman, Sir Roger Williams, may have inspired the bard to celebrate a Welsh military genius in the character of Fluellen. He was described as valiant and wise and worth his weight in gold by the Earl of Leicester, who knighted him in 1586 after the battle of Zutphen.[6] Sir Roger Williams had been with Essex during his campaign in support of Navarre in 1591. Navarre declared, "Glory be to God and the said Sir [Roger] Williams who has not believed by his actions the good opinion that all good people of both nations had of him this long time." Williams became close to Essex, who attended him on his deathbed. He gave all he had to Essex when he died in 1595, just four years prior to the writing of *Henry V.* Several other facts about Sir Roger Williams support his identification as the source for Fluellen: he had fought a duel in 1581, taking up the challenge of another man, just as Fluellen is attacked by Williams in the king's place in the incident with the glove (4.8.1) (Churchyard, 1602, 38). Furthermore Williams was author of *A Brief Discourse of War, with His Opinions Concerning Some Part of Martial Discipline,* published by Thomas Orwin[7] in 1590. Fluellen's endorsement of military discipline in 3.6.53–7 and 3.6.41–2 reflects this. The book was dedicated to the Earl of Essex.[8] Sir Roger Williams was identified by Rowland Whyte as the Soldier in an entertainment in honor of Essex devised by Francis Bacon in 1595 (Jardine and Stewart, 1998, 180). Essex wore a leek in his cap on St. David's Day, so the whole incident of Fluellen and the leek may be seen to have contemporary relevance, given the reference to Essex by the chorus in act 4.

"The General of Our Gracious Empress": The Earl of Essex

Henry V is virtually unique in the canon in having a direct reference to a living contemporary.[9] The chorus of act 5 refers to Robert Devereux, the Earl of Essex, who was leader of the expeditionary force sent to conquer Ireland in 1599.

How London doth pour out her citizens.
The mayor and all his brethren in best sort,
Like to the senators of th'antique Rome,
With the plebeians swarming at their heels,
Go forth and fetch their conqu'ring Caesar in:
As, by a lower but by loving likelihood,
Were now the general of our gracious empress,
As in good time he may, from Ireland coming,
Bringing rebellion broached on his sword,
How many would the peaceful city quit
To welcome him! [5.0.24].

The chorus looks forward to a triumphal homecoming, resembling a Roman Triumph, and we can therefore deduce that the play must have been written between Essex's departure for Ireland on March 27 and his unhappy return in September 1599. Neville was a supporter of Essex and enquired about his progress in his 1599–1600 letters to Cecil, reporting what he had heard from French and other sources. He was reluctant to go as ambassador to France but was persuaded to by Essex. He took with him Ralph Winwood "at my Lord of Essex command" (McClure, 1939, 51, 65). Navarre, for whom Essex had fought ten years earlier, had by then become Henry IV of France, and Neville was to meet him as English ambassador and negotiate the repayment of Elizabeth I's loan from the time of Essex's support.

It has already been mentioned that the play was registered on August 14, 1600, soon after Neville had arrived back to London. Just three months later, on November 15, 1600, with the political isolation of the Earl of Essex, Neville wrote to his secretary Ralph Winwood in Paris, saying, "The Earl of Essex is no **actor** in our **Triumphs** as I wrote was conceived" (Sawyer, 1725, vol. 1, 274). This specifically refers to Essex's continued exclusion from court, in his not being expected to take part in the "running at the Coronation Day" (the annual "tilt," the jousting festivities to celebrate Elizabeth's accession on November 17; see Neville's letter of November 2, 1600 in Sawyer, 1725, vol. 1,). Neville's use of a theatrical metaphor ("actor") and his reference to "our Triumphs" matches Shakespeare's imagery of the play *Henry V* with its direct allusion to Essex receiving a Roman Triumph.

"The topical allusions to the Earl of Essex in Gower's mention of a beard of the General's cut (3.6.75–6) and the Chorus's anticipation of his triumphal return from Ireland (5.0.29–35) have persuaded some that Shakespeare was as active a sympathizer with Essex as was Shakespeare's patron, the Earl of Southampton, to whom he had dedicated his two narrative poems" (Craik, 1995, 75–6). It was, of course, Neville, and not William Shakspere, who was imprisoned with Southampton in the Tower of London after the failed Essex uprising of 1601. While no one ever referred to him as Shakespeare's patron, Southampton was called "Neville's champion"[10] and his "great patron"[11] by his contemporaries.

International Politics

When King Henry V is attempting to woo Princess Katherine, he says, "Shall not thou and I, between Saint Denis and Saint George, compound a boy, half French, half English, that shall go to Constantinople and take **the Turk** by the beard?" (5.2.204). This anachronism has been noted by scholars. The Turks were not in Constantinople until 38 years later, in 1453. The future son of Henry V and Katherine, Henry VI, never attempted a crusade to Constantinople. Shakespeare's contemporary, Robert Devereux, the Earl of Essex, did have Constantinople on his agenda. In his *Civil Wars* Samuel Daniel addressed the earl, saying, "Thou O worthy Essex ... Shouldst have conducted armies, and now stood against the strength of all the Eastern powers." Indeed, Essex sent out spies and diplomats to the Near East, such as Sir Anthony Shirley. Neville undoubtedly knew the Shirley brothers, because in 1604 he served on a special Parliamentary committee concerning the disputed election of Sir Thomas Shirley (Duncan, 1974, 195). A play, *The Travailles of Three English Brothers,* first performed in 1607, illustrated a plan to forge alliances with Persia so as to outflank the Ottoman Empire. This play is about Sir Thomas Shirley and his brothers, Anthony and Robert. The playwrights, John Day, William Rowley and George Wilkins, appear to have imitated scenes from *The Merchant of Venice* (Parr, 1995, 79, 101). The scene between Sophy's niece and her maid (Parr, 1995, 78) may also echo that between Kate and her maid in *Henry V,* as well as recalling Portia and her maid in *The Merchant of Venice* (1.2).

In many of his letters to Cecil in the summer of 1599, Neville reported news he had heard of "**the Turk**," of his sickness, wars, truces, peace treaties, revolts (Sawyer, 1725, vol. 1, 93, 118, 124, 126). On August 8, 1599, Neville wrote to the secretary of state, Robert Cecil, saying:

> **The *Turke*** is sayd to be recovered of his great Sickness, and to have shewed himself publickly in the Moschee.[12] The Peace is treated between him and the Emperour by means of the ***Tartars,*** from when the ***Persians*** have lately recovered a great Country, which they have occupyed during the Warrs against the *Turke,* and here defeated a great Army of them, and slain their *Cham.* The ***Sophi***

hath sent an Embassage to the *Turk* to communicate his good Success therein, and withall to demand Restitution of such Countries as have bin in these late Warrs taken from him [our emphasis; Sawyer, 1725, vol. 1, 88].

In *Henry V* the king also refers to the Tartars, as well as the Turks (2.2.123). It is thought that *Twelfth Night* was written just after *Henry V,* in 1600–1, and in it there is not only reference to the Tartars (2.5), but also to the leader, or Sophy, of Persia, similar to that referred to in Henry Neville's 1599 correspondence. In *Twelfth Night* Fabian swears, "I will not give my part of this sport for a pension of a thousand to be paid from the Sophy" (*Twelfth Night*, 2.5.180). Toby Belch also mentions the Sophy (*Twelfth Night*, 3.4.284). In these exotic references Shakespeare is believed to have been recalling Shirley's journey to Persia (Lothian and Craik, 2005, xxx, 72 note). The correspondence of Henry Neville, the English ambassador to France, demonstrates an awareness of the real historical people on whom these theatrical figures are based. Towards the end of his life Neville "was part of an attempt to open an overland trading route to the Far East across Asia for trading purposes" (James and Rubinstein, 2005, 200). John Chamberlain wrote to Winwood, on May 6, 1613, reporting, "the King ... hath caused Sir *Henry Nevill* to conferr with some of the Councill about it diverse times; wherein they say he showed great Sufficiency, and discoursed at large what commodity might arise by bringing the whole trade of Persia, and the inland Parts of the *East Indies* up the River Hydaspes" (McClure, 1939, 448). Neville invested in the East India Company (Duncan, 1975, 199). We have already noted that there is, among Neville's books, a volume, dated 1594, *Historia della Guerra Fra Turchi et Persiani* (see Chapter 2).

National Politics

Henry V's soliloquy in act 4 (4.1.230–289), when he muses over his sleeping army before the battle of Agincourt, is not to be found in the early quartos of the play (1600, 1602 and 1619) and only appears in the First Folio of 1623. We suggest it is a Jacobean addition. It is a speech with much humility, revealing his contempt for ceremony and his anxiety for the lives of his people. The play's idealized king understands that royal ceremony and the resultant adoration is only the result of "place, degree and form, creating awe and fear" (4.1.251–2). He sees that all the flattery and ceremony is actually powerless to heal a fever or summon sleep. This speech may be seen to be a warning to James I that the monarch was not divine. The lines, apparently addressed to the "idol ceremony," might also be addressed to James:

What kind of god art thou, that suffer'st more
Of mortal griefs than do thy worshippers? [4.1.246–7].

Soon after James I succeeded the English throne, he claimed a divine right to rule (McIlwain, 1918, xxxv).[13] Neville was not a sycophantic courtier giving "poisoned flattery" (4.1.56). He did, however, try to help James achieve a balanced relationship with the House of Commons and create a United Kingdom.

A United Kingdom

Neville accompanied Essex on a diplomatic mission to Scotland in 1583. In the dialogue between the Scotsman Jamy, the Irishman MacMorris, Welshman Fluellen, and the Englishman Gower in act 3 (3.2.78–143) there is a deliberate attempt to portray a "United Kingdom" with the various captains representing the nations that were coming together to establish Britain in James I's reign. This scene, which is not in the 1600 quarto but is in the First Folio of 1623, was possibly devised after the accession of James I to the throne in 1603 and reflects the optimism engendered by the unification with Scotland. The friendly Captain Jamy perhaps echoes a friendly King James. Neville was involved in the negotiations for the Union. However, Neville was dismayed by James's extravagance towards his Scottish friends and was opposed to the excessive promotion of Scottish courtiers. This may explain the bard's residual anti–Scottish view (evident in *Edward III*; see Chapter 2) as when Henry says:

We do not mean the coursing *snatchers* only
But fear the main intendment of the Scot,
Who hath been still a giddy neighbour to us;
For you shall read that my great-grandfather
Never went with his forces into France
But that the Scot on his **unfurnish'd kingdom**
Came pouring like a tide into a breach,
With ample and brim fullness of his force,
Galling the gleaned land with hot assays,
Girding with grievous sieges castles and towns;
That England, being empty of defence,
Hath shook and trembled at th'ill neighbourhood [italics added; 1.2.143].

The italicized parts seem to have been added to the First Folio, to emphasize the power of the Scots. While the description of the Scots as "coursing snatchers" may sound negative, it is perhaps less pejorative than the quarto's "coursing sneakers." It seems that the bard was treading a fine line here between telling the history and possibly offending the new Scottish king. In the 1600 quarto the last line reads, "Hath shooke and trembled at the brute hereof." "Brute" here means "bruit,"[14] i.e., news (although there may be a pun on brute, as in brutality). In his letters Neville used the word "bruit" for news (James, 2008, 250). In the original quarto and First Folio this word is most often spelled "bruite" with a final "e." This spelling is found in Neville's letters and perhaps explains the spelling "brute" in the 1600 quarto of *Henry V.*

The use of the words "his **unfurnish'd** kingdom" in the above passage recalls Neville's letter dated August 7, 1599, in which he wrote that the queen had "**disfurnished** herself to **furnish** them" (i.e., the French).

Sources for Henry V: *Hall and Horace*

While Holinshed was the major source for the play, Hall's *Chronicles* were also used by the playwright. Of the above passage, Craik (1995, 140 note) pointed out that "these lines amplify an argument of Westmoreland's in Hall (not in Holinshed)." Westmoreland, of course, was Ralph Neville. In the play, just 22 lines later, Westmoreland says:

> But there's a saying very old and true,
> "If that you will France win,
> Then with Scotland first begin" [1.2.166].

Neville, annotating Hall's *Chronicle,* wrote in the margin of Folio vii of the Henry V section:

> he that wyll fraunce wynne
> with Scotland he must begynne [Alan and Lubbock, 1954, 137].

The annotated copy of Hall's *Chronicle* was discovered in 1940 by Alan Keen; the first thing he noticed was a passage that occurs in *Henry V.* He saw that the Latin words "In terram salicam mulieres ne succedant" had been underlined. In the play these very words are quoted by the archbishop of Canterbury, who helpfully translates them as, "No woman shall succeed in Salike land" (1.2.39, First Folio spelling). The Hall annotator had written in the margin, "note the exposition."

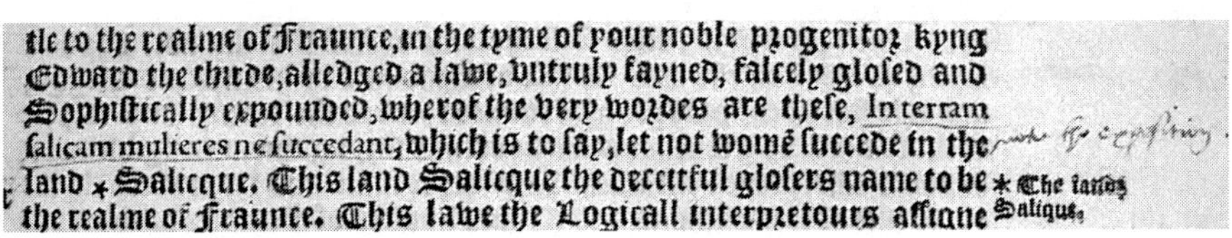
tle to the realme of Fraunce, in the tyme of your noble progenitor kyng
Edward the thirde, alledged a lawe, untruly fayned, falsely glosed and
Sophistically expounded, wherof the very wordes are these, In terram
salicam mulieres ne succedant, which is to say, let not womẽ succede in the
land * Salicque. This land Salicque the deceitful glosers name to be * The landes
the realme of Fraunce. This lawe the Logicall interpretours assigne Salique,

Halle's Chronicle, Henry V, f.iv[b] (by permission of the Trustee of the Tudor Players [Rufford], the owners of the annotated Hall's *Chronicle*).

The text referred to explains:

> which is to say, let not womẽ succede in the land *Salicque. This land Salicque the deceitful glosers name to be the realm of Fraunce. This lawe the logicall interpretours assigne to directe the croune and regalitie of the same region, as who would, say that to that preheminence no woman were liable to aspire, nor no heire female was worthy to inherite.

The asterisk refers to a printed marginal note, "*The lands Salique." Scholars agree that the Hall's *Chronicle* passage was the source used by Shakespeare for *Henry V.* Neville, annotating his copy of *Leicester's Commonwealth*, also made a unique annotation that reads, "**The Lawe Salique in ffraunce.**"

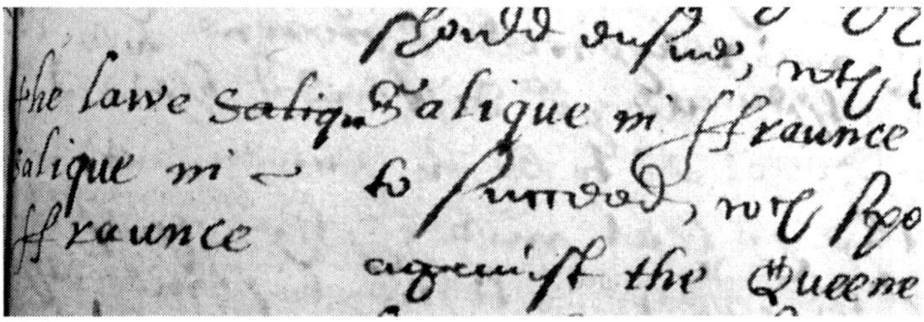

Worsley MSS 47, 39 (by permission of the Eighth Earl of Yarborough and Lincolnshire Archives).

The phrase used in the main text of *Leicester's Commonwealth* is "**the Law Salick in Fraunce**" (original spelling). In *Henry V* the king refers to "**the Law Salike,** that they have **in France**" (1.2.11, First Folio spelling).[15] The archbishop of Canterbury also speaks of "this **Salique Law**" (1.2.91, First Folio spelling). Neville and Shakespeare spell this as "'Salique," as does the Hall marginal note. This identical spelling might seem like coincidence at a time when spelling was not standardized. However, it is precisely the shared spelling of the river "Elue" in the First Folio (as opposed to Elbe: 1.2.52) that proves Shakespeare was reading Hall here (who makes this mistake) and not Holinshed (who corrects it). It seems that *Leicester's Commonwealth* sparked Neville's interest in the "Salique" law, which he then researched in Hall and used in *Henry V* (Casson, 2010, 37, 76). The annotated Hall has many more hand written marginal annotations relevant to the play, and there is good evidence that these were written by Neville (Casson, 2010, 73–94).

Shakespeare's debt to the Latin poet Horace has been noted by Craik (1995, 127 and 230 notes) in two passages in *Henry V.* The first is a simile used by the bishop of Ely (1.1.65) that derives from Horace's Odes (1.12.45–6); the second is an image used by the French king (3.5.52) that derives from

Horace's Satires (2.5.41). There are two small volumes of Horace's poetry amongst Neville's books with passages underlined, showing they had been read. The 1509 volume is heavily annotated in a sepia ink that has faded, and both the above images to be found in *Henry V* are in passages that are annotated. In the first image Ely, speaking of the young Prince Hal, says that he

> Grew like the summer grass, fastest at night,
> Unseen, yet **crescive** in his facility [1.1.65].

In the Horace the words "**crescit** occulto" (growing unseen) have the word "occulto" written above them.[16]

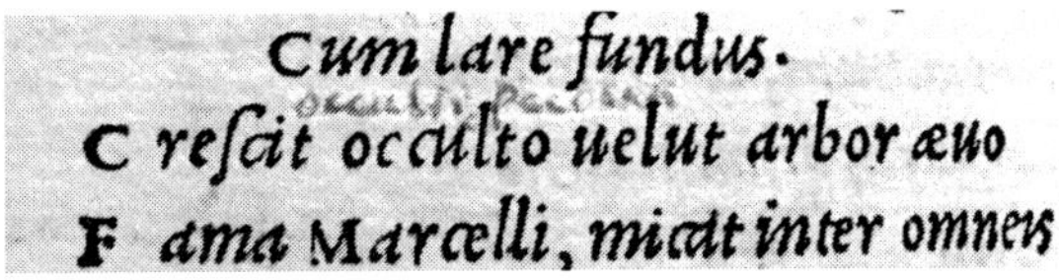

Cum lare fundus.
C reſcit occulto uelut arbor æuo
F ama Marcelli, micat inter omnes

***Horace Poems*, 1509, page 18 (private collection).**

The second passage is a quotation by Horace of another Latin poet, Furius Bibaculus, and Horace changed his line about Jupiter, substituting the name Furius. Neville shows his awareness of this change by noting "Juppiter" in the margin.

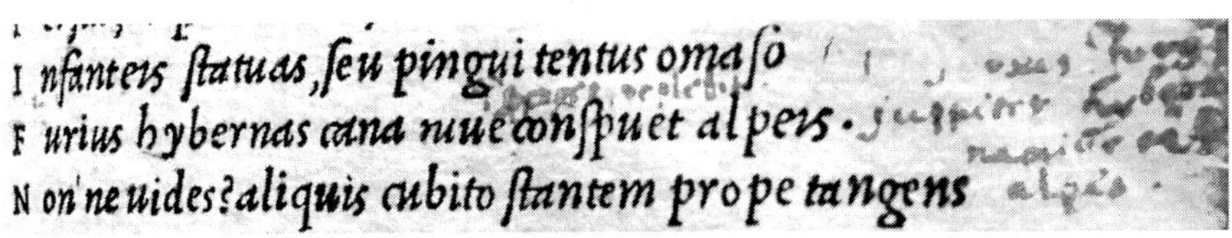

I nfantes ſtatuas, ſeu pingui tentus omaſo
F urius hybernas cana niue conſpuet alpes.
N on ne uides? aliquis cubito ſtantem prope tangens

***Horace Poems*, 1509, page 297 (private collection).**

In both Horace and Shakespeare the image is of the snow in the Alps, and we can clearly see the word "alpes" is the last word in the marginal annotation. Neville referred to Horace in one of his letters (James and Rubinstein, 2005, 164). Neville had travelled through the Alps in 1581.

Neville's Letters of 1599

We are able to compare the vocabulary used by Neville at the same time that Shakespeare wrote this particular play because his letters, written during his ambassadorial service, are preserved in Winwood's *Memorials* (Sawyer, 1725). We will focus first on one letter and then look at others. Because Neville was in France when he wrote these letters and had been there since May, it cannot be argued that his vocabulary had been influenced by having seen Shakespeare's play.

Shared Vocabulary in Neville's Letter of August 1, 1599 and Henry V

Of 1,113 words to be found in Neville's letter of August 1, 1599 (Sawyer, 1725, vol. 1, 82), 329 words (29.5 percent) occur in *Henry V.* The play was mostly written in the period April–August, so this letter was written towards the very end of the period when *Henry V* was first composed. The letter was written from Blois, France. We can see the variety and specific nature of the vocabulary used by Neville and Shakespeare. Many words are common, but when they occur together with more specialized words such as "articles," "yoke," "Roüen," "preservation" and "unprovided," they appear to be a unique combination shared only by Neville and Shakespeare at that time.

The word "**inconveniences**," which is to be found in the letter, was only used once by Shakespeare, in *Henry V.* This unique word occurs in a context of international negotiations in France. He writes, "We spake of the *Article* of the *Treaty or Reglement of Depradations,* which I desyred might be changed, and quallifyed in some sort, as her Majestie might be freed from such **Inconveniences** as had thereby already happened, and were dayly like to happen" (italics in original).

In *Henry V* this word occurs in relation to international negotiations in France. Burgundy says,

> my speech entreats
> That I may know the let, why gentle Peace
> Should not expel these **inconveniences**
> And bless us with her former qualities [5.2.64].

The passages are parallel in situation and language: instead of "we spake" in the letter we have "my speech" in the play. The word "quallifyed" is in the letter, "qualities" in the play. Both are concerned with the inconveniences to a female (the queen in the letter, personified Peace in the play).

The only time Shakespeare used the word "petit" was in *Henry V*. In his letter Neville also used the French word "pettit," writing, "such **pettit** respects of **Profit**." In the prologue to act 3 of *Henry V* there is a reference to "Some **petty** and un**profit**able dukedoms." The alliteration is actually stronger in Neville's letter ("**p**ettit res**p**ects of **P**rofit"). James (2008, 251) also noticed that Shakespeare used the word "**petit**" in *Henry V* when a French soldier asks, "**Petit** monsieur, que dit-il?" (4.4.50). (See addendum 1 at the end of this chapter for lists of words to be found in this letter and *Henry V*.)

Other 1599–1600 Letters

In Neville's letters written on July 13, 1599, and again on July 29, 1600, he used the word **Commissioners**, which is unique to *Henry V* (2.2.61). In both cases the word is in relation to France. Neville wrote about concerns "to establish the Traffick of our English Commodities in France, and all the Conditions appointed to be considered of by especiall Commissioners" (Sawyer, 1725, vol. 1, 64). In the play Henry V asks, "And now to our French causes: Who are the late commissioners?" (2.2.). In the section on Henry V in Hall's *Chronicle*, Neville noted, "The **commission** to req[uire] the crowne of France" (Alan and Lubbock, 1954, 138).

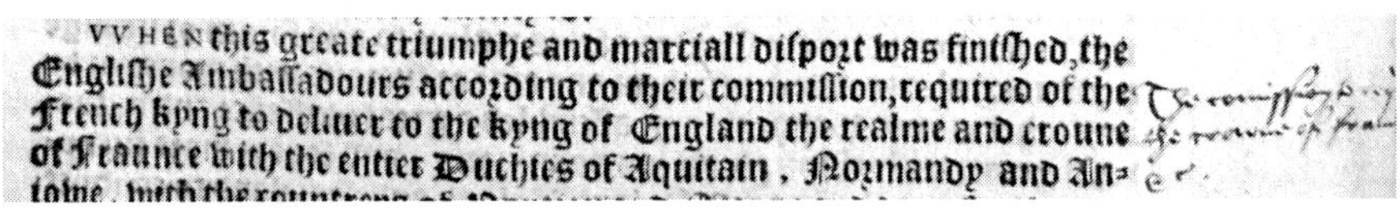
VVHEN this greate triumphe and marciall disport was finished, the Englishe Ambassadours according to their commission, required of the French kyng to deliuer to the kyng of England the realme and croune of Fraunce with the entier Duchies of Aquitain, Normandy and Anioine, with the countreys of

The annotated Hall's *Chronicles* (by permission of the Trustee of the Tudor Players [Rufford], the owners of the annotated Hall's *Chronicle*).

In his letter of May 15, 1599, Neville wrote that he would serve the queen to the "uttermost of my Abillitie." In the play Fluellen says, "my uttermost power" (3.6.9). In this letter Neville reported, "Her Majestie did acknowledge his great Wisdome in discovering the Errours of **his Predecessours**" (Sawyer, 1725, vol. 1, 21). In *Henry V* the archbishop of Canterbury refers to France and sums of money offered to "**his predecessors**" (1.1.81). Shakespeare only used this word three times: the other times are in *Macbeth* and *Coriolanus*, both later than *Henry V*. Neville had been sent to France to regain money lent to Henry IV by Queen Elizabeth.

In the same letter Neville wrote that he had delivered a message of congratulations from Elizabeth I to the French king for surviving an attempted assassination, "for his **Preservation** from the Attempts which had bene against his **Person**" and "her Majesties **Care** of his safety." Confronting his potential assassins, Henry V speaks of "their dear **care** and tender **preservation** of our **person**" (2.2.58). One of these assassins was Sir Thomas Grey, who had married Ralph Neville's daughter (Craik, 1995, 154 note). Immediately after naming Grey, the king speaks to Ralph (i.e., Westmoreland, 2.2.68–70). At the time the play was written, Neville reported to Cecil that he did not trust "the Master of Gray" (Patrick, sixth Lord Gray). In his letter of June 29, 1599, Neville stated that Gray was "**hollow** and venall." The chorus to act 2 lists the assassins and describes them as "a nest of **hollow** bosoms." Neville reported Gray's saying, "He was free and owed no Respect or service to any Prince." Neville warned Cecil that Gray's intelligence was "both untrew and utterly improbable" (Sawyer, 1725, vol. 1, 53). The word "improbable" only occurs once in Shakespeare, in *Twelfth Night* (3.4.129), which was written in 1600 (i.e., after Neville's letter).

In his letter of June 6, 1599, Neville wrote, "my poor and weak **Endeavours**" (Sawyer, 1725, vol. 1, 44). In *Henry V* Burgundy says he has "labour'd with all my wits, my pains and strong **endeavours**" (5.2.25). Both phrases are structurally identical: "my xxxx and xxxx endeavours."

In his letter of June 27, 1599, Neville used the word "irreconcileable" (Sawyer, 1725, vol. 1, 52). Shakespeare never used this word but did use the word "irreconciled" just once, in *Henry V* (4.1.152).

Word Play: A Neville Line

In the revision of the St. Crispin's Day speech in the First Folio, King Henry V declares:

> From this day to the ending of the world,
> But we in it shall be remembered;
> We few, we happy few, we band of brothers,
> For he today that sheds his blood with me
> Shall be my brother; be he **ne'er so vile**,
> This day shall gentle his condition [4.3.58].

Apart from about 14 extra lines added to the speech, the Folio text is almost identical to that in the First Quarto of 1600. But for some reason, the second to last line has been modified:

FROM: For he today that sheds his blood by mine / Shall be my brother; be he **ne'er so base**.
TO: For he today that sheds his blood with me / Shall be my brother; be he **ne'er so vile**.

The change from "base" to "vile" means a loss of powerful alliteration in adjacent lines: band of brothers, blood, brother, be, base, abed. Is there another reason for the change, and what might be gained from it? The words "base" and "vile" have an overlap of meaning. Both can mean "lowly," as is clearly the intention here, but they can also mean "dishonourable" and "unworthy," which is not meant by this passage. The king uses the milder word "base" before the siege of Harfleur, declaring, "For there is none of you so mean and base / that hath not noble lustre in your eyes" (3.1.29–30). The more benign use of "base" is when the guard, Pistol, challenges the disguised King Henry V to identify himself, demanding, "art thou officer? Or art thou base, common and popular" (4.1.37–8). In act 2, scene 1, Bardolph invites his drinking friends Nym and Pistol to join him as "three sworn brothers to France" (2.1.12), paralleling the St. Crispin's Day speech but for "base" commoners (2.1.29). As their conversation becomes more dysfunctional and abusive, Pistol employs the more pejorative term "vile," such as "O viper vile!" (2.1.45), and "O braggard vile" (2.1.60). Perhaps to stress that these "brothers" were too "vile" to be part of "God's will" and "God's peace" of the St. Crispin's Day promise (4.3.23, 31), we are later informed that Bardolph and Nym are both hanged (4.5.75) for looting a church (3.2.46, 3.6.41, 3.6.104).

In other plays Shakespeare generally used "vile" in the pejorative sense,[17] and only in the St. Crispin's day speech (4.3.62) is it meant as the more neutral "lowly" and "of humble birth" (Crystal and Crystal 2002, 483). This may conceal wordplay on the Neville name: "**Ne'er so vile**," contains "**Ne'vile**." Other examples of this word play on "vile" have been found in the sonnets, such as Sonnet 121, "'Tis better to be vile th**en vile** esteem'd" (which contains "**en vile**"). The original spelling of "than" as "then" in the first printing of the sonnets in 1609 means this spelling hides the name "Nevile" in plain sight. The Neville family motto of "ne vile velis" means "wishing nothing base (or vile)" and includes the separation of "ne vile," as in sonnet 121: "en vile."

In his play *Every Man Out of His Humour* (1599) Ben Jonson ridiculed not only *Henry V* but also the playwright himself. Then, sometime between August 14, 1601, and December 21, 1601, Ben Jonson publicly apologized for his satirizing of other poets. This apology was not published until 1616, when *Poetaster* was printed with the *Apologetical Dialogue* attached. The fifteen-year delay was due to the censorship of the apology when the First Quarto version of *Poetaster* was published on December 21, 1601. This censorship was "by Authority." Below is the *Apologetical Dialogue*, which was censored:

> Now, for the Players, it is true, I taxed 'hem,
> And yet, but some; and those so sparingly,

As all the rest might have sat still, unquestion'd,
Had they but the wit, or conscience,
To think well of themselves. But, impotent they
Thought each man's vice belong'd to their whole tribe:
And much good do't 'hem. What th'have done 'gainst me,
I am not mov'd with. If it gave 'hem meat,
Or got 'hem clothes. 'Tis well. That was their end.
Only amongst them, I am sorry for
Some better natures, by the rest so drawn,
To run in that **vile line**.

This has perplexed scholars, as there is nothing obvious that may be considered so offensive as to merit an apology. As Bednarz noted, "the only candidate ever proposed for Jonson's allusion to "some better nature" is Shakespeare (Bednarz, 2001, 24). Yet "better natures" is a term more evocative of nobility than of the common player. Might this, therefore, be the reason for the censorship of this passage until after Neville's death? It appears that this dramatist of a "better nature" was the only one for whom he was particularly sorry. The reason for his sorrow is that this dramatist was "drawn" by "the rest" "to run in that vile line." Yet what was so vile? Or is "**vile line**" an anagram of Neville?

A few months prior to Jonson's public apology, in May 1601, Henry Neville was sent to the Tower of London for his part in the Essex rebellion. Neville remained in the Tower for two years. When questioned by the authorities as to why they had performed *Richard II* on the eve of the rebellion, the actors said they had done it because they were well paid, confirming Jonson's view that they were motivated by the need to eat and clothe themselves.

Conclusion

Neville's life, letters and library books provide external evidence in support of his authorship of *Henry V.* Meanwhile, the playwright's distortion of historical fact to include members of the Neville family in crucial moments of the story makes no sense if the play were written by William Shakspere from Stratford.

Addendum 1

In Neville's letter of August 1, 1599, the following words occur that are also found in *Henry V.*

Single Words

Honourable, yesterday, Monsieur, proposed, first, Things, before, presented, receave, Answer, what, weight, Reason, poore, witts, Answeres, very, good, Words, many, Favours, already, entered, Satisfaction, Answere, last, *First,* touching, done, Dispatch, convenient, Speed, themselves, Particulars, Cause, desired, Inconveniences, particular, enter, other, Course, shewing, equall, indifferent, both, more, proceeding, therein, Majestie, proposed, certaine, Articles, taken, execution, redd, Occasion, ever, think, thrust, upon, told, just, Prince, Sea, besydes, required, nothing, content, contented, secure, eyther, way, purpose, greatest, *all,* Man's, Preservation, Queen, *herself,* Estate, Enemie, armed, against, *such,* Friends, *pettit,* urge, anything, saw, Proofe, rather, Nature, *true,* bear, little, good, thing, wherein, hitherto, Friendship, until, charge, without, returne, reasonable, seemed, Syde, Yoke, Servitude, themselves, Course, never, great, Wrong, Admirall, Officers, Matters, thereupon, Ambassador, Counsaill, since, received, *Spaine,* fresh, withal, Fleet, assembled, Sail, Men, Opinion, possess, send, Way, otherwise, leave, Island, follow, prey, Part, Ireland, England, therefore, unprovided, better, Copy, favour, Kingdom, expressly, because, came, moment, Post, hast(e), consider, looke, Money, hence, till, Year, doubt, Somme, Crownes, fail, ready, paid, Roüen, Army, purpose, Fort, Bridge, Action, House, taken, gone, Isle, meet, having, left, Foot, Horse, labour, means, theirs, joyne, hoped, Person, every, humbly, leave.

Pairs of Words

The same, I might, so long, full of, That they, to give, that very, I should, in Charge, they would, with all, I should, might be, like to, the Matter, only *in,* much more, our Preservation, any longer, and therefore, out of, their own, thought not, put in, were made, a tyme, when they, jealous of, but that, yeald them, Law of, be assured, Power to, the only, between us, should be, could not, the King's, hold the, his whole, will come, your Honor, of Warre, Parts of, the rather, seems to, may make, Yt may, please your, the next, some certaine, shall be, The *Germain,* have built, to defend, The Princes, the rest, the Camp.

Phrases of Three Words

Were able to, in some sort, therefore we must, according to the, the King will, they seem to, some part of, the Duke of.

Near Misses

There are some phrases that, while not identical, are very close and some words that are near misses. For example, in Neville's letter we have "impeach" rather than "impeachment" in the play. In the letter we find "this Action," in the play, "this fair action"; in the letter "my poore witts," in the play, "my wits"; in the letter, "to defend their Bridge," while in the play Fluellen reports that the Duke of Exeter "keeps the bridge most valiantly"; there is "by all means" in the letter and "by the means" in the play. Instead of "we thought not good to" in the play, there is "I thought good to" in the letter.

Shakespeare never used the following words, which occur in the letter: related, secondly, concerned, strengthened, assented, Spaniards.

Chapter 6

Henry VI
(1422–1461; 1470–1471)

> Suffolk: And he of these that can do most of all
> Cannot do more in England than the **Nevils**
> —*Henry VI* part 2 (1.3.73)

The trilogy of *Henry VI* was first written during 1589–1592, though it was certainly revised later. It is possible that part 2 was written first. In the First Quarto edition of the play the name "Nevil" occurs eight times (one of these was cut in the First Folio version). Thus, in the very first play generally accepted as by Shakespeare, the playwright was repeatedly naming one particular family. The Nevilles were a dominant force in the politics of this period, and so any playwright would have been bound to include members of this family in a history play about the Wars of the Roses. Our thesis, however, is that the playwright shows a Neville bias. This bias either foregrounds a Neville in a positive light or puts a Neville into the background to protect his reputation.

An example of the positive Neville bias in *Henry VI* part 2 is when Richard Neville, the Earl of Warwick, is credited with the achievements of his father-in-law Richard de Beauchamp (Warren, 2003, 118 note). This bias was also apparent in part 1 of the trilogy. According to James,

> When we realise too that the placement of Richard Neville here as the Earl of Warwick at this early point in Henry VI's reign is entirely anachronistic, then the evidence for Henry Neville's authorship again scores an extra point. The real Earl of Warwick at the time was Richard **Beauchamp**, Richard Neville inheriting the position at a later date. Yet we can be sure that it is Richard *Neville* who is meant here, because the Duke of York, in a soliloquy, declares Warwick and his father (who is named as the Earl of Salisbury in the play) to be Nevils [James, 2011, 268].

Warwick explicitly offers his support to York:

> Sweet York, begin: and if thy claim be good,
> The **Nevils** are thy subjects to command [*Henry VI* part 2, 2.2.8].

The Duke of York had grown up in the household of Ralph Neville, first Earl of Westmoreland, and married Cecily Neville, his daughter (and the sister of Richard Neville, fifth Earl of Salisbury), and subsequently allied himself to the Nevilles (Saccio, 1977, 129). His ambition was to claim the crown, and the Nevilles were the most powerful allies he could have chosen. He says:

> A day will come when York shall claim his own;
> And therefore I will take the **Nevils**' parts [*Henry VI* part 2, 1.1.239].

Neville by Name

Of all the Nevilles in this trilogy the most important was Richard Neville, the Earl of Warwick, "the King Maker." The Duke of York, speaking to Richard, says:

> And, **Nevil**, this I do assure myself:
> Richard shall live to make the Earl of Warwick
> The greatest man in England but the king [*Henry VI* part 2, 2.2.80].

Warwick's father was Richard Neville, the Earl of Salisbury, whom York praises as "that winter lion" (*Henry VI* part 2, 5.3.2). While Warwick is the dominant power broker in both *Henry VI* parts 2 and 3, his father Salisbury is a rational, moderate and mature figure. In the 1594 version of part 2, *The First Part of the Contention,* he says:

> The reuerence of mine age and ***Neuels*** name,
> Is of no litle force if I command [161].

Shakespeare clearly had second thoughts about using the Neville name in this play, because when he revised the text he cut one of the occasions when the name occurred. In the early version of *Henry VI* part 3, York says:

> bid *Richard* ***Neuill*** Earl of *Warwicke*[1]
> To leaue the cittie, and with his men of warre
> To meete me at Saint *Albons* [*The True Tragedy*].

In the First Folio this becomes, "whet on Warwick to this enterprise" (*Henry VI* part 3, 1.2.37), which is an example of the Neville name being hidden behind a title.

Warwick, Salisbury and York were Henry Neville's ancestors. Suffolk acknowledges that Salisbury and Warwick are especially powerful men when he says:

> And he of these that can do most of all
> Cannot do more in England than the **Nevils:**
> Salisbury and Warwick are no simple peers [*Henry VI* part 2, 1.3.74].

Even while insulting Warwick, Suffolk speaks of "the Nevil's noble race" (*Henry VI,* part 2, 3.2.214). Suffolk, the villain of this play, is captured, and just before he is murdered the lieutenant speaks of

> The princely Warwick, and the **Nevils** all,
> Whose dreadful swords were never drawn in vain [*Henry VI* part 2, 4.1.90].

In effect the Nevilles triumph over their enemy, Suffolk. His actual identity was William de la Pole (or Poole). In part 2 he arranges the murder of Humphrey, Duke of Gloucester, who was lord protector of the realm. Sir Edward Neville, Henry Neville's grandfather, became entangled in the Pole/Courtenay conspiracy in 1538. It was Sir Geoffrey Pole who, under torture, accused Neville of high treason. Neville was executed; Pole was pardoned. Sir Edward Neville was accused by Gertrude Courtney, the Marchioness of Exeter, of dabbling in prophecy, just as Humphrey's wife was accused in *Henry VI* part 2 (Hawkyard, 2004, 490). In both Eleanor's and Edward's cases the accusations of sorcery were politically motivated to destroy them.

We will now look at each of the three plays in turn in order to identify hidden Neville connections.

Henry VI *Part 1*

A central dramatic theme of this first part of the trilogy is the lionization of John Talbot. When he was nine, his mother married Thomas Neville,[2] Lord Furnivall, who became a major influence in his life. Talbot married first Maude Neville and then Margaret Beauchamp, so becoming brother-in-law to Richard Neville, the Earl of Warwick, the key figure in *Henry VI* parts 2 and 3. The bard distorts history in showing Talbot's death in *Henry VI* part 1, when in fact he died in 1453, after the deaths of four characters we see in part 2: the Duke of Exeter (1426), the Duke of Gloucester, Cardinal Beaufort (1447) and the Duke of Suffolk (1450). On page 742 in his copy of *A Catalogue of Honor*, Neville corrected the location of Talbot's death. In *Henry VI* part 1, Talbot's titles are listed (4.7.61). There is a puzzle about how Shakespeare knew of this list, which was on Talbot's tomb at Falais, near Caen, in France. The list was first published in 1599 in Richard Crompton's *Mansion of Magnanimitie*, after the play had been written. Of course, Neville had travelled through France in 1582, before the play was written. Two of the listed titles, Furnivall and Falconbridge, were titles held by members of the Neville family. How closely the Talbots are related to the Nevilles becomes visible when we look at the family tree.

Table 6. The Talbot-Neville Family Tree

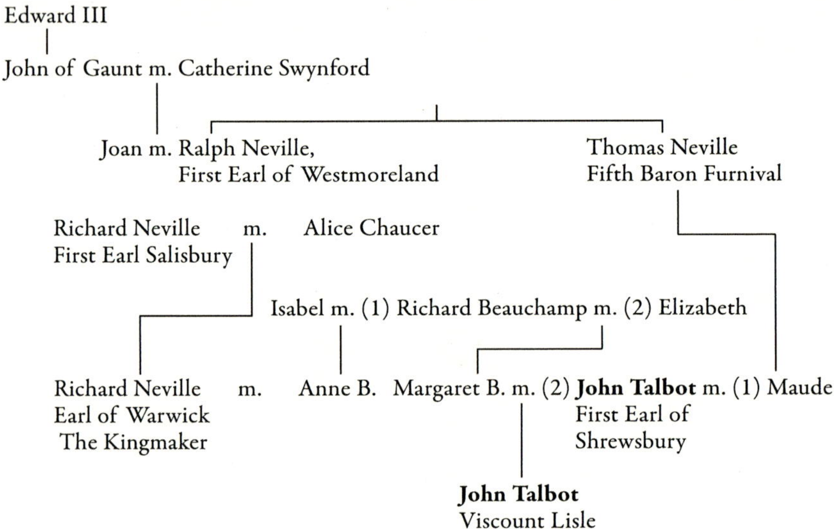

Source: Hattaway, 1990, 203.

Both John Talbots, father and son, appear in *Henry VI* part 1. They died together at the battle of Castillon in 1453.

The older John Talbot's mother was Ankaret Talbot, seventh Baroness Strange of Blackmere. The Stanley family claimed "in their ancestry the two Talbots" (Warren, 2003, 70). Ferdinando Stanley, fifth Earl of Derby, inherited his father's Barony of Strange. His company of actors, Lord Strange's Men,[3] performed a play, "harey vj," possibly *Henry VI* part 1, on March 3, 1592, at the Rose (Warren, 2003, 61). In August that year Nashe celebrated the moving scenes of Talbot's triumphs and death in his *Piers Penniless.* On the Northumberland Manuscript (1596–7) Neville named Nashe and his play *The Isle of Dogs*, and this is evidence that Neville, at the very least, knew of him. Nashe may have contributed to the writing of *Henry VI* part 1 (Warren, 2003, 68). In 1592 Ferdinando was a possible heir to the throne under Henry VIII's will. A play idolizing his ancestor and performed by his acting company was therefore a political act. Jowett (2000, 4) showed how Shakespeare demonstrated a pro–Stanley bias in *Richard III:* he altered his source, More's account, to present Thomas Stanley in a favorable light (Stanley's wife was Eleanor Neville; see Chapter 7). Ferdinando's death in 1594, possibly by poisoning, was a political scandal that opened up the question of who would succeed Elizabeth I. The scene of the dying, imprisoned Mortimer in act 2 raises the issue of the rightful succession to the crown. Speaking to Richard Plantagenet, Mortimer advises, "With silence, nephew, be thou politic" (2.5.101). Elizabeth I had forbidden discussion of the succession to the throne. The Shakespeare plays were a way of speaking, circumventing this embargo, while Neville himself observed a politic silence. The *Henry VI* trilogy explores the dangers to the kingdom of rival claimants to the throne and the catastrophes of civil war. Ferdinando's grandmother, Eleanor, was a daughter of Charles Brandon. Casson (2010, 168) has shown the connections between Brandon, More and the Neville family (see also Chapter 8). Ferdinando's brother, William Stanley, sixth Earl of Derby, has been proposed as a Shakespeare authorship candidate. He was reported as "penning comedies for the common players" in 1599 (Rubinstein, 2012, 134). Thomas Stanley (in *Richard III*) and John Talbot (in *Henry VI* part 1) shared with Henry Neville a common ancestor, Ralph Neville, Earl of Westmoreland, who appears on stage in *Henry IV* parts 1 and 2 (see table 2 and Chapter 4). His grandson, also called Ralph, appears as the second Earl of Westmoreland in *Henry VI* part 3.

Talbot was the Earl of Shrewsbury. Shakespeare's contemporary Earl of Shrewsbury, George Talbot, became keeper of Mary, Queen of Scots, until she was passed, first into the keeping of Ralph Sadler and Neville's father (1584–5), then to Amias Paulet. The duplicitous behavior of the Countess of Auvergne in the play has been seen as a reference to Mary, Queen of Scots (Hattaway, 1990, 65; Scoufos, 1979, 144).

James found an example of the protective Neville bias in the rose garden scene, which is an invented symbolic start to the Wars of the Roses. She noted that Richard Neville, the Earl of Warwick, claims the purest of motives as he plucks the white rose in support of Richard Plantagenet.

> In reality, one major reason for Richard Neville's opposition to Somerset's Lancastrian cause was that Neville was in personal dispute with Edmund, Duke of Somerset, regarding the inheritance of some really big property ... a dispute which had by then led to actual fighting between them, plus the seizure of a couple of castles by Neville in order to prevent Somerset taking them. The writer is therefore crediting Neville with more honour than he had in reality" [James, 2011, 273–5].

Somerset's grandfather, John, first Earl of Somerset, was a brother of Ralph Neville, Warwick's own grandfather (Hattaway, 1993, 225).

Five years before *Henry VI* was on the stage Neville read, copied and noted the banned political tract *Leicester's Commonwealth* (Worsley MSS 47; see Casson, 2010). James discovered this manuscript in the Lincoln Archives and showed that it was a source for the history plays, especially those on the Wars of the Roses (James and Rubinstein, 2005). She noticed the phrase "The red rose and the white," which occurs in *Henry VI* parts 1 and 3 and which Neville wrote in his marginalia:

Worsley MSS 47, 40V (by permission of the Eighth Earl of Yarborough and Lincolnshire Archives).

At the end of this chapter there is a section about *Leicester's Commonwealth* as a possible source for *Henry VI* (see also Casson, 2010).

Henry Beaufort, the Bishop of Winchester, appears in *Henry VI* parts 1 and 2. He was brother-in-law to Ralph Neville, Earl of Westmoreland and father of Richard Neville, Earl of Salisbury, and Cecily Neville. Richard and Cecily had another brother, Edward Neville (1412–76), who was Henry Neville's great, great-grandfather. Winchester, however, is portrayed in a very negative light in the plays and is called proud, haughty and arrogant. Is there any particular reason why Neville might have a negative view of a bishop of Winchester? In 1551 Edward VI granted the Hundred of Wargrave to Neville's father: "When Queen Mary came to the throne in 1554 she returned the Hundred of Wargrave to the Bishop of Winchester and it was not until 1558, the first year of the reign of Queen Elizabeth I, that the original grant to Sir Henry Neville was confirmed by an Act of Parliament. In 1567 he built a fine Tudor residence at Billingbear which became the seat of the Neville family for some 300 years" (Railton, 2006, 1).

Astronomy

Henry VI part 1 opens with an invocation: "Comets ... brandish your crystal tresses in the sky" (1.1.2). Hattaway (1990, 67) pointed out that the word "comet" derives from a Greek word meaning "long-haired star." Neville read Greek and accompanied Henry Savile on travels through Europe, when they met several astronomers. Savile made notes in his journal[4] about comets (folio 34: De Cometis).

The eccentric movements of Mars are referred to by Charles, the Dauphin (*Henry VI* part 1, 1.2.1). In *Henry VI* part 3, York refers to the Antipodes and the Septentrion (the seven stars of the Great Bear: 1.4.134–5). Hattaway (1993, 96) noted that the idea of the Antipodes "was embodied in the Ptolemaic cosmology." Neville owned the *Ptolemiæi Astronomi* (1538), a book on celestial geometry. He gave it to Merton College, Oxford. It is annotated by Neville in Latin and Greek. Neville studied astronomy and geometry at Merton under his tutor Henry Savile. This may explain Shakespeare's statement in Sonnet 14: "I have astronomy."

Henry VI *Part 2*

Henry VI part 2 has two important members of the Neville family center stage, father and son, Richard Neville, Earl of Salisbury, and Richard Neville, Earl of Warwick.

> Now by my fathers age, old **Neuels** crest,
> The Rampant *B*eare chaind to the ragged staffe,
> This day ile weare aloft my burgonet... [*Henry VI* part 2, 5.1.202].

One of Neville's unique annotations on his copy of *Leicester's Commonwealth* is the word "Beares" in an italic hand against a passage in secretary script:

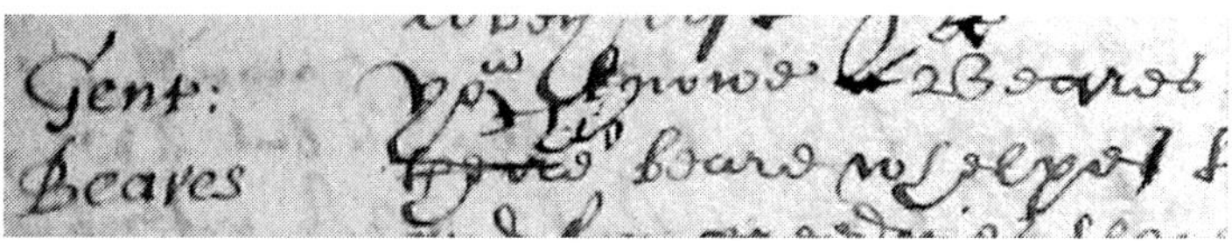

Gent: Beares, Worsley MSS 47, 6V (by permission of the Eighth Earl of Yarborough and Lincolnshire Archives).

This is spelled the same way as the word "*B*eare" (also with a capital "*B*" italicized) in the first printed text of *The First Part of the Contention* (*Henry VI* part 2). In the passage of *Leicester's Commonwealth* the Gentleman speaks of a "beare whelpe," as can be seen in the adjacent text in the above illustration. Richard of Gloucester (son of Cecily Neville) describes himself as a "Beare-whelpe" (First Folio spelling, *Henry VI* part 3, 3.2.161).

The author of *Henry VI* part 2 appears to have taken some poetic license to foreground the Neville name in 5.1.202 (see above). Despite Warwick's declaration, the "rampant bear" was **not** "my father's badge, old Neuels crest." His father, Richard Neville, Earl of Salisbury, did not have the bear emblem, but a bull's head. Rather, it was that of his father-in-law, as Richard Neville attained both his title as Earl of Warwick and the "rampant bear" crest from Richard Beauchamp when he married Beauchamp's daughter, Anne (Warren, 2003, 279 note). Earlier in this scene a similar allusion is made when York commands, "Call hither to the stake my two brave bears" (5.1.144), referring to Salisbury and Warwick. This foregrounding of Warwick and Salisbury is further emphasized in the First Quarto (1594), in scene 3 of the final act. On the stage entry of Warwick and Salisbury, Richard says to his father, York, "See noble father, where they do come, / The only props unto the house of York." This is preparation for York, Salisbury and Warwick to have the last words in the play: thus are they "eternized in all age to come" (5.3.31).

Minor Characters and Their Neville Connections

Eleanor Cobham was mistress and then wife of Humphrey, Duke of Gloucester. After being found guilty of conjuring spirits, Eleanor is publicly humiliated. She is then sent to the keeping of "Sir John Stanley" on the Isle of Man. His first name was actually Thomas (Shakespeare picked up this error from his sources in Hall and Holinshed). He appears on stage in *Richard III.* His brother Sir William Stanley is in *Henry VI* part 3. Thomas became the first Earl of Derby and married Eleanor, the daughter of Richard Neville, the fifth Earl of Salisbury.

The Duke of Buckingham in the play was Humphrey Stafford (1402–1460). He married Anne Neville, daughter of Ralph Neville, first Earl of Westmoreland.

A man surnamed Vaux appears in *Henry VI* part 2 (3.2.371). This was probably William Vaux, a Lancastrian, who was killed at the battle of Tewkesbury in 1471. According to Warren (2003, 220) Shakespeare's chronicle sources do not mention him, so this suggests some special knowledge of the Vaux family, which Neville may well have had. Catherine, daughter of William Vaux, the third baron, married another Sir Henry Neville, who later became the seventh Lord Abergavenny, c. 1615. This suggests at least some familiarity between the families before that date. Sir Nicholas Vaux appears in Shakespeare and Fletcher's *Henry VIII.* His son, Thomas Vaux, was a poet and is misquoted by the gravedigger in *Hamlet* (Casson, 2010, 133).

The Jack Cade Rebellion

In 1903 Eva Bell-Irving published a history of Mayfield. Neville lived in Mayfield from c. 1587 to 1597, the very period when the history plays were written. On March 10, 1588, Neville's first son, Henry, was baptized there (Bell-Irving, 1903, 95). In Chapter 4 of her book Bell-Irving revealed that Jack Cade was "a native of Mayfield or of Heathfield.... We can trace the family later still from deeds at Sunny Bank. The first of these is a grant from Henry Nevill, Lord of the Manor, of lands in Mayfield to Richard Cade of Maighfield, yoman, 81 acres" (Bell-Irving, 1903, 50). Neville therefore would have met Jack Cade's descendants. The hamlet of Heathfield where Jack Cade

> was killed is still called Cade Street. A pillar there bears the inscription: Near this spot was slain the notorious rebel Jack Cade by Alexander Iden, Sheriff of Kent, A.D. 1450.... Cade had hidden at Newick Farm between Mayfield and Heathfield but becoming tired of the monotony, he sallied forth to play bowls in an old garden at Heathfield, when he was surprised and shot with an arrow by Iden. The road which led from Heathfield to Newick used to be called Iden's Way [Bell-Irving, 1903, 54–5].[5]

In Shakespeare's play Cade dies in Iden's garden. Iden calls himself "an esquire of Kent" (*Henry VI* part 2, 4.10.42). The Duke of York reveals,

> I have seduced a headstrong Kentishman,
> John Cade of Ashford,
> To make commotion [*Henry VI* part 2, 3.1.].

Ashford is in Kent. In the play the rebels were from Kent, "the filth and scum of Kent" (*Henry VI* part 2, 4.2.113). One of the rebels is named "Best's son, the tanner of Wingham," and we see a "clerk of Chartham" caught by the rebels (*Henry VI* part 2, 4.2.21; 4.2.78). Wingham and Chartham are villages near Canterbury, Kent (Warren, 2003, 237, 240 notes). Neither Holinshed nor Hall, Shakespeare's main historical sources, mentions Wingham or Chartham. Shakespeare shows special local knowledge, which Neville would have had. However, the bard does not refer to the rebels as being from Sussex, nor does he mention Mayfield or Heathfield. (Hall mentions Sussex.) The omission of these geographical details may be regarded as an example of a negative Neville bias as the playwright shifted the scene away from Mayfield into Kent to obscure the location and avoid identification.

One of Jack Cade's followers is called John Holland in the First Folio (4.2 and 4.7). Editors have speculated that this was the name of an actor (Warren, 2003, 236 note). However, while the name occurs elsewhere in the *Chronicles*, no rebel is called John Holland in Holinshed's account of the Jack Cade episode. John Holland therefore appears to be a creation of the author. In the play, Holland observes Cade's growing megalomania and sagely predicts, in asides, "sore" and "stinking laws" (4.7.7 and 11). Holland is critical of the nobility, saying: "It was never merry world in England since gentlemen came up"

(4.2.9); "The nobility think scorn to go in leather aprons" (4.2.13); "Let the magistrates be labouring men; and therefore should we be magistrate" (4.2.18).

At the time of the writing of this play, Henry Neville was lord of the manor in Mayfield.[6] He was also a justice of the peace, so would have known the people's opinions of magistrates. In 1593 Neville granted a lease to a yeoman called Alexander Muddle of Wadhurst, and Muddle made leases of tithes and corn to a John Holland in 1597.[7] We wonder whether Neville drew inspiration from an outspoken man whom he had met as a local character when he wrote John Holland into *Henry VI* part 2. However, given the name was a common one that occurred elsewhere in the *Chronicles*, this may simply be coincidence.

Within twelve years of writing the play, Neville would be reluctantly associated with a rebellion against the government and later become a leader of the popular party in the House of Commons. Neville, however, was not in favor of outright rebellion, and Shakespeare's bias against Cade's "rabblement" is explained when we identify the bard as a member of the governing class (Saccio, 1977, 124).

Henry Neville's Notebook and Vocabulary

Neville was conducting historical research while imprisoned in the Tower: his notebook, Worsley MSS 40, dated 1602, is in the Lincoln Archives. This contains Neville's annotations about laws, coronation ceremonial, noble families' pedigrees and the history of Parliament. In one note he referred to Grafton, who was one of Shakespeare's sources for *Henry VI* part 2 (Warren, 2003, 31).

According to McQuain and Malless (1998, 222). Shakespeare was the first to use "torture" as a verb. In *Henry VI* part 2 it is indeed Richard Neville, the Earl of Salisbury, who uses the word (3.2.249). Henry Neville himself used "The torture" in a letter dated June 29, 1599 (Sawyer, 1725, vol. 1, 55).

Henry VI *Part 3*

Richard Neville, Earl of Warwick, plays the role of Kingmaker in this play. In the first scene he steps into this role and does so using imagery from falconry and forestry (1.1.63). Henry Neville was a forester and had learned falconry from his father, eventually serving on a parliamentary committee about the sport.

The Marquess of Montague was John Neville, third son of Richard Neville, Earl of Salisbury, who appeared in *Henry VI* part 1. He was Richard Neville's brother and is so identified by Warwick five times in the play without naming him as a Neville (2.1.167; 4.8.14; 5.2.34; 5.1.4; 5.2.34). Somerset identifies Montague as Warwick's brother (5.2.42). A messenger (the Post) also identifies him as Warwick's brother when delivering a letter to the latter in France (3.3.164). That Montague is mentioned twenty times in the play draws attention to him without naming him as a Neville. John was also an ancestor of Henry Wriothesley, the Earl of Southampton, Shakespeare's patron, to whom he dedicated his major poems.

Another of Warwick's brothers, George Neville, the archbishop of York, is mentioned as keeping Edward IV in protective custody after his capture by Warwick (4.3.53; 4.4.12; 4.5.5; 4.6.68). That he is mentioned four times draws attention to him without naming him as a Neville. Edward escaped and reclaimed the crown. Henry Neville's father was Mary, Queen of Scots' custodian in 1584–5 and so would have known about keeping a royal prisoner in custody and guarding against possible escape attempts.

The second Earl of Westmoreland in this play is Ralph Neville, grandson of the Ralph Neville in *Henry IV.*

John de Vere, the thirteenth Earl of Oxford in the play, married Margaret Neville, sister of the Kingmaker. When Richard Neville, the Earl of Warwick, meets him in France he is at first hostile, but when Warwick changes sides they become allies.

William Hastings, Lord Hastings in the play, married Katherine Neville, daughter of Richard Neville, fifth Earl of Salisbury. Shakespeare names Hastings as Richard (4.7.1). Hastings was loyal to Edward IV. He appears in *Richard III* (see Chapter 7).

The Duke of Norfolk in the play is John Mowbray. He married Catherine Neville, the sister of Cecily (Hattaway, 1993, 227).

Edward, George, Rutland and Richard are all sons of Richard Plantagenet, the Duke of York and Cecily Neville. Rutland's death in *Henry VI* part 3 is made all the more cruelly poignant by the playwright's trick of reducing his age from seventeen to that of a child accompanied by his tutor. Shakespeare shows a distinctly Yorkist/Neville bias, raising York and his son to the level of tragic figures (Saccio, 1977, 160). Cecily Neville became the mother to two kings—Edward IV and Richard III—and appears herself in *Richard III*, in which Rutland's death is again recalled (see Chapter 7). George, her other son, who is created Duke of Clarence on stage (in act 2, scene 6), married Isabel, daughter of Richard Neville, the Earl of Warwick, the Kingmaker. Shakespeare followed his sources, Hall and Holinshed, in thinking Edward, Prince of Wales, married Anne Neville; however, they were only betrothed, and Edward died at Tewkesbury before they could be married. Anne is mentioned but not named in the play (3.3.242; 4.1.117). The bard also confuses her as Warwick's eldest daughter and Isabel the younger. He corrected this error in *Richard III* (Hattaway, 1993, 150 note). That Anne is a half hidden Neville in *Henry VI* part 3 is another example of the protective Neville bias, and we can now uncover the reason for this concealment.

Edward IV: Just Lascivious or a Rapist?

Shakespeare portrays Edward IV as a sexual predator. He is described as "wanton Edward" (1.4.74), "lustful Edward" (3.2.129) and "lascivious Edward" (5.5.34). A central moment in the play is when Richard Neville, the Earl of Warwick, suddenly changes from Edward's ally to his enemy. The reason given in the play is that Warwick felt humiliated by Edward's marriage to Elizabeth Woodville when he was abroad negotiating a betrothal to the French king's daughter. However, there were darker reasons for the split between the men. In *Henry VI* part 3 Warwick confronts Edward IV with his offences including "th'abuse done my niece" (3.3.8). Hall reported: "whether he would have **deflowred** his daughter or his nece, the certainty was not for both their honors openly knowen" (for full text see the addendum at the end of this chapter). Shakespeare used the word "deflower" in *The Rape of Lucrece* and in *Titus Andronicus* (published the same year, 1594). Marcus says, "some Tereus[8] hath **deflowred** thee" (2.3.26, First Quarto spelling). Edward IV had attempted to rape a young female Neville just over one hundred years before the *Henry VI* trilogy and *The Rape of Lucrece* were written. Clearly the bard had read about this in either Hall or Holinshed, who both mention it.

James (2011, 85) first found reference to Edward IV's sexual abuse in Bulwer-Lytton's novel *The Last of the Barons.* He had researched that reign exhaustively and was able to show that the most likely victim of the king's rapacity was Warwick's daughter Anne, as no niece was present at that time; and so reference to her was an attempt to screen the identity of the actual victim. Anne was a teenager at the time of the attack. Shakespeare later shows us Anne being further seduced by Richard III: he was Edward's brother and so could be regarded as guilty both by association and his own nature. The major political consequence of this rape was that Richard Neville revolted against Edward IV and dethroned him (albeit temporarily and at the eventual cost of his own life). Shakespeare followed Holinshed, who suggested the cause of the break between the Kingmaker and the king was Warwick's offence at Edward's marriage to Elizabeth Woodville when he was in France negotiating a marriage to the Lady Bona. Holinshed (1587, vol. 3, 284) stated:

> All men for the most part agree, that this marriage was the onlie cause, why the earle of Warwick conceiued a hatred against king Edward, whome he so much before fauoured. Other affirme other causes: and one speciallie, for that king Edward did attempt a thing once in the earles house, which was much against the earles honestie (whether he would have defloured his daughter or his neece, **the certaintie was not for both their honours openlie revealed**) [emphasis added].

Holinshed continues, copying his source, which is Hall (see addendum below). The date of the assault is uncertain. Holinshed has the date 1465 in a marginal annotation.

Hall and Bulwer-Lytton both suggested the rape was the real cause of the break. Bulwer-Lytton (1891, xvi) stated, "Here was, indeed, a wrong never to be forgiven, and yet never to be proclaimed." Shakespeare's suggestion that it was the Bona marriage debacle continued the cover-up of King Edward's shameful sexual behavior. However, in *Henry VI* part 3, Warwick does obliquely refer to Edward's nature in his not being "contented with one wife" (4.3.37). Hall suggested that Warwick had bided his time until he was ready in order to hide the shame to himself and his daughter. Richard Neville, the Earl of Warwick, was a first cousin of Neville's great-grandfather (James, 2008, 352).

The incidents of royal sexual abuse by Edward III (see Chapter 2) and Edward IV are parallel: both kings are called Edward, both make attempts on the Earl of Warwick's daughter, both mix sex and politics. The parallel is stronger when we know that the original source for the Countess of Salisbury story was Jean Le Bel's *Vrayes Chroniques*, which accused Edward of violently raping the Countess (Melchiori, 1998, 23, 186). This explains why the bard chose to dramatize the Countess of Salisbury story in *Edward III.* The Neville family had held the titles of the earldoms of Salisbury and Warwick. Edward IV was Neville's great, great-grandfather's nephew through Cecily Neville. It can also explain why Shakespeare took a negative view of Edward IV. Only a Neville had reason to both highlight and conceal Edward's predatory sexual behavior when the victim was a member of the Neville family. Furthermore, both the rape and Edward's marriage had wider political implications: "Edward ... married the Lady Grey (Elizabeth Woodville) in order to build up an alliance that would check the power of Warwick and the Nevilles" (Hattaway, 1993, 16). Certainly the bard casts the Woodvilles in a negative light, so revealing another apparent Neville bias.

The Disappearing Falconbridge

Shakespeare, as we saw in Chapter 1, had a habit of using the name Falconbridge in early plays. It occurs in *Henry VI* parts 1 and 3. It is a name with Neville connections. In part 3 when Queen Margaret says, "Stern **Falconbridge** commands the narrow seas," she is referring to William Neville, Warwick's uncle, who was admiral of the Channel fleet in 1462. Hattaway (1993, 61, 83 note; Cairncross, 1964, xxii) also lists two other Nevilles: the bastard Thomas, who was vice admiral, and his father Lord Falconbridge, who also went to sea. Falconbridge does not appear on stage and some editors substitute Montague (John Neville). Here is another omission that may be an example of the protective Neville bias when the bard omits a Neville to avoid shaming a family member. Thomas eventually led a rebellion in support of Richard Neville, the Earl of Warwick, against Edward IV in 1471 and was beheaded. This rebellion by the bastard Falconbridge does not feature in the *Henry VI* trilogy but was dramatized by Thomas Heywood in *The First and Second Parts of King Edward IV*, which was published in 1599. That play does not show Thomas in a good light.

Leicester's Commonwealth *and the* Henry VI *Trilogy*

Leicester's Commonwealth is concerned with the succession to the throne. Neville's family had been intimately involved in this issue. Neville's father had been a witness of Henry VIII's will, which is explicitly mentioned in *Leicester's Commonwealth*. There are several Nevilles mentioned in the text. Richard Neville, the Kingmaker, is prominent. One passage tells: "Two Nevilles took upon them to join with Richard of York to put down their most benign prince King Henry VI, and after again in the other side to put down King Edward IV, it was not upon want of advancement, they being Earls both of Salisbury and Warwick and lords of many notable places besides" (Peck 135–6/*91*).

In *Leicester's Commonwealth,* Leicester is likened to Richard Duke of York.

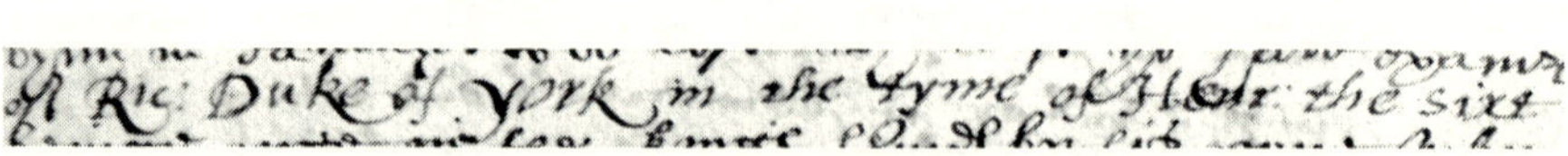

Worsley MSS 47, 19 (by permission of the Eighth Earl of Yarborough and Lincolnshire Archives).

In 1584, when this was published, Leicester was indeed powerful, and Elizabeth had no heir so the succession was undecided. Leicester was seen by some as a potential usurper or kingmaker should Elizabeth die. Leicester, however, died in 1588. The succession was still undecided in the early 1590s when the plays were written. By then Leicester had been replaced as the queen's favorite by Robert Devereux, the Earl of Essex. Neville had met Essex in 1583 and had become a supporter. Would Essex become a kingmaker? Hattaway (1993, 55) suggested that events in *Henry VI* part 3 "parallel recent contemporary history: in the period 1589 until 1591 three forces of English soldiers were sent to France in support of the Huguenot Henry of Navarre. From October 1591 until January 1592 Englishmen under the command of the Earl of Essex participated in another, unsuccessful, siege of Rouen." We see a siege of Rouen in *Henry VI* part 1. Talbot triumphantly takes the city. The capture of the city is, however, fictitious. Shakespeare clearly wanted to show a successful siege of Rouen on stage when this did not happen in reality. He would have heard about the campaign from his father-in-law, Henry Killigrew, who served with Essex and was knighted by him in France in 1591. Killigrew knew France well, having been there as early as 1556, and in 1562 he had led a military contingent at Rouen. Neville himself had been in France in 1582 and owned a French book, *Discources Politiques et Militaires,* dated 1587, dedicated to Henry of Navarre, whom he later met as King Henry IV in 1599 when he was ambassador.

Neville copied and annotated *Leicester's Commonwealth* before the *Henry VI* trilogy focusing on the Wars of the Roses was written (Worsley MSS 47; see Casson, 2010). Members of the Neville family fought on both sides of this conflict, and their triumphs, disasters and suffering are shown on stage in the *Henry VI* trilogy. The earliest of these plays was first printed as *The First Part of the* ***Contention*** *Betwixt the Two Famous Houses of York and Lancaster.* In his copy of *Leicester's Commonwealth* Neville made a marginal annotation: "the calamitie of Engl: by the **contencōn** betweene York & Lancast: with the contynuance thereof." The printed version is: "The miserie of England by the **cōtentiō** betvv York and Lācaster." What is immediately apparent is that Neville is using alliteration: "**calamity**, **contention**,

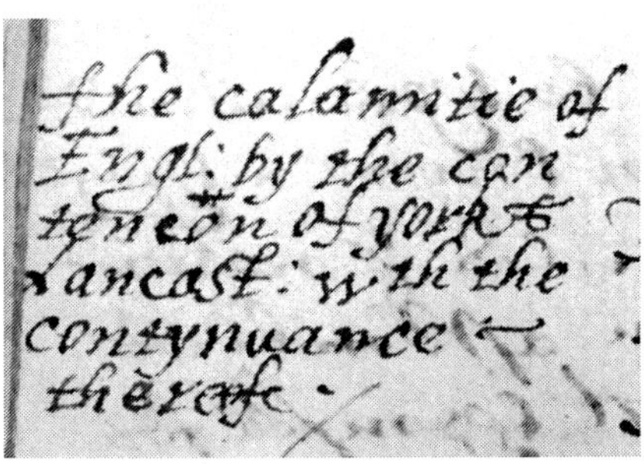

Worsley MSS 47, 40V (by permission of the Eighth Earl of Yarborough and Lincolnshire Archives).

continuance." The main text of *Leicester's Commonwealth* at this point reads, "our **country**'s **calamity** by that **contention**" (Peck, 144/*96*), so we can see that Neville picked up this alliteration from the text—not from the printed annotation—but varied it with an additional word, "**continuance.**" Neville used "**continuance**" in a letter dated May 15, 1599, and twice in a letter of May 26, 1599 (Sawyer, 1725, vol. 1, 21, 36); he used the word "**contention**" in a letter dated June 27, 1599 (Sawyer, 1725, vol. 1, 51). The words calamity, contention, continuance all occur in the *Henry VI* trilogy.

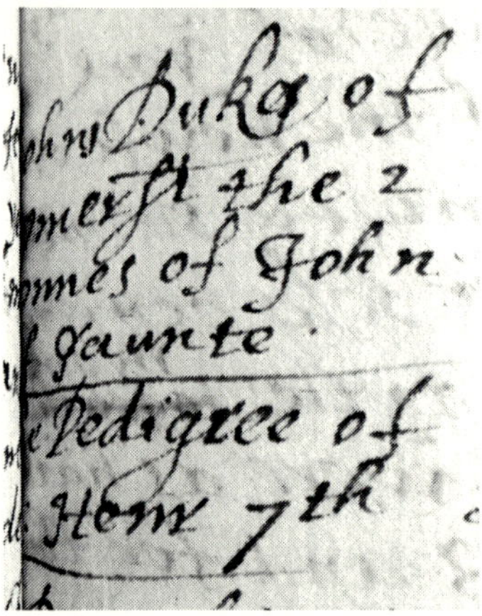

Worsley MSS 47, 43 (by permission of the Eighth Earl of Yarborough and Lincolnshire Archives).

Neville's annotation: "the 2 Sonnes of **John of Gaunte** The **pedigree** of K. Henr: 7th" is echoed in two plays: "he from **John of Gaunt** doth bring his **pedigree**" in *Henry VI* part 1 (2.5.76) and "**John of Gaunt** ... a **pedigree**" in *Henry VI* part 3 (3.3.81–92). In Worsley MSS 47, Neville, annotating independently of the printed text, followed on with a list of the descendants of Edward III: "the yssue of **K: Edw 3** Rich 2." The text reads, "**William of Hatfeild a sonne of Edw 3**," followed by "**Lyonell Duke of Clarence**": The text at the top of the next page continues, "**Edmund of Langley the first duke of Yorke**" (shown below).

In *Henry VI* part 2, Richard, Duke of York, lists the descendants of Edward III:

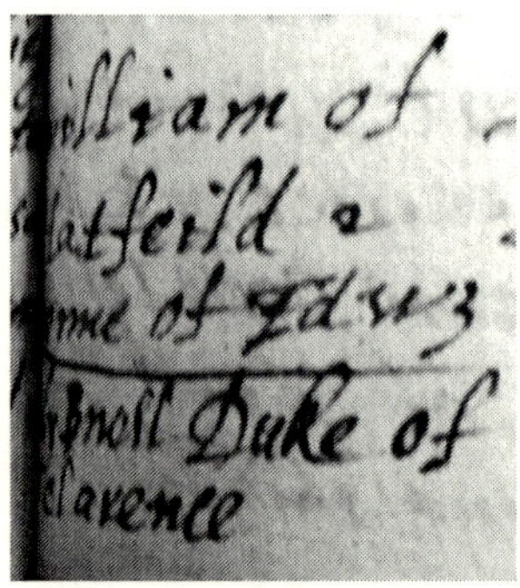

***Right:* Worsley MSS 47, 43. *Below:* Worsley MSS 47, 43V (by permission of the Eighth Earl of Yarborough and Lincolnshire Archives).**

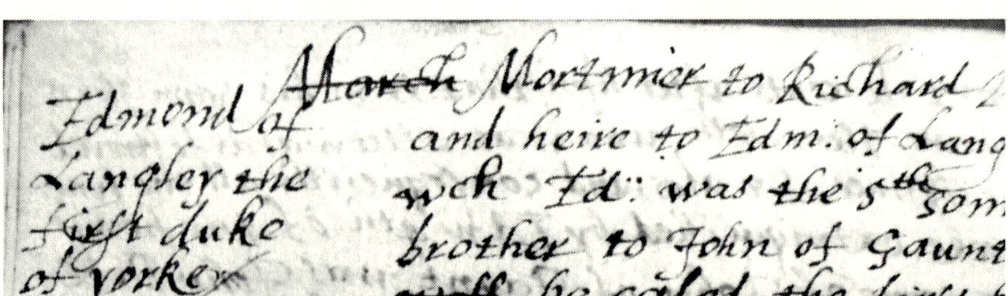

> **Edward the Third**, my lords, had seven sons:
> The first, Edward the Black Prince, Prince of Wales;
> The second, **William** of **Hatfield**, and the third,v
> **Lionel Duke of Clarence**: next to whom
> Was John of Gaunt, the Duke of Lancaster;
> The fifth was **Edmund Langley, Duke of York** [2.2.10].

These names with their titles are all listed in the same order as in Neville's annotations. Later in the scene we hear, "But **William of Hatfield** died without an heir" (2.2.33). The speaker is Richard Neville, Earl of Salisbury. Also present is his son, Richard Neville, Earl of Warwick. "**Lionel Duke of Clarence**" is mentioned four times in *Henry VI* parts 1 and 2. Langley is mentioned three times by Shakespeare, twice as "**Edmund Langley, Duke of York**" (*Henry VI* part 1, 2.5.85; part 2, 2.2.15).

One of Neville's annotations reads: "The Battle of Tadcaster on Palme Sundaye Barnett and **Tewxburie**," whereas the printed version is: "The battaile by Tadcaster on palme Sõdaye, An. 1460." Neville repeats the spelling "**Tewxburie**" in his version of the text. The battle of Tadcaster is otherwise called the battle of Towton (Peck, 1985, 214 footnote 203), which Shakespeare dramatizes in *Henry VI* part 3, act 2, scene 3. Neville notes the battle place-names of Barnet and Tewkesbury. We find these in *Henry VI* part 3. The First Folio spelling of these is in the following passage:

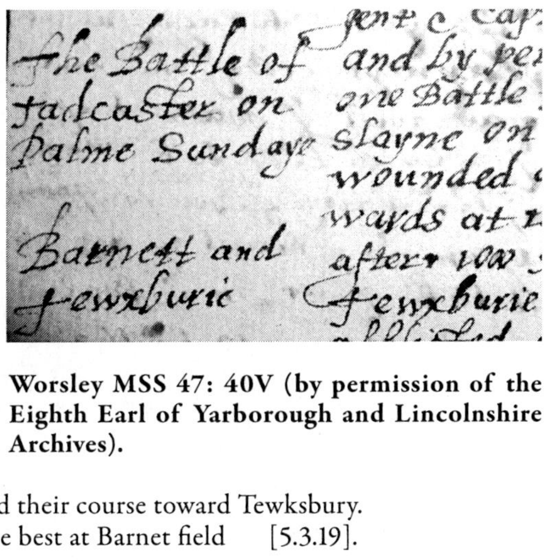

Worsley MSS 47: 40V (by permission of the Eighth Earl of Yarborough and Lincolnshire Archives).

> That they doe hold their course toward Tewksbury.
> We hauing now the best at Barnet field [5.3.19].

In the 1595 version of *Henry VI* part 3, *The True Tragedy of Richard Duke of York*, one of these place names is spelled differently: **Tewxburie**. (Barnet is not mentioned.) The spelling in the early version of *The True Tragedy* matches Neville's annotation. Furthermore Neville noted, "Henr: the 7th his **descent**."

In *The True Tragedy* there is "Henries lineallie **discent**" whereas the Folio version is "Henry lineally descends" (3.3.87). Again Neville's note is closer to

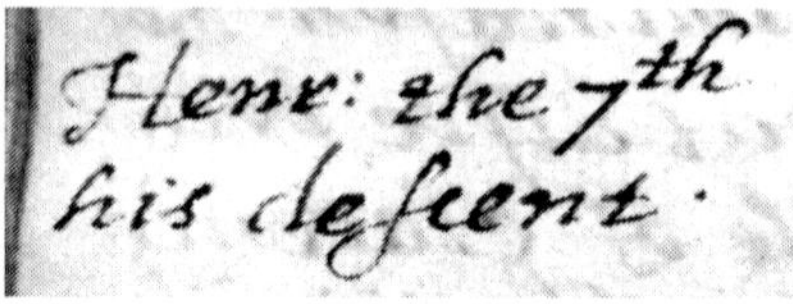

Worsley MSS 47, 41V (by permission of the Eighth Earl of Yarborough and Lincolnshire Archives).

The True Tragedy word, which makes sense when we consider that Worsley MSS 47 must date to 1585, just before Shakespeare wrote the first versions of the *Henry VI* trilogy (Casson, 2010, 42, 45, 53–56).

Rare Vocabulary Used by Shakespeare and Neville

In making his manuscript copy of *Leicester's Commonwealth* Neville copied one printed marginal note: "Nevv mẽ most contẽptuous" as: "newe men most **contumelious.**" Shakespeare used this rare word more times than any other writer of the period. "**Contumelious**" is to be found in *Henry VI* part 1 (1.4.38) and *Henry VI* part 2 (3.2.204). In *Henry VI* part 2 Queen Margaret is speaking to the Earl of Warwick, Richard Neville. (See Casson, 2010, for many more examples of Neville's using rare vocabulary that Shakespeare subsequently used, in his copy of *Leicester's Commonwealth.*)

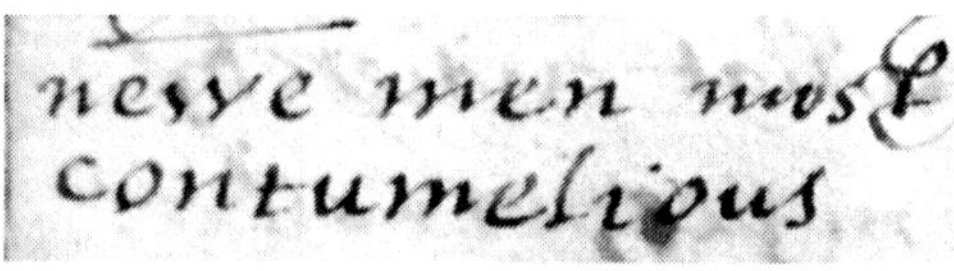

Worsley MSS 47, 55V (by permission of the Eighth Earl of Yarborough and Lincolnshire Archives).

Other Authors of Henry VI

A number of other playwrights have been proposed as having had a hand in *Henry VI,* including Nashe, Peele and Gager. Nashe and his controversial play *The Isle of Dogs* is listed on the Northumberland Manuscript, which was owned by Neville. Peele, as we have seen in Chapter 1, co-wrote *Titus Andronicus* and *The Troublesome Raigne of John.* William Gager produced plays at Oxford with Peele's support. Gager wrote a poem praising Peele. They were at Christ Church College, Oxford, and both were supporters of Robert Devereux, the Earl of Essex. Gager dedicated his play *Meleager* to Essex when it was published in 1592. Evidence for Gager's hand in *Henry VI* part 2 includes a passage that appears to be sourced from *Meleager* (Brook, 1951):

> Methinks the realms of England, France, and Ireland
> *Bear that proportion to my flesh and blood*

As did the fatal brand Althaea burnt
Unto the prince's heart of Calydon [Henry VI *part 2, 1.1.230].*

Althaea and the mothers of Calydon are listed in the *Meleager* dramatis personae, and these lines describe the great climax of Gager's play. Browning (2012) pointed out the reference to the village of Melford in *Henry VI* part 2 (1.3.24). William Gager was born and bred in Melford. In c. 1580 Gager's uncle, Edward Cordell, sent instructions to him regarding the disposal of a buck sent from Windsor "where the Neville family managed the forest."[9] This suggests Gager could have known the Nevilles. He was at Oxford 1574–93. Whether Gager had a hand in the *Henry VI* part 2 or not, Henry Neville shared with him time at Oxford University (1577–8), support for Essex and, as Shakespeare, co-authorship with Peele.

Conclusion

The *Henry VI* trilogy contains much evidence of the Neville bias, and there is external evidence for Henry Neville's interest in this history in his hand-written copy of *Leicester's Commonwealth.* This manuscript predates the writing of the plays.

Addendum

Edward Hall's *The Union of the Two Noble and Illustrate Families of Lancastre and Yorke,* also called Hall's *Chronicle,* was first published in 1542. The passage about Edward IV's offence is on folio vi verso of the section "iiii yere of Edward IV." The original spelling has been retained.

> And farther it erreth not from the truthe that Kyng Edward did attempt a thyng once in the erles house whiche was muche against the erles honestie (whether he would have deflowred his daughter or his nece, the certaintie was not for both their honors openly knowen) for surely such a thyng was attempted by kyng Edward, which loved well both the loke and to fele feyre dammosels. But whether the iniury that the erle thought he had taken at kyng Edwardes handes, or the disdayne of authoritie that the Erle had under the kyng, was the cause of dissolucion of their amitie and league, truthe it is that the privie intencions in their hartes brake into so many small peces, that England, Fraunce, and Flaunders, coulde never ioyne them again, during their naturall lyfes.

THE erle of Warwyke being thus moved, inflamed, and set against the kyng, lest in his fury, his purpose might be espied and broughte to naught, determined himself, covertly dissymulynge, so long to suffer all such wronges + iniuries, as were to hym done, till he might spye a tyme convenient, + a world after his awn appetite, for the setting furth of his enterprise, and accomplishing of his purpose.

CHAPTER 7

Richard III (1483–1485)

I am a villain. Yet I lie: I am not.—*Richard III* (5.3.192)

Richard III is the fourth play of the first tetralogy, preceded by *Henry VI* parts 1, 2 and 3. It was written circa 1592. This four-part epic on the Wars of the Roses was not simply an education in English history; it was also a warning of the woes of civil war and a justification of the Tudor overthrow of the Plantagenet dynasty.

Henry Neville's surname and family motto is on the top left corner of the front page of the Northumberland Manuscript, which is the earliest document to list the play, *Richard III*, and the name "William Shakespeare," dating from 1596–7. This was before the play was published with the author identified as "William Shake-speare" in 1598. While in the Tower of London after the Essex rebellion, Neville, conducting historical research recorded in the Tower notebook, 1602, referred to Richard III, specifically noting, "d. Glouster in nominee Rex." Neville also mentioned Richard III in a speech in Parliament in 1607, saying that how dangerous diplomatic relations between the Scots and French might be, "we may guess by the example of Richard III" (Duncan, 1974, 209; see Appendix A). Neville took a consistently negative view of Richard. In the copy of *Leicester's Commonwealth*, which he made in 1585, Neville added a marginal annotation, "Rich: Duke of gloucester an vsurper."

In correcting his copy of *A Catalogue of Honor* about twenty years later he inserted the word "usurped" to described his kingship (shown on next page). Shakespeare's play ends with Derby offering the crown to Richmond:

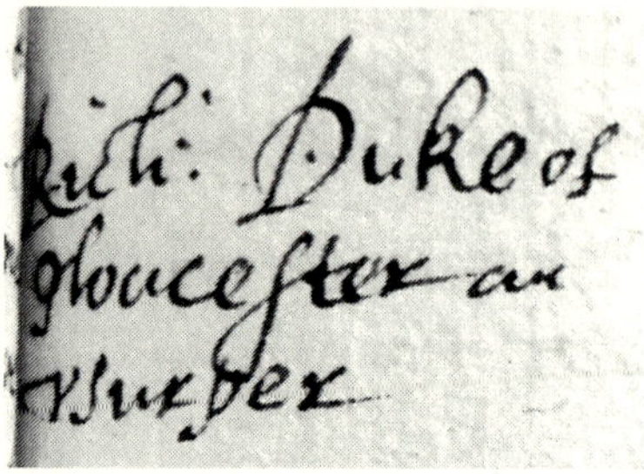

Worsley MSS 47, 57 (by permission of the Eighth Earl of Yarborough and Lincolnshire Archives).

Lo, here, this long-**usurped** royalty
From the dead temples of this bloody wretch
Have I pluck'd off, to grace thy brows withal
[5.5.4].

In his final history play, *Henry VIII* (see Chapter 8), Shakespeare wrote of "Th'usurper Richard" (1.2.197). This play, dated 1612–13, would have been written just after Neville's annotation in *A Catalogue of Honor.*

This extremely negative portrayal of

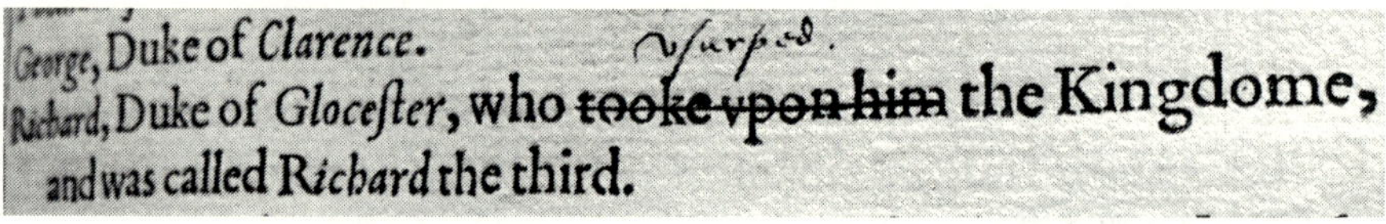
George, Duke of *Clarence.*
Richard, Duke of *Glocester*, who ~~tooke vpon him~~ usurped the Kingdome,
and was called *Richard* the third.

***A Catalogue of Honor,* 351 (private collection).**

Richard, which originates in Sir Thomas More's biography, justified his overthrow. More's works were published by his nephew William Rastell in 1557. In his annotated copy of *Leicester's Commonwealth* Neville showed he had read the *Graunde Abridgement,* a 16th century legal encyclopaedia written by William's father, John Rastell (Casson, 2010, 98, 167). John Rastell, More's brother-in-law, was a lawyer, playwright and publisher. The More and Neville families knew each other. Neville's grandfather, Edward, and John Rastell both went to the Field of the Cloth of Gold in 1520. Edward Neville's brother, Thomas, was one of More's under-sheriff colleagues in the court for "poor men's causes." Thomas Neville was elected speaker of the House of Commons, was knighted, and became a royal counsellor. He was speaker from 1515 and was followed, in 1523, by Sir Thomas More. The More and Neville families knew each other: Neville's servants were mentioned in a comic Christmas entertainment at More's house in 1525 (Guy, 2009, 56, 165). Sir Thomas Neville was Henry Neville's great-uncle.

In his annotated manuscript copy of *Leicester's Commonwealth*, which was a possible source for Shakespeare's history plays, including *Richard III,* Neville added a telling detail to the text. In the printed text we read, "Edward V and his brother, who after were both murdered in the Tower" (Peck, 151/*101*). Neville, however, named the brother as "Rich: d: of york" in his annotation of *Leicester's Commonwealth.*

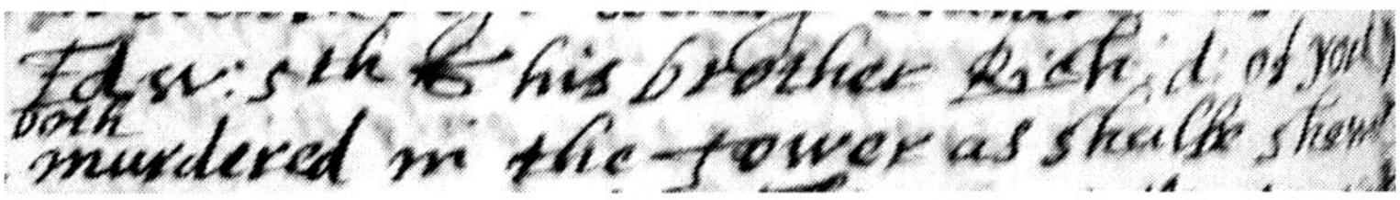
Edw: 5th & his brother Rich: d. of York
both murdered in the tower as shall be shewed

Worsley MSS 47, 43V (by permission of the Eighth Earl of Yarborough and Lincolnshire Archives).

In *Richard III* the young Prince Edward greets his brother, naming him, "Richard of York" (3.1.96), just as Neville had noted. We later hear of the murder of the two princes in the Tower (Casson, 2010, 97).

Furthermore, Neville also noted "Doct Shawe" against a passage about Richard III in *Leicester's Commonwealth* (Peck, 146/*98*).

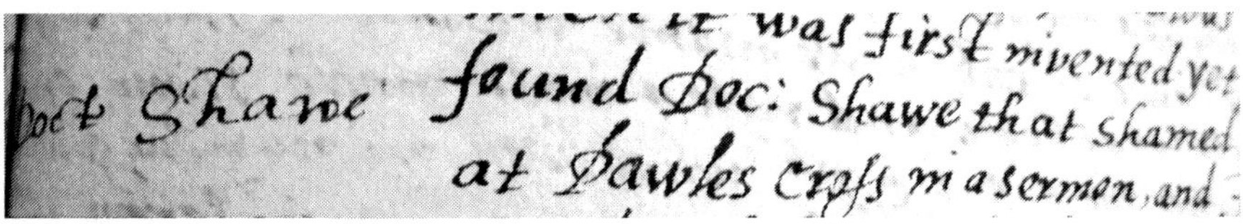
Doct Shawe
it was first invented yet
found Doc: Shawe that shamed
at Pawles Crofs in a sermon, and

Worsley MSS 47, 41 (by permission of the Eighth Earl of Yarborough and Lincolnshire Archives).

In the First Folio edition (1623) of *Richard III* we find Richard saying, "Go, Lovel, with all speed to Doctor **Shaw**" (3.5.97). Dr. Ralph Shawe delivered a sermon on June 22, 1483, in which he said that Edward IV was illegitimate (Given-Wilson and Curteis, 1984, 3). Neville, being illegitimate himself, had reason to be interested in this detail. Indeed he had reason to be interested in many of the characters that appear in *Richard III*, as he was related to most of them. (Table 7 on next page.)

The Women in Richard III

Richard III was the son of Cecily Neville and Richard, Duke of York. Cecily appears in the play as the duchess. Richard married Anne Neville. Shakespeare gives both these women prominent roles in the play. Perhaps only a Neville would foreground these two women while omitting another woman who would have been a sensational figure on the stage: Jane Shore.

Women are generally invisible within the historical chronicles. An exception is the commoner, Jane Shore. Her sorry tale of being charged by Richard III with witchcraft and treason was portrayed by Thomas Churchyard in *The Mirror for Magistrates* (1563). From the very start of the play, as the "wanton

Table 7. Twenty Characters in *Richard III*

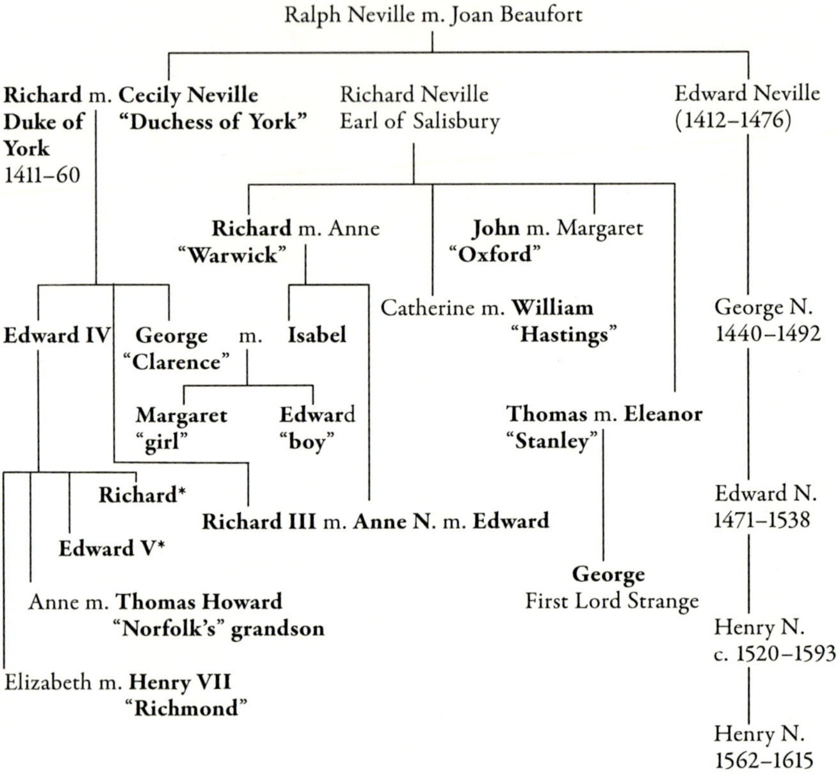

Notes: Characters in **bold** are mentioned or appear in the play. Names used in the play are in quotation marks, i.e., "Warwick." "Norfolk," John Howard, died at Bosworth fighting for Richard III. The Tudor "Norfolk" was Thomas Howard (1473–1554)—see Chapter 8. *Princes murdered in the Tower.

ambling nymph" (1.1.17), she is persistently present in the wings (1.1.73, 74, 93, 98; 3.1.185; 3.4.71; 3.5.31, 51), but she never appears on stage. Yet *Richard III* is the only history play to have five significant female characters: the Duchess of York, Queen Elizabeth, Queen Margaret, Lady Anne, and the Duke of Clarence's daughter. These noblewomen develop a coalition against Richard III and might seem to act on Jane Shore's behalf. Richard sets up this gender war. Early in the play when deceiving his brother, Clarence, as to who was responsible for the malevolent influences that had imprisoned him, Richard blames "men ruled by women" (1.162). He refers to "gentlewomen" who "are mighty gossips in our monarchy" (1.1.82–3) while Clarence and himself "are the queen's abjects" (1.1.106). A sisterly coalition is developed between Duchess of York (Cecily Neville), Queen Elizabeth (Woodville, widow of

Cecily's son, Edward IV), Lady Anne (Neville, wife of Prince Henry and daughter of Richard Neville) and Queen Margaret (Anne Neville's mother-in-law) (2.4, 4.1, 4.4). One could imagine that it is the curses of these women that defeat Richard III at Bosworth Field. Anne is one of the ghosts who damn Richard and bless Richmond before the battle.

In contrast, there is no mention of Ralph Neville (c. 1456–99), the third Earl of Westmoreland, who was one of five earls who fought *with* Richard III at Bosworth in 1485 (Ross, 1981, 159). His support for Richard is commemorated in the "Ballad of Bosworth Field," composed within ten years of the battle:

> The Erle of Lincolne wold not spare,
> The Erle of Northumberland ready bowne,
> The Erle of Westmoreland great othes sware,
> All they said Richard shold Keepe his crowne [58.232].[1]

This is an example of the negative Neville bias that removes a member of the family from the story when to present him on stage would be potentially damaging to the family's reputation.

The Duchess Cecily Neville and the Lady Anne Neville

Neville continued to be interested in Anne Neville, annotating Milles' 1610 *A Catalogue of Honor* with notes about her son. Perhaps this interest was stimulated by the fact that Neville's own wife was called Anne. The first scene of the play reveals Rich-

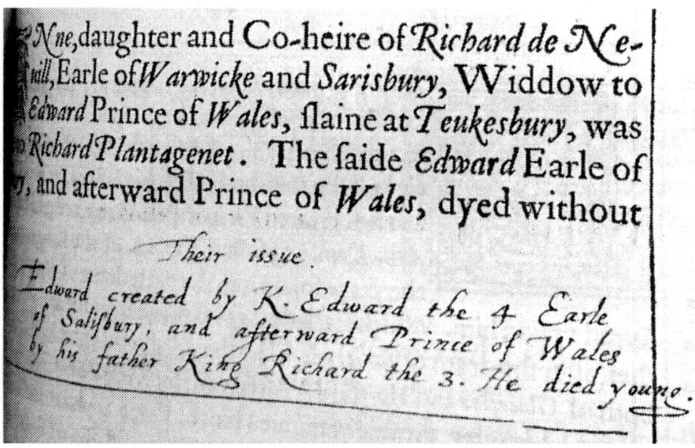
Nne, daughter and Co-heire of *Richard de Ne-*
vill, Earle of *Warwicke* and *Sarisbury*, Widdow to
Edward Prince of *Wales*, slaine at *Teukesbury*, was
Richard Plantagenet. The saide *Edward* Earle of
, and afterward Prince of *Wales*, dyed without
Their issue.
Edward created by K. Edward the 4 Earle of Salisbury, and afterward Prince of Wales by his father King Richard the 3. He died young.

***A Catalogue of Honor*, 387. The large "A" of "Anne" is hidden down inside the spine of the book (private collection).**

ard's (Duke of Gloucester, soon to become King Richard III) most cynical and politically motivated plan to seduce "Warwick's youngest daughter" (1.1.153), even though "I killed her husband [Edward, son of Henry VI] and her father [Richard Neville, the Earl of Warwick]" (1.1.154). Historically, these killings occurred in 1471 at the battles of Tewkesbury and Barnet, respectively (as seen in *Henry VI* part 3). After a long lament by Lady Anne over the body of her dead father-in-law, King Henry VI, in the second scene of the play, she is accosted by Richard, who proceeds to seduce her. After his conquest of Lady Anne, Richard sneers:

> Was ever woman in this humour wooed?
> Was ever woman in this humour won?
> I'll have her, but I will not keep her long [1.2.232].

Although the wooing scene is fictitious, Richard married Anne in 1472. She thus becomes the third queen in this play, but the coronation is seen more as an execution:

> And I with all unwillingness will go.
> O, would to God that the inclusive verge
> Of golden metal that must round my brow
> Were red-hot steel, to sear me to the brains.
> Anointed let me be with deadly venom
> And die ere men can say, "God save the queen" [4.1.57].

In 1485 she died under suspicious circumstances (Ross, 1981, 145; Hicks, 2007, 194). In the play, after marrying and murdering Anne, Richard declares himself "a jolly thriving wooer" (4.3.43), and pursues a plan to woo his niece to consolidate his claim on the throne (4.4). However, his mother, the Duchess of York (Cecily, née Neville), confronts her son, declaring that she regrets not "strangling thee" in her "accursed womb" (4.4.137–9). She then curses him, saying:

> Therefore take with thee my most grievous curse,
> Which in the day of battle tire thee more
> Than all the complete armour that thou wear'st.
> My prayers on the adverse party fight,
> And there the souls of Edward's children
> Whisper the spirits of thine enemies
> And promise them success and victory.
> Bloody thou art, bloody will be thy end;
> Shame serves thy life and doth thy death attend [4.4.188].

From the time that his own mother curses him, Richard III's wooings and warrings fail. Earlier in the play, he had accused Queen Margaret, Queen Elizabeth and Jane Shore of being witches who had cursed him (1.3.164; 3.4.70–1). Indeed, Queen Margaret advises Queen Elizabeth on cursing: "Better thy loss makes the bad causer worse. / Revolving this, will teach thee how to curse" (4.4.122). The bard redeems the mother, Cecily Plantagenet, née

Neville, by having her curse her son. This contrasts with the mother of Richmond (the future Tudor king Henry VII), who blesses "Derby—I, by attorney, bless thee from thy mother, / Who prays continually for Richmond's good" (5.3.84). The author of *Richard III* ensured that while the last Plantagenet king was condemned and character-assassinated, the reputations of his mother and wife, both Nevilles, remained intact.

His mother's curse does not stop Richard III attempting to cajole Queen Elizabeth into assisting in his wooing of her daughter. Perhaps it was the success of the scene about Anne Neville's wooing that encouraged the bard to embellish this scene (4.4), adding 68 more lines to the First Folio (4.4.223–235 and 288–342), compared to the First Quarto. This scene, with the line "prepare her ears to hear a wooer's tale" (4.4.327), has similarities with the king's wooing of the countess in *Edward III* (c. 1593), via her father: "command her, woo her, win her any ways / to be my mistress" (2.1.344). In Chapter 3 we showed how the Countess may be identified with Margaret Pole and her father with Warwick, Richard Neville.

The Guiltless Wife, Isabel Plantagenet, née Neville, and Her Children, Edward and Margaret

Richard declares, "His [the Duke of Clarence's] daughter meanly have I match'd in marriage" (4.3.37) to "some poor gentleman" (4.2.52). Clarence's daughter was Margaret Pole, née Plantagenet. Horace Walpole noted that it was King Henry VII who married her to "the insignificant Sir Richard Pole, because he was safe."[2] The bard then ascribed this cynical Tudor ploy to the Plantagenet tyrant, Richard III. Earlier in the play, when Clarence is arrested, he pleads his case for his family, saying, "O spare my guiltless wife and my children" (1.4.72). Scholars have noted the anomaly that his wife was already dead by the time Clarence was arrested and killed in 1478. She died soon after giving birth in 1476 and was buried with her child. It appears, however, that the dramatist was keen to include another Neville woman in this play. Her name was Isabel, oldest daughter of Warwick and sister of Lady Anne.

Scholars have been perplexed as to why the patently incorrect line, "O spare my guiltless wife and my children" (1.4.72), was included in the First Folio (1623), whereas the First Quarto, published in 1597, was more historically correct. This First Quarto is often supposed to be a "bad" quarto derived from the unauthorized publication of the play from a promptbook, and therefore more prone to error than the First Folio. It is possible that the inclusion of this historically incorrect line in the First Folio was due to a relaxation of censorship. The children referred to are Edward and Margaret Plantagenet, whose mother was Isabel Neville and paternal grandmother was Cecily Neville. They feature in act 2, scene 2, as innocent young orphans, emphasizing Richard's cruelty. *Richard III* is imbued with Tudor propaganda to justify the overthrow of the last Plantagenet king, and to this end many sins are piled on King Richard's shoulders, the least of which is blaming him for Margaret's marriage to the "insignificant" Sir Richard Pole, mentioned above. But the implication that the deaths of the "brats of Clarence" (3.5.107) could be attributed to Richard III was more likely to raise the question, "What did happen to Clarence's children?" In contrast to Jacobean censors, Tudor censors would have wished to avoid the recollection of recent Tudor history.

Clarence's son, Edward, whom Richard says he has imprisoned ("pent up close," 4.3.36), was kept prisoner in the Tower of London by the Tudor king Henry VII from 1485, when Edward was ten years old, till 1499, when he was beheaded. Likewise, the Tudor censors would not relish stirring up memories of the execution of Clarence's sixty-seven-year-old saintly daughter, Margaret, in 1541, by the Tudor king Henry VIII. Not only was she widely regarded as innocent, but the eleven blows of the incompetent executioner's axe needed to hack off her head were seared into the memories of many contemporaries and their descendants (see Chapter 2). In act 2, scene 2, Margaret shares in the lamentations of Cecily and Queen Elizabeth, and becomes a part of the sisterly coalition. In his copy of *Leicester's Commonwealth* Neville made notes on George, Duke of Clarence, and his daughter Margaret, Countess of Salisbury (Casson, 2010, 215; see Chapter 2). These annotations predate the play by up to seven years.

The Mighty Warwick, Richard Neville, and His Brothers-in-Law, Oxford, Hastings and Stanley

Richard Neville, the Earl of Warwick, stalks all four scenes of the first act of *Richard III.* He is mentioned or alluded to in every scene (1.1.153, 1.2.159, 1.3.135, 1.4.49). In act 2 he is referred to as "mighty Warwick" (2.1.111). Even before she becomes queen to King Richard III, Lady Anne (née Neville) is aware that King Richard "hates me for my father, Warwick" (4.1.85).

Hastings and Stanley are major characters in this play, but they are portrayed as unwilling supporters of Richard III. Hastings lives in terror. In the first scene, Richard determines Hastings' fate, saying, "He cannot live, I hope, and must not die / Till George be packed with post horse up to heaven" (1.1.145). Hastings is eventually beheaded by Richard for supposed conspiracy. William Hastings (1431–83) was a brother-in-law to Warwick, having married Catherine Neville (see Table 7). At the time this play was written, in 1592, his great, great-grandson was Henry Hastings, third Earl of Huntingdon (1539–1595). He was dedicatee of Thomas Hoby's influential translation of Castiglione's *The Courtier* (1561), and therefore probably Hoby's patron. Hoby was the uncle of Henry Neville's wife.

Henry Hastings was personally mentored by Reginald Pole, the Archbishop of Canterbury and son of Margaret Pole. Huntingdon's mother, Katherine Hastings, née Pole (1511–1576), and his aunt, Winifred Hastings, née Pole (1525–1580), were daughters of Margaret Pole's son, Henry, and Jane Neville. Henry and Jane were beheaded with Henry Neville's grandfather, Edward Neville, in a purge by Henry VIII.

Although the third Earl of Huntingdon had no children, his namesake and the only son of his nephew, Francis, was Henry Hastings, who became the fifth Earl of Huntingdon (1586–1643) by the time of the publication of the First Folio. He was a patron of playwrights John Fletcher and Francis Beaumont. He was also married to a descendant of another prominent character in *Richard III.* Henry Hasting's wife, Elizabeth Stanley (1588–1633), was the daughter of Ferdinando Stanley, the fifth Earl of Derby.

Stanley, who appears as the first Earl of Derby in *Richard III,* was a brother-in-law to Warwick. His wife was Eleanor Neville, sister of Richard Neville, the Earl of Warwick. As Richard's servant, Catesby, says, "He will do all in all as Hastings doth" (3.1.168). The loyalty of Thomas Stanley to Richard III was only maintained by threats and terror. For example, "Stanley, look to your wife. If she convey / Letters to Richmond, you shall answer for it" (4.2.90). The loyalty of Eleanor Stanley, née Neville, to the Tudor cause is thus revealed. Stanley's support for Richard III was also founded on his son, George, being held hostage by Richard, and even then Stanley rebelled against the king (5.4.344). By virtue of his marriage in 1482, George Stanley became Lord Strange, and was ancestor of Ferdinando Stanley (1559–1594), who, as Lord Strange, was patron of Strange's Men. This company performed Shakespeare's *Henry VI* in 1592, about the time *Richard III* is thought to have been written.

A major supporter of Henry Tudor, the Earl of Richmond, was the thirteenth Earl of Oxford, John de Vere. In the play he makes only one heroic

Table 8. William Hastings, His Descendants and the Nevilles

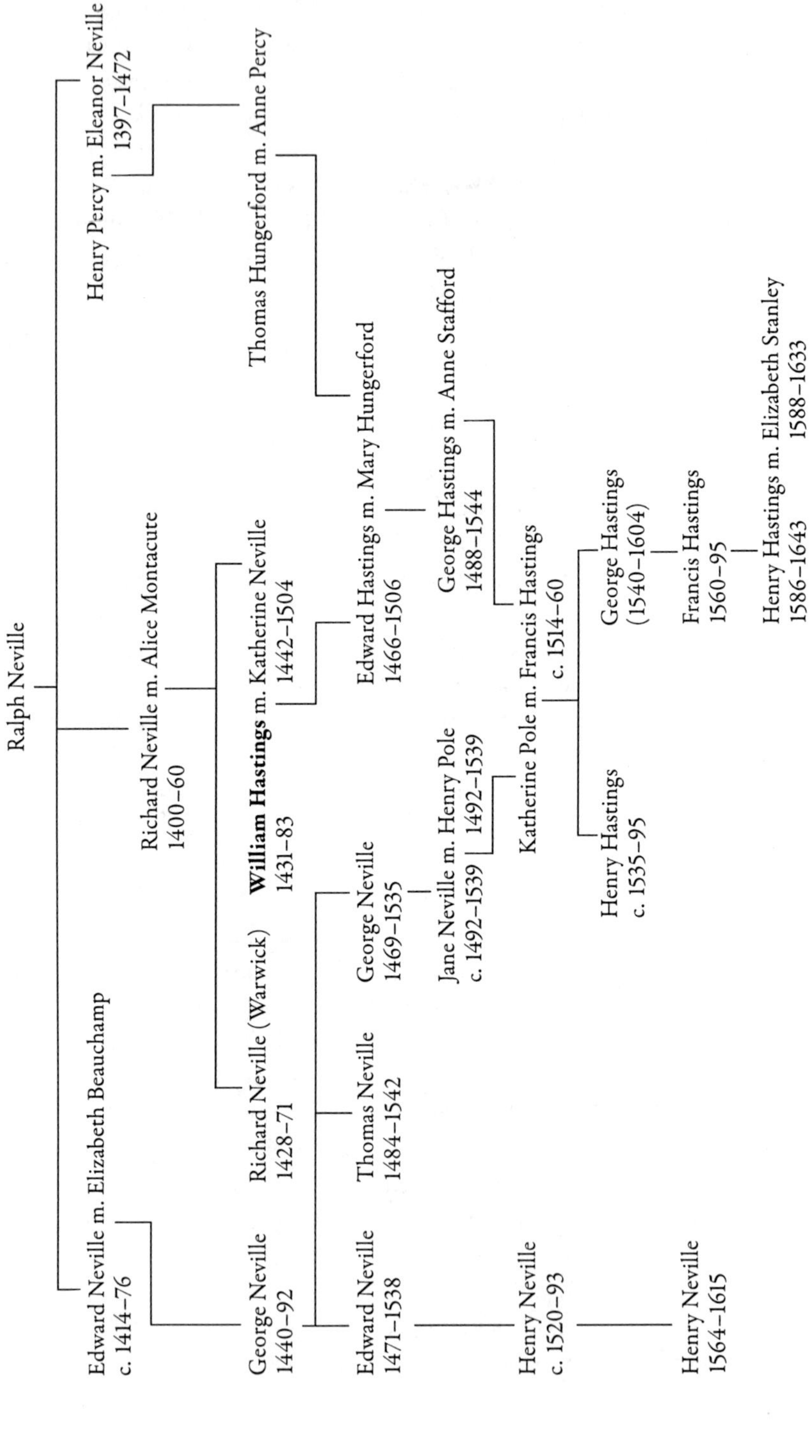

statement, "Every man's conscience is a thousand men, / To fight against this guilty homicide" (5.2.17). His modest role in the play ignores the fact that he became lord chamberlain and officiated at the coronations of Henry VII and Henry VIII, and was ancestor of Edward de Vere, seventeenth Earl of Oxford. He was a brother-in-law to Richard Neville, having married Margaret Neville. Had Edward de Vere been the author of the Shakespeare plays, he might have given his ancestor more lines!

Henry Wriothesley, Henry Neville and the Gift of the Encomium of Richard III

The period 1592–1593 was a time of wooing. *Richard III* is thought to have been composed in 1592, as it was performed in 1593. Richard's wooing of the widow Lady Anne, in act 1, scene 2, and of Richard's niece, Elizabeth, via the widow Queen Elizabeth, in act 4, scene 4, are breathtaking in their eloquence, deceit and cynicism. *Edward III,* probably written in 1593, also portrays a corrupt and cynical wooing by a king, though this time he is full of lust. In 1592/3, the bard wrote the poem *Venus and Adonis,* which he dedicated to Henry Wriothesley, the Earl of Southampton, and also wrote sonnets that, many scholars agree, were to encourage the nineteen-year-old to marry his guardian's granddaughter. His guardian was Lord Burghley (William Cecil). Neville had met Wriothesley as a boy when the latter was being educated at Burghley's. Neville had previously attended the school there.[3] The bard apparently failed in his mission, and it was rumored that Wriothesley was fined £5,000 for his disobedience in not marrying his guardian's granddaughter.[4] But the bard and the earl continued as friends. Henry Neville and Southampton were in the Tower of London 1601–3 and remained friends for the rest of their lives (James and Rubinstein, 2005; James, 2008). In 1612 Southampton was reported to be Neville's "champion" in Parliament (in a letter dated November 4, 1612, from John Chamberlain to Dudley Carleton [Hamilton, 1992, 166] and in 1613 Southampton was called Neville's "great patron" (McClure, 1939, vol. 1, 401). Likewise, Neville was described as Southampton's "Dear Damon" (1613), a reference to the legendary friends Damon and Pythias (James and Rubinstein, 2005, 246).

Southampton was a keen theatergoer, "going to plaies every day" in 1599 (Collins, 1746, ii. 132). In 1603 he dedicated to Henry Neville a manuscript defending Richard III. This document was based on *The Encomium of Richard III,* which was originally written by Sir William Cornwallis the younger.

Southampton made specific revisions of the document referring to "undiscreete Croniclers and witty **Play-makers**," and how "wee must still make him [Richard III] more Cruelle infamous in pamphlets and **playes**." The mystery of why Southampton would dedicate a defense of Richard III to Neville is resolved if we accept that Neville was the author of the play that so comprehensively blackened Richard's reputation. (See Appendix A for a thorough study of *The Encomium*.)

Richard III and Robert Cecil

Henry Neville married Anne Killigrew, daughter of Catherine Killigrew née Cooke. Catherine's sister, Mildred, was the mother of Robert Cecil, and another sister, Elizabeth, was the mother of Edward Hoby. In the same year that Sir Edward Hoby accompanied Essex on the campaign against Cadiz in 1596, he invited Sir Robert Cecil to supper and to see a play about a King Richard. Whether this was *Richard II* or *Richard III* is unclear, but both plays are controversially about the usurpation of the throne. Although Robert Cecil's father, William, lived till 1598, he was seriously incapacitated by a stroke in 1592 and the reins of political power fell into Robert Cecil's hands. Supporters of Robert Devereux, the Earl of Essex, compared Robert Cecil to Richard III (O'Callaghan, 1998). Robert Cecil, like Richard, was physically challenged. Elizabeth I is said to have referred to him as "my elf" and "my pigmy." The Spanish ambassador Antonio Perez dubbed Cecil "microgibbus" ("little hump": Jardine and Stewart, 1999, 163). Cecil was described as "a slight crooked, hump-backed young gentleman, dwarfish in stature" (Motley, 1856). Contemporaries associated Cecil with Richard III. John Chamberlain reported a ditty to Dudley Carleton:

> While two Great Rs both crouchback stood at the helm,
> The one spilt the blood royal, the other the realm [Crofts, 1991].

In a letter to Neville dated September 13, 1600, Ralph Winwood reported that Sir Thomas Erskin had referred to Cecil as "the Crookback'd Secretary" (Sawyer, 1725, vol. 1, 256).

Baynard Castle and Crosby Place

As the young Duke of Gloucester and as lord protector, Richard's official functions were conducted at his mother's London residence, Baynard's Castle.

Cecily Plantagenet, née Neville, lived there from 1460. Baynard's Castle is mentioned twice in the play; Richard meets the mayor, aldermen and citizens of London there and is offered the crown by Henry Stafford, the Duke of Buckingham. Buckingham's maternal grandmother was Anne Neville (a daughter of Joan Beaufort) who was from the same line of John of Gaunt's descendants as Henry Neville. Buckingham was second cousin to Anne Neville, Richard's queen.

Richard's more sinister gatherings are at Crosby Place. Richard invites the newly wooed Anne Neville to Crosby Place (1.2.212). It is also where Richard briefs the two murderers to kill his brother George, the Duke of Clarence (1.3.345). Later, Richard assigns William Catesby to determine if Hastings is prepared to collaborate in Richard's plan for the crown and the execution of those who stand in the way. Catesby is to report back to Richard at Crosby Place (3.1.190).

According to the Holinshed *Chronicles*, "Crosbies in Bishops gate Street [was] where [Richard as] the protector kept his household" before he became king (Holinshed, 1587, 712). When *Richard III* was being written, Henry Neville's aunt, Cecily Cioll, née Gresham, lived at Crosby Place (and did so until she died in 1609). Cecily and Elizabeth (Henry Neville's mother) were daughters of John Gresham. Cecily's husband, Germain Cioll, had been a leaseholder of the property since at least 1554, and he was the owner from 1561 to 1566. After 1566, Mr. Cioll kept a lease on a portion of it for his wife. Neville therefore would have known this, his aunt's property.

Oddly enough, the property was named after Sir John Crosby, who was knighted in 1470 by Edward IV for defending London from Thomas Neville, the Bastard of Falconbridge. Shakespeare mentioned this Falconbridge in *Henry VI,* part 3 (1.1.239).

Conclusion

Henry Neville had a significant interest in the reign of Richard III, expressed in notes in extant manuscripts and in a political speech in Parliament. This observation is reinforced by Southampton's dedication to Neville of his version of the *Encomium* on Richard III (see Appendix A). Neville's family environment and genealogy gave him the depth of knowledge from which to compose *Richard III.* Indeed, the author of this play appears to have deliberately foregrounded members of the Neville family, even when some, such as Warwick and his daughter Isabel, were dead.

CHAPTER 8

Henry VIII (1509–1547)

His overthrow heap'd happiness upon him;
For then, and not till then, he felt himself,
And found the blessedness of being little.
—*Henry VIII* (4.2.64)

The Famous History of the Life of King Henry the Eight is the last of the history plays in the First Folio. It dates from 1612–1613 and was on stage as a new play in the summer of 1613. This was over thirteen years after Shakespeare's previous history play, *Henry V,* written in 1599. Not only had the monarch changed, but Shakespeare had changed considerably. The bard had travelled through the fearful landscapes of his great tragedies and the problem plays into the sunnier romances, and now he was at the very end of his writing career, with only one last play, *The Two Noble Kinsmen,* to create. These last plays were co-written with John Fletcher. *Henry VIII* was first published with the authorship attributed to William Shakespeare and no acknowledgment of any other writer. Since 1850, when James Spedding attributed sections to John Fletcher, textual and computer analysis has enabled scholars to identify more exactly which sections were probably written by Shakespeare and which by Fletcher. We will focus more on the sections that are by Shakespeare.[1] *Henry VIII* is not just a costumed pageant, though the spectacular nature of the play was remarked upon at the time and the special effects led to the burning down of the Globe Theatre on June 29, 1613. As we will show, it is also a play with hidden political meaning for Henry Neville.

Henry VIII: A Rich History

The life of Henry VIII was long, varied and dramatic. He had six wives, two of whom he divorced and two executed. He broke with Rome, dissolved the monasteries and made himself head of the Church of England. He had legitimate and illegitimate children, three of whom became monarchs themselves. He fought wars with Scotland and France. His reign included political intrigue, major cultural upheaval, the uprising of the Pilgrimage of Grace and many executions.

Shakespeare's play is remarkable for what the bard left out, focusing instead on a selection of episodes, beginning with a peace treaty in France; showing the falls of Buckingham and his persecutor, Wolsey; Henry's struggle to divorce Queen Katherine; and the rise of Cranmer and Cromwell; and ending in the coronation of Henry's new wife Anne Bullen and the baptism of the future Queen Elizabeth I. What is strange in a play subtitled *All Is True* is quite how much is not true, is distorted, omitted or hidden.

The Hidden Nevilles

It is generally accepted that this play was co-authored by Shakespeare and John Fletcher. Analysis of the text has shown that the first scene was written by the bard. The play opens with a description of the Field of the Cloth of Gold. Three members of the Neville family were present at this glittering occasion in 1520, when the kings of France and England met to feast and establish a brief peace treaty: Ralph Neville, fourth Earl of Westmoreland, George Neville, fifth Baron Bergavenny, and his younger brother Sir Edward Neville.

Edward Stafford, third Duke of Buckingham, was also present, but the playwright invents an illness that prevented his attendance so that the Duke of Norfolk can describe it to him and get his reaction. In fact it was Norfolk who was not present at the Field of the Cloth of Gold. This is the first untruth in *All is True*. All these characters in this first scene have close family connections, as we can see when we look at the family tree (on the next page).

In the play people convicted of treason and subsequently executed are named and presented positively. In 1604 Neville persuaded the House of Commons to establish a committee to consider the whole question of what amounted to treason. He had personal experience of the danger of people unwittingly finding themselves accused of treason. In the play characters such

Table 9. Act 1, Scene 1, of *Henry VIII* and Henry Neville's Family

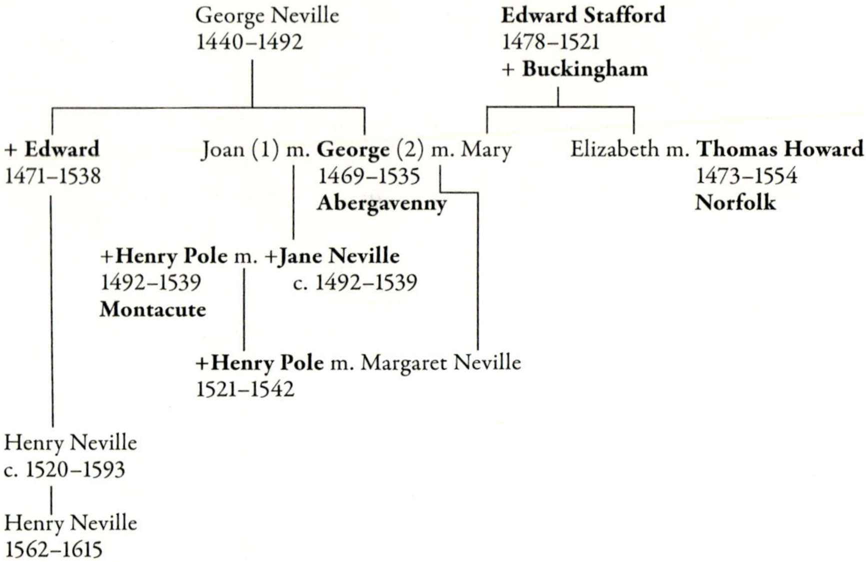

Notes: + indicates persons executed. Characters in **bold** are mentioned or appear in the play.

as Cromwell, Surrey (Norfolk's son) and Anne Boleyn, who were all eventually executed, are treated kindly and given human faces. Initially, one might feel an injustice is being done to them, because their executions are not mentioned. But the playwright has given them vivid life on stage. Most radical is the presentation of the unjust trial and beheading of Buckingham. Shakespeare, as author of *Richard III* and possibly of *Thomas of Woodstock,* had shown the elimination of two other dukes of Buckingham (see Chapters 3 and 7; Casson, 2009, 178). These dukes were of royal blood, being descended from Edward III and therefore a threat to the reigning monarch, as possible heirs, should the king not have a son. Henry VIII's anxiety about siring an heir may have been a factor in his eliminating Buckingham. In the play Buckingham is betrayed by his surveyor, who testifies that his master had said, "If the king dies without issue, he'll carry it so to make the sceptre his" (1.2.134). Edward Stafford was the third Duke of Buckingham. His father appears in *Richard III*, and in *Henry VIII* Buckingham remembers his father, acknowledging that he suffered an extra-judicial killing:

> I had my trial,
> And, must needs say, a noble one; which makes me,
> A little happier than my wretched father [2.1.119].

Buckingham's second daughter, Katherine, married Ralph Neville, fourth Earl of Westmoreland. Buckingham's youngest daughter, Mary, married George Neville, fifth Baron Bergavenny. George appears on stage with Buckingham, his father-in-law, in the first scene as Lord Abergavenny. George was the older brother of Edward Neville, who was the grandfather of Henry Neville.

Henry VIII also shows the arrest of George Neville, Lord Abergavenny, and Henry Pole, Lord Montacute, and this is recorded in Holinshed's *Chronicles* (1587, 863):

> After the apprehension of the duke, inquisitions were taken in diverse shires of England of him so that by the knights and gentlemen, he was indicted for high treason for certain words spoken by the same duke at Blechingly, to the Lord Abergavenny and therewith was the same lord attached **for concealment** and so likewise was the Lord Montacute, and both **led to the Tower**. Sir Edward Neville, brother of the said Lord Abergavenny, was forbidden the king's presence [emphasis added; see also Halio, 1999, 85, note].

Henry Neville himself was sent to the Tower **for concealing** what he knew about the Earl of Essex's plans in 1601.

George, Lord Abergavenny, was imprisoned but released and participated in Anne Boleyn's coronation. Henry Pole, Lord Montacute, was later executed in the same purge as Edward Neville. Henry Pole married Jane Neville and was therefore son-in-law to George (Richardson, 2011, 244).

The arresting officer in the play is Charles Brandon (act 1, scene 1). In his copy of *Leicester's Commonwealth* Neville had made a unique annotation about Charles Brandon, Duke of Suffolk (Casson, 2010, 216). On the Brandon page of *A Catalogue of Honor,* Neville corrected the text, stating Charles was Duke of Suffolk (not Somerset). These annotations predate the play.

In *Henry VIII* Charles appears as Brandon in the first scene and then, in act 2, scene 2, as the Duke of Suffolk. His first marriage was to Margaret Neville, daughter of John Neville, first Marquess of Montagu, although for the period covered by the play, he was married to Henry VIII's sister, Mary Tudor.

An. Dom. 1513.

Suffolk

Harles Brandon (ſonne of *William*
Garter, Maiſter of the Horſe (w
led) was by *Henry* the 8. (whoſe
the French king he had marrie
after Duke of ~~*Somerſet*~~ Suffolk on Can
of king *Henry* the eight. In whi
of a ſolemne Tilt and Turney t
the Dolphin; This Duke, the

***A Catalogue of Honor,* 1610, 542 (private collection).**

The first scene is the only appearance of Abergavenny and the only mention of Montacute. One might wonder why they feature at all in this play. What is important about these characters to warrant specific and prominent mention? Lord Abergavenny makes a peculiar comment that may explain the purpose of his role. After Buckingham complains to Abergavenny about Cardinal Wolsey's presumption in imposing immense costs on those whom he proposed should attend the king at the Field of the Cloth of Gold, Abergavenny agrees, saying:

I do know
Kinsmen of mine, three at least, that have
By this so sicken'd their estates, that never
They shall abound as formerly [1.1.80–83].

We know that George Neville, Edward Neville (his brother) and Ralph Neville,[2] attended the Field of the Cloth of Gold and so may have "sickened their estates" in meeting the costs. However, we hypothesize that this reference to three kinsmen effectively ruined during Henry VIII's reign could be to Abergavenny's brother, his daughter and his grandson. His daughter is the previously mentioned Jane Neville who married Henry Pole (Lord Montacute), and her son was also named Henry Pole (Table 9). Abergavenny's brother was Edward Neville. These three were beheaded by Henry VIII after the demise of Wolsey in 1530, long after this scene. Whether Abergavenny's reference to three kinsmen is to those who attended the Field of the Cloth of Gold or to the trio of executed members of the family, the common figure is Edward Neville. This discreet reference to him can be seen as another indication of the playwright's identity.

Sir Edward Neville (1482–1538)

Edward Neville was a close friend of Henry VIII. Hall (1809, 517) in his *Chronicle* reported Edward's part as the knight Valiaunt Desire in a theatrical pageant at the end of the Christmas period of 1510. Later, for May Day, he took part in another theatrical celebration (Hall, 1965, 520). "Neville was not only a notable masquer. He was also an accomplished singer with a liking for merry songs. He possessed a talent for extemporary verses, often of current topicality" (Hawkyard, 2004, 489). It seems that verbal creativity and theatricality were hereditary traits in the Neville family (Casson, 2009, 175). Edward took part in embassies to France (in 1518 and 1532).

At a banquet given by Cardinal Wolsey in 1527, Edward appeared disguised in a masque and "the cardinal was deceived, or pretended to be, in identifying Neville in his vizard as the King" (Hawkyard, 2004, 489). Edward physically resembled Henry VIII so Wolsey's misidentification is understandable. A version of this incident occurs in *Henry VIII.* In act 1, scene 4, masquers enter a banquet at Cardinal Wolsey's house. One of them is the king himself, disguised. The cardinal guesses the royal person is present: he asks the lord chamberlain,

> WOLSEY: Pray, tell 'em thus much from me:
> There should be one amongst 'em, by his person,
> More worthy this place than myself; to whom,
> If I but knew him, with my love and duty
> I would surrender it.
> CHAMBERLAIN: I will my Lord. (*He whispers with the masquers.*)
> WOLSEY: What say they?
> CHAMBERLAIN: Such a one, they all confess,
> There is indeed; which they would have your grace
> Find out, and he will take it.
> KING HENRY VIII: (*Unmasking*) Ye have found him, cardinal [1.4.77].

Halio in his edition of *Henry VIII* (1999, 106, footnote) identified this incident as the occasion involving Edward Neville. The words underlined in the above speeches are taken directly from George Cavendish's *Life of Cardinal Wolsey,* which was composed in 1554–8. Whereas the play has Henry VIII unmasking in response to the cardinal, Cavendish's account continues with Wolsey saying,

> Me semys the gentilman w^{t} the blake beard shold be even he / And w^{t} that he arrose out of hys chayer and offered the same to the gentilman in the blake beard (w^{t} his Cappe in his hand) The person to whom he offered than his Chayer / was **sir Edward Neveyll** A comely knight of a goodly personage that **myche more resembled the kynges person** in the Maske than any other/ The kyng heryng & perceyvyng the Cardynall so disseyved in his estymacion and choys cowld not forbear lawyng/ but plucked down his visare & **mr Neveylles** & dasht owt [emphasis added; Sylvester, 1959, 27].

George Cavendish's *Life of Cardinal Wolsey* was not published during Shakespeare's lifetime but was available in manuscript form. Scholars, such as Halio, are unsure how either Shakespeare or Fletcher was aware of this manuscript and how they obtained a copy. It is easier to understand how Henry Neville would have his own copy of a document that so flatteringly portrays his grandfather.

Despite the close dependence on the Holinshed *Chronicles,* the play avoids mention of Lord Abergavenny as George Neville. It avoids mention of

Edward Neville being "forbidden from the king's presence." It also avoids mention of Edward Neville's direct involvement in the masque scene. Yet all these Neville figures are hidden in the background, and revealing them illuminates the political meaning of the play.

The Nevilles and their cousins, the Courtenays, supported Katherine[3] of Aragon, and this led to the execution of Edward Neville and many of his relatives. Katherine is portrayed very sympathetically in the play, so it seems the playwrights were consciously redressing the wrong done to her and those who supported her.

The Tower Notebook

James and Rubinstein (2005, 44 and 218–221), identified the Tower notebook of 1602 as a source for Anne Boleyn's coronation (act 4, scene 1). In this Neville made notes on coronation rituals from Richard II onwards. These include some that we see in *Henry VIII*; for example, this stage direction: "Then under a canopy borne by four barons of the Cinque Ports, Anne the new Queen." In the Tower notebook Neville annotated the text in three places about the barons of the Cinque Ports carrying the canopy. One of these states, "Barons 5 ports claym to Cary the Canapie on 4 Lances gilt staves. 4 men at a lance."

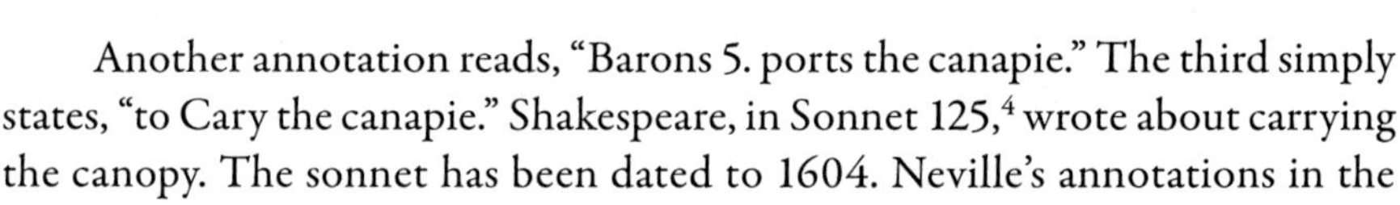

Worsley 40, The Tower notebook (by permission of the Eighth Earl of Yarborough and Lincolnshire Archives).

Another annotation reads, "Barons 5. ports the canapie." The third simply states, "to Cary the canapie." Shakespeare, in Sonnet 125,[4] wrote about carrying the canopy. The sonnet has been dated to 1604. Neville's annotations in the Tower notebook date from 1602–3. In the 1604 quarto of *Hamlet* the word is spelled "Canopie." In the 1599 quarto of *Romeo and Juliet* it is spelled "Canapie."

The Politics of the First Decade of James I's Reign

The politics of the first ten years of James's reign were about the power of the king's favorites, the Union of Scotland and England in Great Britain, and the conflict between the monarch and parliament. Henry Neville was involved in all of these. From 1606 Robert Carr emerged as James I's favorite and was eventually made Viscount Rochester and then Earl of Somerset. He had been introduced to court by Sir Thomas Overbury. As Carr and Overbury became more important in managing government business for James, they conducted correspondence in which they used codenames for significant figures. Henry Neville was named "Similis" because he looked like Henry VIII and Thomas Howard, Earl of Suffolk, was called "Wolsey" (Somerset, 1997, 90). Immediately we can see that these historic figures had contemporary relevance.

Neville's Political Life, 1612–13

The play opens with three dukes discussing the spectacular Field of the Cloth of Gold. Abergavenny and Buckingham complain of the enormous expense of this diplomatic extravaganza (1.1.80–85). Whereas Elizabeth I was notoriously parsimonious, James I was extravagant and had to return again and again to Parliament to ask for more money. "Neville hated excessive expenditure by the government and the burden it placed on the tax payer" (Duncan, 1974, 201).

The Field of the Cloth of Gold peace treaty was a failure. Neville was doubtful about James I's peacemaking with Spain, calling him "Jacobus Pacificus" in a letter to Winwood in 1606 and saying, "The kingdom generally wishes this peace broken" (Duncan, 1974, 201). Complaining of the failure of the Field of the Cloth of Gold, Norfolk says:

> France hath flawed the league and hath attached
> Our merchants' goods at Bordeaux [1.1.95].

As ambassador, and years later, Neville was much concerned about the difficulties of English merchants in France, as is evident in his letters (for example a letter dated June 4, 1606: Sawyer, 1725, vol. 2, 217).

In *Henry VIII* Norfolk, describing the jewels on display, said the wealth "made Britain India"[5] (1.1.21). Britain was the name proposed for the newly united kingdoms of England and Scotland, so the use of Britain here would have been an anachronism in Henry's reign but appropriate for the union under James I. Neville was involved in the negotiations from 1606. *Cymbeline* dates from 1609–10 and refers to Britain twenty-three times.

The only time the word "secretary" occurs in the Shakespeare canon is in *Henry VIII*, where it is used five times, especially about new secretaries taking over the role: at least one of these is in a scene accepted as by Shakespeare. This reflects Neville's political ambitions in 1613. Many people expected Neville to become the secretary of state that year, following the death of Robert Cecil in 1612. Cecil had not handled the Commons successfully, and Neville was confident that he would be able to persuade the Commons to be more cooperative. In a letter dated August 6, 1613, Henry Wriothesley, the Earl of Southampton, expressed his confidence that Sir Henry Neville would become secretary (Stopes, 1922, 363). In the autumn of 1612 Neville had proposed that he and Ralph Winwood share the role of secretary[6] (Duncan, 1974, 243). In the play there is a touching scene in which Wolsey, knowing his power is gone, hands over to Cromwell:

> Seek the King—
> That sun I pray may never set—I have told him
> What and how true thou art. He will advance thee [3.2.415].

The play *Henry VIII* is mainly about the rise and fall of powerful people: the prologue invites us to see "how soon this mightiness meets misery." Despite the damning portrait of Wolsey in the first half of the play (see section "Wolsey and the Cecils," below), the writers are sympathetic to Wolsey and Cromwell in the latter half of act 3, scene 2, even allowing Wolsey a final realization that the loss of political ambition releases him from an oppressive grandeur. This scene between Wolsey and Cromwell has no source in the historical records (Halio, 1999, 9). This passage is thought to have been jointly written by Shakespeare and Fletcher. Given that Cromwell became the first Earl of Essex, Neville may have appreciated the irony of Wolsey's fall precipitating Cromwell's rise, although Cromwell, like Robert Devereux, the second Earl of Essex, was later executed. In the play two of the figures who fall, Buckingham and Katherine, proclaim their innocence, and Cranmer is threatened by enemies despite his innocence. This could be both a reflection of Neville's experience of being unjustly accused of treason (he was arrested in 1604 on the basis of a rumor and then released) and a warning to Winwood of the perils of high office.

One motive for presenting a spectacular pageant play in 1613 may have been the marriage of Princess Elizabeth, James I's daughter, to Frederick, the Elector Palatine. They were seen by many as the Protestant hope of Europe. That the play ends in a scene of rejoicing at the birth of Elizabeth, who is promised a glorious future, suggests it was written as a compliment to James I's daughter (Halio, 1999, 16). Indeed the wedding of Princess Elizabeth may be obliquely referred to in the play when, at Anne Boleyn's wedding, her hair is stated to be "adorned with pearl" (4.1.36.28). Holinshed does not mention pearls in Anne Boleyn's hair but they "were prominent in Princess Elizabeth's headdress in 1613" (Halio, 1999, 173 note; see also 170 note).

Frederick and his new wife left England in April, arriving in Heidelberg in June 1613. On July 6 William Trumbull, the English ambassador, wrote that Neville was in Brussels to see "the Procession of the Sacrament of Miracles, the Princes and this Court in its Glory" (Sawyer, 1725, vol. 3, 467). Henry Wriothesley, the Earl of Southampton, was also in the Netherlands that summer, intending to visit Brussels "very privately" (according to a letter from Sir John Throckmorton to Trumbull). He returned to England in August (Stopes, 1922, 362; Casson, 2009, 219). They may both have accompanied the royal party. Frederick and Elizabeth lived in Heidelberg Castle, where Frederick built a theater for the performance of Shakespeare's plays.[7] There is a tradition that the members of the Globe Theatre Company stayed there when their theatre was destroyed by fire.[8]

Contemporary Politics in Henry VIII

We have suggested that Shakespeare's history plays use history as metaphor for the present. From the above it is clear that the bard may also have been using aspects of Henry VIII's reign as metaphors for contemporary political struggles. It appears that from the beginning of this play, history is being manipulated to draw parallels between George Neville and Henry Neville; Buckingham and Robert Devereux; Wolsey and Robert Cecil. Furthermore, there is evidence that the play also refracts contemporary political struggles through the lens of historical power shifts of Henry VIII's court. The playwright is exploring how the monarch can manage these; the issues were very much topics of 1613 because after Salisbury's death the tectonic plates at court were shifting. With Robert Cecil gone, Neville could look back to the earlier struggles between Essex and Cecil that had had such an impact on him and reflect on the current situation.

Buckingham, Surrey and Essex

Robert Devereux, Earl of Essex, was appointed Lord Deputy of Ireland and sent there to quell a rebellion in 1599. Essex, who was involved in a political power struggle with Robert Cecil, wrote at the time, "I am not ignorant what are the disadvantages of absence" from court (Gajda, 2012, 148). In *Henry*

VIII Wolsey uses a similar strategy to get Surrey out of the way so that he cannot help his father-in-law Buckingham.

> 1st Gentleman: Then deputy of Ireland; who, remov'd,
> Earl Surrey was sent thither, and in haste, too,
> Lest he should help his father.
> 2nd Gentleman: That trick of state
> Was a deep envious one.
> 1st Gentleman: At his return
> No doubt he will requite it. It is noted,
> And generally, whoever the king favours,
> The cardinal instantly will find employment,
> And far enough from court too [2.1.42–49].

This policy of weakening a rival courtier's influence is denounced by Surrey himself in act 3 (3.2.260). This was also true of Neville's friend and supporter Thomas Overbury, who was offered the post of ambassador in Russia and turned it down, resulting in his imprisonment in the Tower from April 21, 1613. A similar strategy can be seen in *Henry VIII* when a Dr. Pace, who had been the secretary of state before Wolsey, was posted abroad by the cardinal, who

> fearing he would rise, he was so virtuous,
> Kept him a foreign man still; which so grieved him
> That he ran mad and died [2.2.121–129 and 134–135].

Neville knew how maddening it was to be an ambassador. Pace was recalled from Venice in 1536, but his death occurred six years **after** Wolsey's death. This reference to his death in the play is therefore an anachronism. One might wonder why the playwright put this reference in, if not to reflect his personal experience as an ambassador and concern for his friend and ally Overbury.

The characterization of Buckingham and Norfolk's sage advice to him in the first scene of *Henry VIII* may be a reflection on the rash behavior of Essex. A furious Buckingham is about to confront his enemy Wolsey. Norfolk advises him:

> Stay, my lord,
> And let your reason with your choler question
> What 'tis you go about. To climb steep hills
> Requires slow pace at first: anger is like
> A **full-hot horse**, who being allow'd his way,
> Self-mettle tires him...
> Be advis'd;
> Heat not a furnace for your foe so hot

That it do singe yourself. We may outrun
By **violent swiftness** that which we run at,
And lose by **over-running** [1.1.129–136].

After Essex negotiated a truce with the Irish in 1600, Elizabeth refused to accept the terms. Essex feared she was ill advised by Cecil and felt he must speak to her and ensure that his views were understood. Essex left Ireland for Wales on the 24th of September, then with "**full-hot horse**" and "**violent swiftness**," rode day and night and rushed into the queen's bedchamber at Nonsuch Palace on the 28th of September. Essex was mud-splattered. The queen had not finished dressing. The earl's rash intrusion resulted in him being placed under house arrest, and within six months he would be executed as a traitor.

One of Essex's fears was that there would be a Catholic heir to the throne. In *Henry VIII* the analogy between Buckingham and Essex is highlighted when Buckingham accuses Wolsey of treason in secret negotiations with foreign powers. He speaks of how

> Charles the emperor ... privily deals with our Cardinal.... I am sure the emperor ... paid ere he promised ... when the way was made, And paved with gold, the emperor thus desired, that he would please to alter the king's course ... thus the cardinal does buy and sell his honour as he pleases, and for his own advantage [1.1.174–192].

"Charles the emperor" here refers to Charles V (1500–1558) of the Spanish Empire and the Holy Roman Empire. Simpson (1874, 426) noted, "There is no foundation for Buckingham's charge that Wolsey was bribed by the Emperor.... The invention seems to regard some of James's ministers who were in the pay of Spain." In 1605 Robert Cecil, the Earl of Salisbury, was a pensioner of Spain.[9] In 1611, one year before Prince Henry died, Robert Cecil proposed a marriage for the prince to Phillip III of Spain's sister, Anne. This caused anxieties in England about the possibility of a Catholic monarch. Essex had been a supporter of a protestant succession, of James I, and had feared Cecil supported the succession of the Infanta Isabella of Spain.[10]

Essex was a popular nobleman. In the play Buckingham is also popular with the people:

this duke as much
They love and dote on; call him "bounteous Buckingham,
The mirror of courtesy" [2.1.50].

After his abortive rebellion Essex was tried and executed. The government wished to minimize the public outrage and prevent Essex's becoming a martyr. King Henry describes similar fears at the trial of Buckingham, in act 1:

It grieves many:
The gentleman is learn'd, and a most rare speaker,...
This man so complete,
Who was enroll'd 'mongst wonders, and when we,
Almost with ravish'd listening, could not find
His hour of speech a minute; he, my lady,
Hath into monstrous habits put the graces
That once were his, and is become as black
As if smeared in hell [1.2.110–124].

The main prosecution witness against Buckingham, his own surveyor, reports his saying to Lord Abergavenny:

First, it was usual with him, every day
It would **infect** his speech, that if the king
Should without issue die, he'd carry it so
To make the sceptre his [1.2.133].

Soon after the execution of Essex, the government published a declaration in which Essex supposedly confessed to treasons that were a "leprosy that had **infected** farre and neere."[11] There are some similarities between Buckingham's long farewell speech and that given by the Earl of Essex before his execution. Both wish the monarch that condemned them to death a long life; both speak of having had a trial; both refer to angels. (For the Earl of Essex's speech see Salisbury, 1906, part 11, 83.)

Wolsey and the Cecils

In 1874, Richard Simpson drew attention to the close parallel between the contemporary politics of Shakespeare's time and the politics portrayed *Henry VIII*:

> This degradation of the nobles was felt to be one of the most serious facts of the time. Under the Cecils the peers had come to be mere parasites of the court, feeding upon the people by their monopolies, helpless to protect the Commons against the Crown, and only powerful as the instruments of its tyranny. Essex, involved in the net, vainly struggled against the toils" [Simpson, 1874, 430].

Henry Neville was of a noble family and had experienced firsthand the physical, spiritual and financial degradation of his class. The noblemen in *Henry VIII* complain that Wolsey has been given power despite his humble origins (he was son of a butcher). He was

not propp'd by ancestry, whose grace
Chalks successors their way, nor call'd upon

> For high feats done to the crown; neither allied
> To eminent assistants [1.1.59].

Likewise, the Cecils were not noble but were middle-class crown servants. In reading *Henry VIII,* Simpson (1874, 431) recalled Philopater, who in 1592 wrote that William Cecil and the queen had made nothing of the ancient nobility: "Cecil so oppressed them, bred such quarrels amongst them, so impoverished them, and loaded them with debt, that he was thenceforth free from all fear about them."

In the play Wolsey is accused of increasing taxes, just as Robert Cecil as the Earl of Salisbury imposed new taxes in 1610. Queen Katherine speaks to King Henry of Wolsey's exactions:

> your subjects
> Are in great grievance: there have been commissions
> Sent down among 'em, which hath flaw'd the heart
> Of all their loyalties: wherein, although,
> My good lord cardinal, they vent reproaches
> Most bitterly on you, as putter on
> Of these exactions [1.2.20].

Again and again Katherine complains:

> These exactions,
> Whereof my sovereign would have note, they are
> Most pestilent to the bearing; and, to bear 'em,
> The back is sacrifice to the load [1.2.48].
>
> The subjects' grief
> Comes through commissions, which compel from each
> The sixth part of his substance, to be levied
> Without delay [1.2.57].

Act 1, scene 2, is most unusual for this appeal against excessive taxation of the common man. This section of the play is believed to be by Shakespeare. However, "Katherine's appeal on behalf of the commons is unhistorical and seems to have been invented by Shakespeare to arouse sympathy at once for the Queen" (Halio, 1999, 87, note). We have already seen that there were members of the Neville family who were supportive of the queen. In James I's reign Henry Neville was deeply involved in negotiations about the crown's expenditure and raising the necessary income. In 1610 he spoke fearlessly to James, stating, "Where your majesty's expense growth by the Commonwealth we are bound to maintain it. Otherwise not. In this one parliament we have already given four subsidies and seven fifteenths, which is more than ever was given by any parliament" (Duncan, 1974, 223).

The play was completed in 1612. We suggest that it was partly written in response to Robert Cecil's death on May 24, 1612. With Cecil's death there was an outpouring of vitriol against him not dissimilar to that expressed against Wolsey in the play when Katherine says, "they vent reproaches most bitterly on you" (1.2.23–4). The posthumous libels against Cecil included one calling him

> Oppression's praiser, Taxation's raiser...
> The country's scourger, the cities' cheater
> Of many a shilling [Crofts, 1991, 49].

Another libel depicted Cecil as a spider: "Dissembling smoothfaced dwarf ... I know your crockback's **spider-shapen**" (Crofts, 1991, 47). Wolsey is described as drawing power to himself, "**spider-like,** out of his self-drawing web" (1.1.62). Several libels referred to Cecil as a fox. In the long poem by Richard Niccols, *The Beggar's Ape,* circulating in 1610, Cecil was symbolized by a "sly" and "**subtle**" fox. In the play Cardinal Wolsey is described as "cunning" (1.1.168), "**subtle**" (1.1.160) and a "holy **fox**" (1.1.158).

The contrast between Buckingham and Wolsey may also reflect the different public images of Essex and Cecil. Whereas Buckingham is described as "bounteous," Wolsey is said to be hated:

> All the commons
> Hate him perniciously, and, o' my conscience,
> Wish him ten fathom deep [2.1.50].

Neville may well have been ambivalent about Cecil. They were related. Cecil's influence may have saved Neville's life after the Essex rebellion. In a letter of March 21, 1601, Cecil wrote to Winwood, "Of *Sir* Henry Neville's *Fortune no man taketh more care then I do,* being tyed there unto by all the Lawes of Friendship and Nature" (italics in the original: Sawyer, 1725, vol. 1, 307). After his release from the Tower, Cecil had become godfather to Neville's son, who was christened Robert in 1604. However, Cecil never completely rehabilitated a man whom he may have seen as a potential rival for office, so Neville's career was blighted. Essex had suggested to Neville that he might become secretary of state if he was successful in ousting Cecil. However polite they were to each other after the debacle, their relationship would remain strained. Halio (1999, 31) noted that the play demonstrated a prevalent ambivalence: each character has weaknesses and strengths. Anne's spectacular coronation is framed by scenes of disillusionment and rejection: "they put into significant perspective the pomp and glory of monarchs and further encourage an ambivalent attitude" (Halio, 1999, 35). Neville at the end of his career still enjoyed the ceremonial (as his trip to Brussels in 1613 suggests) but also knew its hollowness, that the "insubstantial pageant" would fade and leave nothing behind (*The Tempest*, 4.1.155).

Surrey, Norfolk and Suffolk

Given the playwright's use of titles to identify characters in the play it is not difficult to become confused about the historical identity of the dukes of Norfolk and Surrey over the period from 1520 (the Field of the Cloth of Gold) to 1533 (Princess Elizabeth's christening) during Henry VIII's reign. From 1524 to 1533 the Earl of Surrey was Henry Howard (1516/7–1547), who pioneered the English sonnet. However, in the play Surrey is identified as the son-in-law of Buckingham, and so must be Henry's father, Thomas Howard (1473–1554). The Duke of Norfolk at the beginning of the play in act 1 might therefore be considered the latter's father, Thomas Howard (1443–1524). Both Thomases, father and son, were excluded from the Field of the Cloth of Gold in act 1, with the senior Thomas being appointed guardian of England during the king's absence and the junior Thomas, as already mentioned, effectively banished to Ireland as lord lieutenant. Norfolk, Surrey and Suffolk make more sense as a group. The titles of Norfolk, Surrey and Suffolk in Shakespeare's own time were all identified with the Catholic Howard family.

After the death of Robert Cecil in 1612, a major, influential courtier was Henry Howard (1540–1614), the Earl of Northampton and Lord Privy Seal. He was the son of the sonneteer Earl of Surrey, Henry Howard (1516/7–1547); his older brother was Thomas Howard, fourth Duke of Norfolk (1536–1572), whose son was Thomas Howard (1561–1626), first Earl of Suffolk and Lord Chamberlain. Norfolk, Surrey and Suffolk are identifiable titles of the Howard faction in the government of King James I. "This faction dominated both the court and Privy Council" (Hamilton, 1992, 66).

In her book *Shakespeare and the Politics of Protestant England,* Hamilton described the play *Henry VIII* as presenting "the story of Henry VIII, England's archetypal story of the struggle against impure religion in contemporary England and, more particularly, in ways that discredit the powerful Howard faction at court—a faction dominated by Catholics" (Hamilton, 1992, 164). Hamilton suggested that the playwright tarnished the Howards by their association with the ambitious villain Wolsey. We have already noted that Overbury and Carr used the name Wolsey as code for Thomas Howard, the Earl of Suffolk, in their correspondence. More damaging is the Howard faction's portrayal as supporters of Gardiner, Bishop of Winchester, in the prosecution of the reformer Archbishop Cranmer. There is little evidence that this was actually the case in either Holinshed's *Chronicles* or Foxe's *Book of Martyrs.* The writers of *Henry VIII* were hinting that the Howards were supporters of the Roman Catholic Church who, by implication, had tried to kill the whole royal family in the Gunpowder Plot of 1605.

The faction opposing many of the Howard policies included "Henry Neville and two parliamentary radicals, the Earl of Pembroke and," as Chamberlain wrote to Carleton on November 4, 1612, Neville's "champion, the Earl of Southampton" (Hamilton, 1992, 166). After 1603 Southampton, who had earlier been allied with Essex, became associated with Pembroke. Together they formed a faction at court in opposition to the Howards. In that alliance, both Southampton and Pembroke supported Henry Neville for the position of secretary (Hamilton, 1992, 27). Southampton was the dedicatee of Shakespeare's earliest publications, *The Rape of Lucrece* and *Venus and Adonis*, while Pembroke was a dedicatee of the First Folio. Shakespeare's views thus match those of Neville's patrons (Hamilton, 1992, 22).

Wolsey, Cranmer and Neville: Mayfield and Blackfriars

Henry Neville had a personal connection to Cardinal Wolsey and Cranmer. The palace in Mayfield, where Neville lived close to his ironworks, was an old monastic property that had once housed Wolsey. It came to the Nevilles on the death of Sir Thomas Gresham, who was Elizabeth Gresham's uncle. Elizabeth was Neville's mother. According to Duncan (1974, 66) it was a favorite residence of the archbishops of Canterbury until turned over to Henry VIII by Cranmer in 1545. It was then that John Gresham purchased it. So Neville had lived in a house owned by two important characters on stage in *Henry VIII.*

In the play King Henry chooses the location for the hearing about the legality of his marriage to Katherine:

> The most convenient place that I can think of
> For such receipt of learning is **Blackfriars** [2.2.138].

Henry Neville was baptized and grew up in Blackfriars, near the Office of the King's Revels, where his father was "instrumental in devising Court entertainments" (James 2008, 203–5). Indeed, Neville's father asked permission for

Richard Farrant to use part of the Blackfriars property. Farrant created the first Blackfriars Theatre for the child actors of the Chapel Royal. This was the very room in which Henry VIII and Katherine had faced each other and where Shakespeare's play was eventually performed. Neville would have known this room from childhood.

The Protestant Writers: Shakespeare and Fletcher

At the end of act 3, power is shifting. In particular, Wolsey is replaced as the king's religious adviser with the appointment of the archbishop of Canterbury, Thomas Cranmer. In addition, the king has secretly married Anne Boleyn. A divorce from Queen Katherine can be assumed when she is called "the princess dowager" (4.1.23). In acts 4 and 5, episodes from the Holinshed *Chronicles* have had their order shuffled. In act 4 the death of Queen Katherine in 1536 is reported **before** Anne Boleyn gives birth to Princess Elizabeth, in 1533, in act 5. In the first scene of act 5, the protestant Cranmer becomes the hero of the play and uses the king's ring to save himself from accusations of heresy. This episode dates from 1546, thirteen years after the baptism of Elizabeth that ends the play. These are further examples of the subtitle *All Is True* being somewhat wide of the mark.

Cranmer was burnt as a heretic during Mary Tudor's reign, and Foxe's *Book of Martyrs* is the source for the ring episode. Mary is mentioned only twice in the play in offhand references (2.4.173, 4.2.133). In contrast, the rousing final speech is given by Princess Elizabeth's godfather, Thomas Cranmer. This would suggest that the authors had strong Protestant sympathies. Wolsey, who is mostly portrayed as self seeking, abusing his position for gain as he pursues his ambition to become pope, is an archetype of the corrupt Catholic Church. He in turn describes Anne Bullen as a "spleeny Lutheran" (3.2.100).

Neville was described as a Puritan during the period of his ambassadorship and was certainly anti–Catholic in the period following the Gunpowder Plot. John Fletcher's father was Richard Fletcher, who was the Church of England bishop of London when he died in 1596. John Fletcher was born in 1579 in Sussex, the very area where Neville began working on his inherited iron foundry when he returned from his European travels in 1582. John Fletcher's mother was a relative of Neville. It is therefore possible that he knew Richard Fletcher, the father, and may have watched John grow up. Another reason for Neville to sympathize with Fletcher was their mutual connection with the Earl of Essex. Fletcher's uncle Giles (his guardian after his father's death) was, like Neville, caught up in the Essex rebellion by which the family were impoverished.

Henry Neville possessed the only known manuscript of *A King and No King* by Beaumont and Fletcher, and it was this copy that was offered for publication in 1619. Walkley's dedicatory epistle to the "Worthy Knight, Sir Henry Nevill," introduced the play. In it, he said that Neville had encouraged the writers (Bliss, 2004). Whether this epistle was addressed to Sir Henry (who died in 1615) or to his son (who shared his name and lived 1588–1629), it is documentary proof of a relationship between Fletcher and the Nevilles. It is reasonable to assume that Neville had originally received the play from Fletcher and that his son later offered it for publication. *A King and No King* was first performed in 1611 in the same season as *The Tempest.* That year Fletcher had also written *The Tamer Tamed*, the only sequel to a Shakespeare play (*The Taming of the Shrew*). It was following this that Fletcher began to cooperate with Shakespeare: all the plays they co-authored, *Cardenio, Henry VIII*, and *The Two Noble Kinsmen,* follow on.

Fletcher's collaborator, Francis Beaumont, retired in 1612–13 to Kent, at precisely the time Fletcher started to work with Shakespeare. Beaumont and Fletcher's main patron was Henry Hastings, the fifth Earl of Huntingdon (1586–1643), who, like Neville, was a humanistic Puritan leader and member of the Virginia Company (Cust in Underdown, 1995, 92–3). Henry was a great, great, great-grandson of Margaret Pole, Countess of Salisbury (see Chapter 2 and Appendix B). Henry Neville served on a parliamentary committee in 1604 with Hastings' great uncle, Francis Hastings (c. 1545–1610), whose grandmother was the executed Jane Pole, née Neville. Table 8 in the previous chapter ("William Hastings, his descendants and the Nevilles") illustrates how Henry Neville and Henry Hastings were related through Henry Pole and his wife, Jane Pole. A close relationship between the Bard and Henry Hastings (1586–1643) has already been proposed with evidence suggesting that Shakespeare wrote a masque hosted by Henry Hastings and his wife, Elizabeth, in 1607 (Levy, 1988).

Francis Beaumont wrote about the "Fraternity of Sireniacal Gentlemen" at the Mermaid Tavern in a verse letter to Ben Jonson c. 1612:

> What things have we seen,
> Done at the Mermaid? Heard words that have been
> So nimble and so full of subtle flame
> As if that everyone from whom they came
> Had meant to put his whole wit in a jest,
> And had resolved to live a fool the rest
> Of his dull life [Halliday, 1964, 313].

Legend has it that Shakespeare frequented the Mermaid, but no one mentioned his attendance in contemporary documents. John Fletcher was a named member. William Strachey (whose account of a shipwreck in Bermuda was a source for *The Tempest*) was also a member. A Latin poem,[12] written during 1608–11, recording a special meeting of the Mermaid Club at the Mitre Tavern, mentions Henry Neville, John Donne and Inigo Jones amongst others, but not Shakspere from Stratford. A contemporary translation tells us:

> *The Miter* is the place decreed,
> For witty jests and cleanly feed,
> The betterest of any.
> There will come, though scarcely current,
> And John *ycleped Made;* [John Donne]
> *Ne let* Sir Henry *count it vile* [Sir Henry Neville]
> Will come with gentle speed;
> Inego *Ionicke-pillar.* [Inigo Jones]

This barely disguised play on Neville's name puts him between a poet and the architect of Jacobean masques. When we recognize his secret identity as the playwright and poet Shakespeare, his appearance in this company makes perfect sense.

Conclusion

It is remarkable that given the enormous number of incidents Shakespeare could have chosen to dramatize from the reign of Henry VIII he focused on those that relate to the fortunes of members of the Neville family. In a play subtitled *All Is True* it is also remarkable how the playwright distorts history to fit his plot and in doing so protects members of the Neville family while highlighting issues of concern to Henry Neville. What is true is that the play includes echoes of Neville's own life experience, or at least the previous fourteen years (1599–1613). This adds weight to the argument that Henry Neville was the true author with John Fletcher, a friend and fellow Mermaid Club man.

Chapter 9

The Other History Plays
A Hidden Neville Leitmotif

Et tu Brute—*Henry VI* part 3

Et tu Brute—*Julius Caesar* (3.1.78)

Shakespeare wrote other history plays: the Roman plays. These include *Titus Andronicus, Julius Caesar, Anthony and Cleopatra, Coriolanus* and *Cymbeline,* all of which use history (more or less fictionalized) to explore political themes of relevance to Elizabethan and Jacobean audiences. To these we can add *The Rape of Lucrece.* None of these, of course, contain any hidden member of the Neville family. They do, however, contain a leitmotif that has a hidden Neville connection, which is symbolized by the name Brutus. This theme first appears in *Henry VI* and *King John*:

> Great men oft die by vile bezonians:
> A Roman sworder and banditto slave
> Murder'd sweet Tully; **Brutus' bastard** hand
> Stabb'd Julius Caesar [*Henry VI* part 2: 4.1.135].

This is the famous Brutus who was reputed to be the illegitimate son of Julius Caesar, who had had a long-term love affair with Servilia, Brutus' mother. There are many bastards in Shakespeare, starting with Falconbridge in *The Troublesome Raigne/King John.* In Chapter 1, we showed the hidden Neville connection with Falconbridge. In *The Troublesome Raigne* there is a specific reference to the rape of Lucrece in the context of the Falconbridge story.

> Upbraid me rather with the Roman Dame
> That shed her blood to wash away her shame [1.1.406].[1]

In Chapter 2 we showed how the rape of Lucrece was also referred to in *Edward III*, and the possible hidden Neville connections in the bard's recurring theme of royal rape were further explored in Chapter 6. In *Titus Andronicus*, Tarquin's rape of Lucrece is again recalled when Lucius promises his sister Lavinia, who has been raped, that he will return to avenge her:

> If Lucius live, he will requite your wrongs;
> And make proud Saturnine and his empress
> Beg at the gates, like **Tarquin** and his queen [3.1.297].

Titus himself also refers to Lucrece:

> What Roman lord it was durst do the deed:
> Or slunk not Saturnine, as **Tarquin** erst,
> That left the camp to sin in **Lucrece**' bed? [4.1.62].

Marcus also vows revenge, referring again to Lucrece:

> that chaste dishonour'd dame,
> Lord Junius **Brutus** sware for **Lucrece**' rape [4.1.90].

Here is another Brutus, who is a significant figure in Shakespeare's long poem, *The Rape of Lucrece.* His full name was Lucius Junius Brutus, so it is immediately apparent that Shakespeare is deliberately creating a parallel between the Lavinia/Lucrece rapes and the political consequences that result in a Lucius revenging the crime. Lucius Junius Brutus appears at the end of the poem and is transformed from a fool, who hid himself in madness/stupidity during the Tarquin tyranny of his uncle, into a purposeful revolutionary.

> **Brutus**, who pluck'd the knife from Lucrece' side,
> Seeing such emulation in their woe,
> Began to clothe his wit in state and pride,
> Burying in Lucrece' wound his folly's show.
> He with the Romans was esteemed so
> As silly-jeering idiots are with kings,
> For sportive words and uttering foolish things [1807].

Brutus is identified in the initial prose argument that precedes *The Rape of Lucrece*:

> Junius **Brutus**, ... finding Lucrece attired in mourning habit, demanded the cause of her sorrow. She, first taking an oath of them for her revenge, revealed the actor, and whole manner of his dealing, and withal suddenly stabbed herself. Which done, with one consent they all vowed to root out the whole hated family of the Tarquins; and bearing the dead body to Rome, **Brutus** acquainted the people with the doer and manner of the vile deed, **with a bitter invective against the tyranny of the king**: wherewith the people were so moved, that with

one consent and a general acclamation the Tarquins were all exiled, and **the state government changed from kings to consuls** [emphasis added].

Here the political aspect of the poem is revealed. Lucius Junius Brutus was the founder of the Roman Republic. His stratagem of hiding in madness is recalled in *Henry V:*

And you shall find his vanities forespent
Were but the outside of the Roman **Brutus**,
Covering discretion with a coat of folly [*Henry V,* 2.4.37].

The strategy of hiding in madness under a tyrannous regime is employed by Hamlet and by Edgar in *King Lear.* Like Junius Brutus, Hamlet must survive his uncle's tyranny. The other Brutus is recalled by Polonius:

I did enact Julius Caesar: I was killed i' the
Capitol; **Brutus** killed me [*Hamlet,* 3.2.102].

Lucius Junius Brutus, founder of the Roman republic, was claimed as an ancestor by Marcus Junius Brutus, the most famous of Caesar's assassins. The two Brutuses are linked in *Julius Caesar* when Cassius, trying to persuade Brutus to join the conspiracy, refers to Lucius Junius Brutus:

There was a Brutus once that would have brookt
Th'eternal devil to keep his state in Rome
As easily as a king [*Julius Caesar,* 1.2.158.].

Cassius also arranges for papers praising Brutus to be stuck onto a statue of his ancestor:

good Cinna, take this paper,
Where Brutus may but find it; and throw this
In at his window; set this up with wax
Upon old Brutus' statue [1.3.142].

Brutus later says:

My ancestors did from the streets of Rome
The Tarquin drive, when he was call'd a king [2.1.53].

They are again linked because both shared the name Junius.[2] Brutus' servant in the play is called Lucius. Lucius is also the name given to Titus' son, and he is the triumphant avenger at the end of *Titus Andronicus.* In the names chosen for specific roles we see Shakespeare weaving the leitmotif of the rape of Lucrece and Brutus into several plays. Furthermore in *Titus Andronicus* Lucius is compared to Coriolanus:

> **Lucius**, son to old Andronicus;
> Who threats, in course of this revenge, to do
> As much as ever **Coriolanus** did [4.4.65].

A Junius Brutus appears in *Coriolanus* (1.1.215):

> The more prominent of the two tribunes in the play is given the name Junius Brutus—that is, the name of the revolutionary founder of the Roman republic, and author of the bitter and calculating invective that appears at the end of *The Rape of Lucrece.* Shakespeare does have a classical warrant for this gesture: Plutarch's life of Coriolanus identifies the first two tribunes as Junius Brutus and Sicinius Vellutus, a detail he seems to have taken from **Dionysius of Halicarnassus** (it is not attested in any other source).... The great villain of the play, who ejects Coriolanus from Rome, is associated with the conniving figure who ejects Tarquin from the city in Shakespeare's poem (the two events, it is worth noting, are only separated by fifteen years) [emphasis added: Armitage et al., 2009, 265].

There is an extant 1546 volume of Dionysius of Halicarnassus on Roman history, in Greek, annotated by the young Henry Neville. He noted that the writer had missed out Ancus Martius and Tarquinius Collatinus (shown below). The name Ancus Martius is to be found in *Coriolanus* (2.3.235), and Dionysius of Halicarnassus's *Roman Antiquities* is an acknowledged source for the play (Parker, 1998, 18). Collatinus is named in the argument of *The Rape of Lucrece,* being Lucretia's husband (his full name was Lucius Tarquinius Collatinus). Ancus Martius was the name of the fourth king of Rome. His successor was Lucius Tarquinius Priscus, who was the grandfather of Lucius Tarquinius Superbus: the rapist of Lucrece and the last king of Rome. Coriolanus was contemporary with Tarquinius Superbus and this is referenced in the play when Comminius says:

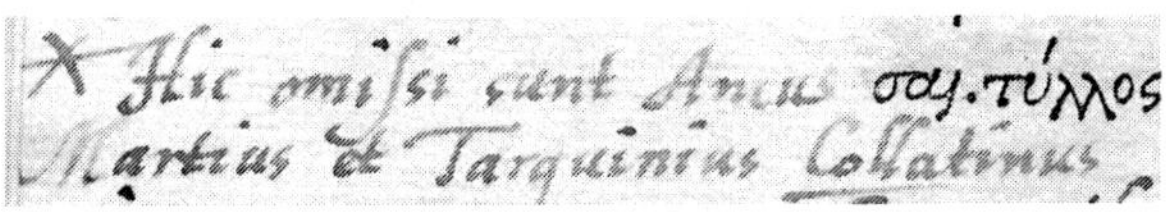

Dionysius, 45. "Hic omisi sunt Ancus Martius et Tarquinius Collatinus" (private collection).

> Tarquin's self he met,
> And struck him on his knee [*Coriolanus,* 2.2.94].

Coriolanus, like Tarquin, is expelled from Rome by a Junius Brutus. The leitmotif is an idée fixe. It recurs in *Macbeth* and *Cymbeline.* Macbeth speaks of "Tarquin's ravishing strides" (2.1.56). In *Cymbeline* Iachimo compares his own invasion of Imogen's bedroom to Tarquin's rape of Lucrece:

> Our Tarquin thus
> Did softly press the rushes, ere he waken'd
> The chastity he wounded [*Cymbeline,* 2.2.12].

Lucius is the name of the Roman ambassador and general of the Roman army in *Cymbeline.*

Neville and Brutus

There is documentary evidence that Henry Neville as a young man was interested in Brutus and the rape of Lucrece. Books owned and annotated by Neville still exist. One of these is a volume of Ovid, Shakespeare's favorite poet.

Ovid is mentioned by name in *Titus Andronicus*, and Lavinia, struggling to reveal her rape, throws Ovid's *Metamorphoses* on the floor and then writes the word "stuprum" (rape) in the sand (4.1.73). The annotator of a 1518 volume of Ovid underlined a passage that uses this word.

In the Dionysius of Halicarnassus the young Neville noted, on page 74, that during the Neptune Games, the youth of Rome raped virgins:

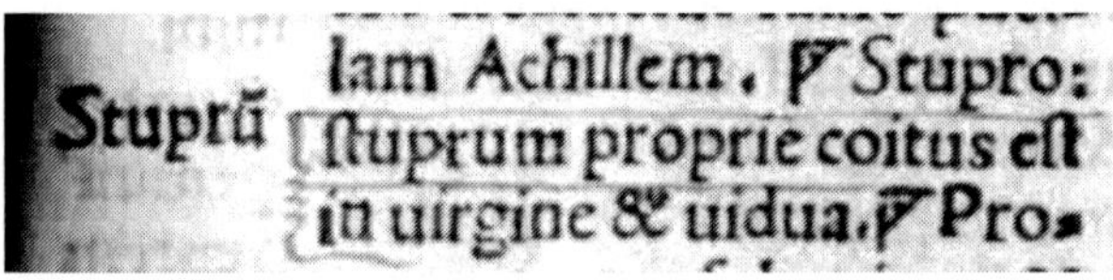
Stuprũ
Iam Achillem. ¶ Stupro: stuprum proprie coitus est in uirgine & uidua. ¶ Pro.

Ovid's *Ars Amatoria* and *Remedia Amoris,* 14 (private collection).

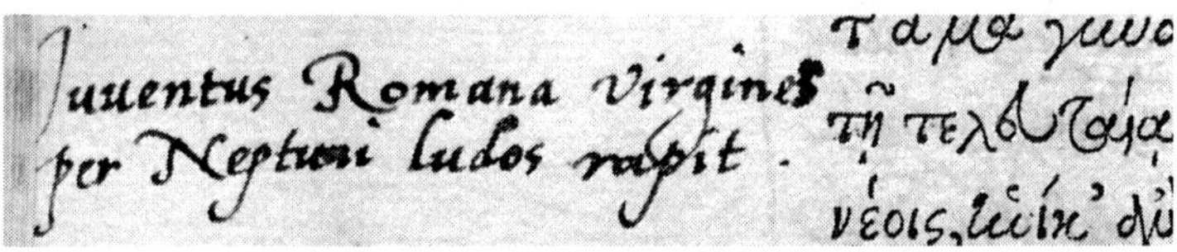
Iuuentus Romana Virgines per Neptuni ludos rapit.

Dionysius of Halicarnassus, 74. "Iuventus Romana virgines per Neptuni ludos rapit" (private collection).

On the next page he has also noted that the number of virgins raped was 683 (shown on right). This early interest in rape later leads on to page 181, where the name of Proud Tarquin: "L. Tarquinius Sup_-bus" is noted:

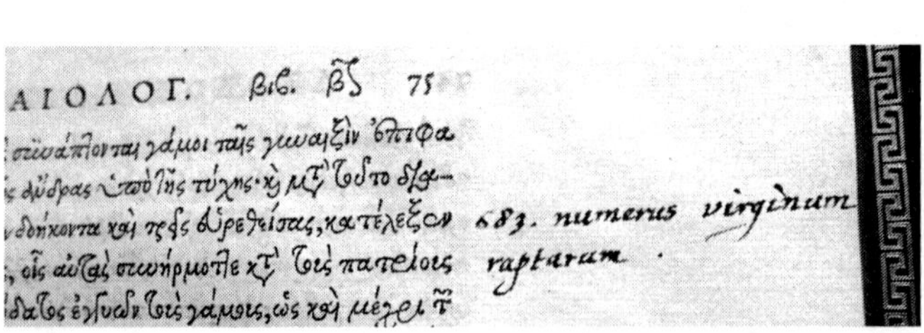
683. numerus virginum raptarum.

Dionysius, 75. 683. "Numerus virginum raptarum" (private collection).

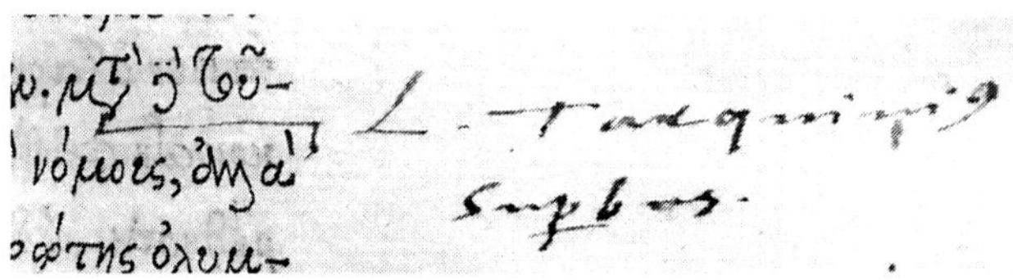

Dionysius, 181. "L. Tarquinius Sup_bus" (private collection).

Another annotation on page 136 again draws attention to L. Tarquinius. The argument at the start of *The Rape of Lucrece* opens with the words: "Lucius Tarquinius, for his excessive pride surnamed Superbus." Another book in Neville's library is John Lydgate's *Fall of Princes*. This rare manuscript was originally owned by Mary Sidney. "Elizabeth Nevell" added her name below, so she must have borrowed or been given the book. She was Neville's mother. James (2011, 91) showed this was a possible source for *The Rape of Lucrece.*

Why then in the 1590s was Neville making notes about rape? Apart from working through the ancestral trauma of Anne Neville's rape by Edward IV (see Chapter 6), he was using this material to reflect on the current political situation. If the history plays use history as metaphor, then the theme of a woman's chastity as a political matter points us to the Virgin Queen, Elizabeth I. While her decision not to marry concentrated power in her own hands, it led to the dangerous question of who would succeed when she died. During her reign there were a number of possible suitors, starting with Robert Dudley, the Earl of Leicester. He was seen as potentially usurping the throne in the 1584 political tract *Leicester's Commonwealth*, where there is an implicit reference to the aftermath of the rape of Lucrece (see Chapter 1). In complaining about Leicester's intolerable sexual appetite "upon men's wives" the writers refer back to how in previous times "offences ... were extremely punished in princes themselves, and that not only in the person delinquent alone, but also by **extirpation of the whole family** for his sake, as appeareth in the example **of the Tarquinians** among the Romans" (Peck, 87/*61*).[3] The theme of threatened chastity that has political consequences can therefore be seen to concern the right succession to the throne and whether this should be by election (as in *Titus Andronicus*), invasion (*King John*), conquest (*Henry IV*), usurpation (*Richard III*) or some other method. Elizabeth had banned discussion of the succession. The *Lucrece* poem and the history plays were an indirect method of exploring the political consequences of Elizabeth's chastity. This link between Elizabeth I and Lucrece is confirmed by Henry Chettle who, in 1603, wrote in *England's Mourning Garment,* addressing Shakespeare as *Melicert:*

Shepheard, remember our *Elizabeth,*
And sing her Rape, done by that ***Tarquin,*** Death.

This preoccupation with chastity in marriage also matches Neville's experience of being illegitimate: his father was not apparently married to his second wife, Elizabeth Gresham, when Henry was conceived in 1561–3. A marriage settlement was achieved only in 1586. Thus it is not difficult to see the connections with Neville's own life when we consider that his own father made love to his mother before they were married and Neville had to bear the secret lifelong shame of bastardy. A similar obsession is manifest in the Shakespeare canon (Casson, 2010, 138). This was the "birth-hour's blot" (*Rape of Lucrece,* 537) and "bed-blotting shame" (*Edward III,* 2.1.458) that is evidenced by the recurring blot image cluster in Shakespeare (see Chapter 1 and Casson, 2009; 2010) and the frequent appearance of significant bastards in the plays, culminating in Edmund who cries, "Gods stand up for bastards!" in *King Lear* (1.2.22). Neville served on a parliamentary committee concerned with "bastardy."[4]

There is a major volume of the works of Appian on Roman history, in Greek, dated 1551, amongst Neville's books, and it contains many annotations by Neville about Brutus, Cassius, Anthony and Caesar. In *Julius Caesar* Brutus addresses the crowds at Caesar's funeral. "Brutus' speech to the people on the Capitol" is a translation of the Latin annotation, "Bruti ad populû[m] in capitolio δημηγορια" (Neville starting in Latin and switching to Greek in one annotation):

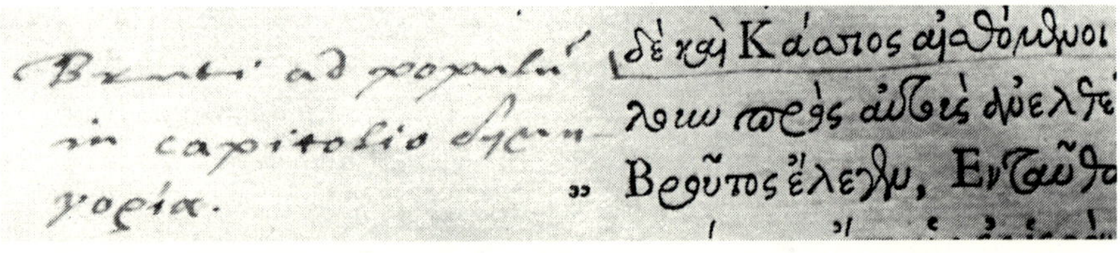

Appian. "Bruti ad populus in capitolio δημηγορια" (private collection).

In Shakespeare's *Julius Caesar* Brutus uses the words "in the Capitol" as he is speaking to the people (3.2.38). Appian's *Civil Wars* is a recognized source for Shakespeare's *Julius Caesar.*

The play culminates in the Battle at Philippi. On page 234 of the volume of Appian there is an annotation that, when translated, reads, "The War at Philippi waged by Octavius and Anthony against Brutus and Cassius":

Defeated in battle, Brutus kills himself (5.5.51). Another annotation states, "Brutus lays hands on himself. Portia, his wife eats a hot coal."

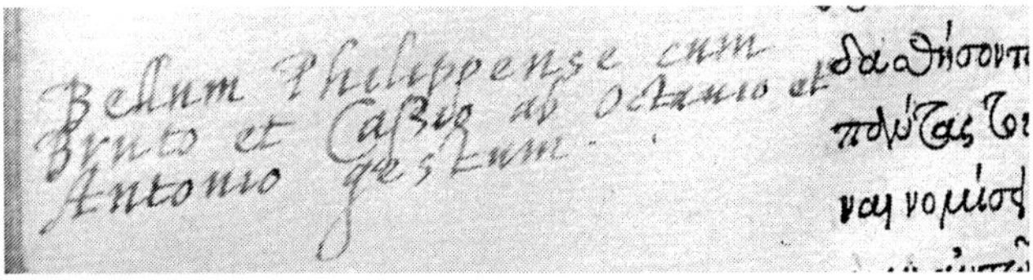

Appian, 234. Bellum Philippense cum Bruto et Cassio ab Octavio et Antonio gestum" (private collection).

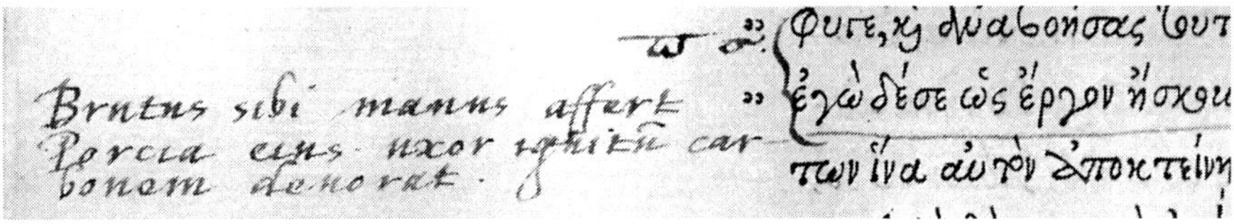

Appian, 238. "Brutus sibi manus affert Porcia eius uxor ignitu carbonem devorat" (private collection).

In the play we hear how Portia "swallowed fire" (4.3.154) and see Brutus' suicide. The obvious difference in the handwriting between these annotations suggests that they were made at different times, the latter being the earlier. I suggest the earliest annotations were made when, from 1577, Neville was a student at Oxford, where his tutor, Savile, taught Greek. His knowledge of Roman history would therefore long predate his decision to write the poem and the play.

In his copy of *Leicester's Commonwealth,* Worsley MSS 47, dated circa 1585, Neville added to the text of the printed annotation. The text states:

> The example of Iulius Cesars destruction.
> To much cõfidence very perilous in a Prince [Casson, 2010, 225].

Neville copies this as:

> To much confidence verie perilous ni a Prnice.[5]

When in 1599 Shakespeare wrote *Julius Caesar* he remembered this annotation. Calphurnia warns her husband:

> Your wisdom is consumed in confidence [*Julius Caesar,* 2.2.49].

Neville continued his annotation:

> This was the distruction of Julius Cesar by Marc: Brutus.[6]

He adds the name Marcus Brutus. No other copyist of the known manuscript editions of *Leicester's Commonwealth* added "Marcus Brutus" to their version

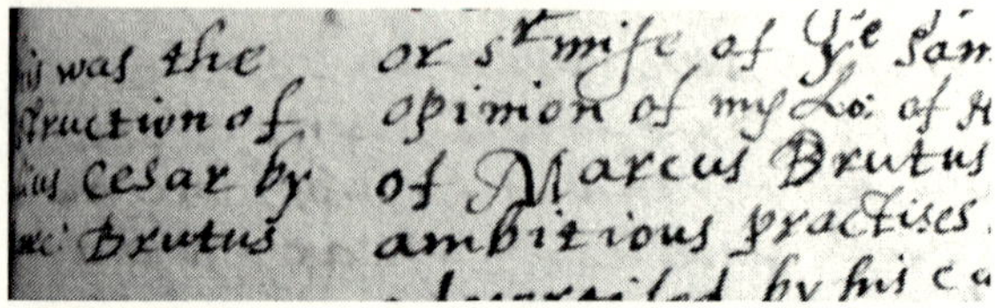

Worsley MSS 47, 58 (by permission of the Eighth Earl of Yarborough and Lincolnshire Archives).

of this annotation (Dwight Peck, personal communication, October 20, 2013). Other evidence also suggests that *Leicester's Commonwealth* was a source for *Julius Caesar* (Casson, 2010, 18).

This chapter opened with "Et tu Brute," quoted in both *Henry VI* and *Julius Caesar*. Richard Eedes (1555–1604) used these words in his 1582 Latin play *Caesar Interfectus*. Neville may have seen this play as he returned from his continental travels in 1582. Eedes certainly met Neville in 1583 when they were both travelling in the North and recorded the meeting in his poem *Iter Boreale* (see Chapter 2). Both went to Oxford University in the 1570s, so they could have met then.

"Brutus" and Henry Neville

For this comparison we collapse the two Brutuses into one. The double role of "Brutus" and Henry Neville share the following characteristics:

1. They were both possibly illegitimate.
2. They were both politicians, concerned about monarchy, involved in government.
3. They both hid: Lucius Junius Brutus in folly or madness; Neville hid his authorship of a document presented in Parliament in 1614 (James, 2011, 21) and, we contend, of the works of Shakespeare.
4. They were both involved in conspiracies. For both the outcome was a disaster.
5. Neville's ancestors were both prosecutors and victims of the civil wars of the Roses. His interest in them was evident in Shakespeare's history plays. Brutus was also the victim of a civil war.
6. Rape and the political consequences of the act were issues of concern to both.
7. They both feared for their wives' sanity: Brutus' wife committed suicide; Neville expressed concern for his wife in letters to Cecil while he was incarcerated in the Tower after the Essex rebellion.

Neville's identification with Marcus Junius Brutus, bastard son of Caesar, is understandable. Despite the warning he gave to the Essex faction (and himself) in *Julius Caesar*, he was unable to prevent this archetypal pattern being played out. Unlike Brutus he survived and the last plays (*Pericles, A Winter's Tale*) show how deeply shamed, grieving men are eventually forgiven and restored to their family. This pattern matches the life experience of Henry Neville, who was released from the Tower and reunited with his family. The traumatic imprisonment lasting more than two years, during which both Neville and his wife suffered great distress and life-threatening illnesses as well as the threat of financial ruin.

Conclusion

The Brutus leitmotif is inexplicable if the writer was William Shakspere from Stratford. With Henry Neville as the writer this leitmotif illuminates the multiple meanings of the recurrent references to the Brutus themes. Again it is the combination of the personal (illegitimacy) and the political (the succession to the throne and the right governance of the realm) that matches Neville's ancestral experience: his family had been at the heart of government for centuries and had suffered under tyrannical kings, in civil wars and from royal rape. Henry Neville was not the first bastard in the family, and other Nevilles had been involved, right up to Elizabeth I's reign, in rebellion, treason and civil war.

Chapter 10

Neville's Trial Statement and *Hamlet*

I am forbid to tell the secrets of my prison-house.—*Hamlet* (1.5.13)

In this book we have shown how Neville's and Shakespeare's covert support for the Earl of Essex informed the history plays from the very beginning, as is evident in *The Troublesome Raigne of King John*, in which an Earl of Essex was made ruler of the realm and even his leadership of a rebellion prefigured (Chapter 1). *Henry V* looked forward to celebrating Essex's triumphal return from Ireland (Chapter 5). *Julius Caesar* warned the Essex faction of the dangers that would result from assassination and civil war, however noble the motives of those involved (Chapter 9). The subsequent debacle of the Essex rebellion was a tragedy for Essex and a catastrophe for Neville and his family. While his brief period as an ambassador ensured Neville a footnote in historical records, it was his involvement in the Essex rebellion and subsequent trial that brought him onto the stage of history as dramatically as any protagonist in the Shakespeare history plays.

In 1601 Henry Neville was on trial for his life. Having been implicated in the rebellion by the earls of Essex and Southampton at their trials, Neville was arrested in Dover on his way back to be Elizabeth I's ambassador in France. At first under house arrest,[1] he was later moved to the Tower of London and spent the rest of Elizabeth's reign in prison, being released on James I's orders in 1603. His life was saved by a combination of factors: the slight role he had played in the rebellion, at the least being cognizant of something being planned and not disclosing this to the authorities, at the most, waiting at Court for the outcome (possibly being ready to take the role of secretary of state had Robert Cecil been forced out of office); his previous good conduct as ambassador; and his close relationship with Cecil.

Shakespeare's writing takes a sudden turn towards darkness and tragedy in 1601. Though this may be seen to be prefigured by the rather dark comedy of *Twelfth Night*, nevertheless the break is real. Tragedy follows tragedy, and the problem plays of *Troilus and Cressida* and *Measure for Measure* suggest Shakespeare was feeling bitter and cynical. This fits Neville well, as he lost a great deal by the earls' betrayal, whereas the authorship of William Shakspere from Stratford provides us with no explanation. Some scholars have seen Achilles and Patroclus in *Troilus and Cressida* as angry, satirical portraits of Essex and Southampton. Certainly there is a strong correlation between the tragedy of *Hamlet* and the Essex rebellion. Robert Devereux's father, Walter, the first Earl of Essex, was believed to have been poisoned by the Earl of Leicester, who married his widow,[2] just as Claudius poisons Hamlet's father and marries the widowed Gertrude. Neville was aware of the rumor that Walter had been poisoned. In his copy of *Leicester's Commonwealth* he made a marginal annotation, "the poysonnig of my Lo: of Essex" (Casson, 2010, 193).

In the play Hamlet describes Denmark as a prison. It opens on the bitterly cold battlements of a castle, reminiscent of the Tower of London. A ghost haunts the first scenes, just as the ghost of Essex might have haunted the prisoners' imaginations so soon after his execution. Neville's own grandfather had been executed in the Tower and for two years, 1601–3, he would have worshipped in the chapel where Edward Neville was buried.

Hamlet is believed to have been written during the years 1599 to 1601, even if there were earlier versions that are not extant. Chambers (1944, 68–75) reviewed the evidence and favored 1601 as the year *Hamlet* was written. It was registered in July 1602. It was first published, with the comment "latelie Acted by the Lord Chamberleyne his servantes," in what may be a crude, possibly unauthorized, quarto in 1603. A fuller version was printed in 1604. Since Neville was released from prison in 1603, this sequence of a poor edition being followed a year later by a more accurate version is understandable, as Neville would have been able to ensure the corrected *Hamlet* went safely to the printers.

With Neville revealed as the author we can now compare his statement at his 1601 trial with the text of *Hamlet* and see immediately the rich echoes of ideas, vocabulary, phrases and argument. This statement was the most important of his life: he had to convince his judges and the authorities that he was not a conspirator, guilty of treason, but an honorable man whose error was a pardonable omission. He therefore needed to use all his powers of rhetoric and eloquence to persuade. Other Neville letters of this period also contain rare vocabulary found in the play. We explore these to provide further evidence of Neville's authorship. As a control we have chosen four letters of 1601 written by Edward de Vere, Earl of Oxford, another authorship candidate (for the texts see addendum 2 at the end of this chapter).

Neville's deposition is undated but it must be after Essex's death (February 25, 1601), because he is referred to as "the late Earl." In Winwood's *Memorials* it is placed before a letter from Cecil dated March 1, 1601 (Sawyer, 1725, vol. 1, 302). Three letters from Winwood, who was in France, to Cecil follow: two dated March 16, 1601, in which he clearly is not aware of Neville's arrest, and another the following day, March 17, 1601, that shows he has just heard the news. It seems likely, then, that Neville's statement dates from early March 1601. Sawyer, in a footnote, stated that it "is all of his own hand and was I think sent to Mr. *Winwood* into *France,* for I found it amongst his Papers."

A total of 426 words occur both in *Hamlet* and Neville's trial statement (which contains 1379). This amounts to 30.9 percent, nearly one third of the statement sharing vocabulary with the play. This is an underestimate, as we have not counted small words such as "you" or "the." We now present the whole of Neville's trial statement so readers can hear the echoes of *Hamlet* for themselves. This statement is copied from Winwood's *Memorials*, volume 1, using the same italics, spelling and capitals but modernizing the Elizabethan long "*f*" as a small "s."

Sir Henry Nevill's *CASE*

Although *I mean not to justify my self altogether from Blame,* but do freely and willingly acknowledge *an Offence,* and submitt my self to her Majestie's Mercie; *yet my own Soul witnessing to her self, that it was ever loyall and faithfull to her Majesty, and consequently abhorring more then Death, the Imputation of that Fault, and loathsome Crime of Falshood and Treason;* I do only desire, that my fault may not be barely or nakedly censured, *but examin'd together with all the Circumstances that did accompany it;* which are the best means to try, not only the Actions, but the Intentions of all Men, as far as it is possible to penetrate.

I have already acknowledged to the Lords of her Majesties Privy Councill, that I was intreated by Mr. *Cuff,* in the late Earl of *Essex* his Name, to meet with the Earle of *Southampton* and Sir *Charles Davers;* by them to understand some Project which he had in Consultation, touching his own good, and the good of the State, and to give my Advice in it; *with assurance, that nothing should be proposed, which I might not hear with due respect to my Alleigance;* for so the Words of the Messenger did import. After some ten Days delay on my part, and often Sollicitation, I went to *Drury-House* on *Candlemas-day,* and met with them; where their Project being opened unto me, I objected both against the Nature and the Difficulties of it, *gave no Approbation, or promise of partaking,* but only said *I would advise of it.* After which, *I never spake with them, nor heard from them;* and when Mr. *Cuffe* came soon after unto me, I utterly refused to have any part or hand in the matter; and being requested to come, and speak with the Earle of *Essex* himself about the third day after, *I refused it, because indeed I would have nothing to doe with him,* finding that he had such Conceits working in his Mind. *The bare and simple Truth of my Case is this.* Where-by it appeareth, *First,* that it was not a matter that originally entred into my Thoughts, *but that I was enticed, and in a manner enforced to hear it.* For with these Protestations and Assurances, how could I well have refused, *and who might not have been abused as well as I?* And *if these Assurances had been performed, what Offence had it been to have heard what had been proposed?* Secondly it appeareth, that at the first Proposition I gave not Approbation, but rather made opposition to it, and afterwards refused absolutely to have any hand or felowship in it; which will I hope sufficiently argue, *that neither originally, nor by perswasion, any disloyal thought against her Majesty did ever settle in my minde.* For the better Evidence whereof, I desire that these Circumstances may be considered. First that I never had any Inwardness with the Earle of *Essex,* nor any Dependency on him, nor any Obligation to him, when he was in his highest Fortunes; but had rather Cause of unkindness and discourtesy offered me by him sundry times, as I have shewed my Lords of the Councill of. And if it be objected, that I went to see him in *October* last, and might then begin a Friendship and Inwardness with him; besides, that I avow there passed nothing of that kinde, but generall Complements between us; let all Men consider, *what kind of Inwardness that was like to be,* seing that in four Months after, he lying in *London,* and my self likewise, *I never so much as once saw him, or had any Communication with him.* Secondly, I desire that it may be remembred, that this Meeting at *Drewry-House* was not till *Candlemas;* whereas her Majesty had signed my Privy-Seal and all my Dispatches, at the least four days before; and in Truth if I could have got my Money (which I laboured with all earnestness both my *Lord Treasurer* and Mr. *Skinner,* and was at length forced to signify to Mr. *Secretary* that I could not get it, albeit my Journey staid upon nothing else,) I fully purposed to have set forward upon the *Thursday* after *Candlemas-day* at the farthest, *and if that had been so, undoubtedly I had never met with them.* Now then *my Dispatches being ready signed,* and my self making all the hast I could to set forward within so few days, *what likelyhood is there that the Earle should build upon any thing from me, in that I was not likely to see the Issue of?* Especially, which I desire may be noted as the Third Circumstance, being the Matter was delivered to me *as an undigested Conception, and not as a Resolution;* and besides that, *they never imparted to me their Articles whereof they did deliberate.* Fourthly it may be considered, *that after that Conference, I never saw them that had broken the Matter to me, nor ever heard from them.* Which argueth, *that they found little Comfort at my hands, and made smal Account of me in the matter;* as it appears likewise in this, that when they made their *desperate Attempt* upon the *Sonday,* and sought to gather unto them all those of whom they had any Hope whatsoever, though it were but by Presumption, *they never sent to me nor made me acquainted with it, as the Lord knoweth,* and as I hope they all testifyed; which is a plaine Argument *that they had not any Confidence in me.* Nay rather, considering that *Cuffe* never came to me, after that I refused to come to my Lord; and how *unequally* (that I may not say *uncharitably*) my Lord dealt with me in his Confession; wherein he delivered matters to charge me, but nothing to discharge me, although both alike known unto him; and how he hath added some things nothing pertinent to this matter, and only of purpose to aggravate as it seems; I have Cause to think that he took offence against me for my refusall, *and perhaps afterwards conceived that I was the Revealer of it.* But howsoever, I do freely and from my Heart, *acknowledge my Offence in concealing of it,* and do humbly implore her Majesties Pardon and Mercy for it; *but protest it was not from any Malice or Discontent against the State, for who had more Interest therein then I? Nor any desire that the Attempt should succeed, for who could have more disliked it than I? Nor any personall Affection to my Lord, for I never had any particular Obligation to him:* But partly *upon Contempt* of the Matter, being *so weak and unlikely a Project* (neither formed nor resolved of) as I hoped would have proved abortive, and vanished of it self, whensoever they should have laid aside the Passion of Discontentment and examined it with reason; and partly upon an *Imbecillitie and Weakness of my own Nature,* (if so it be to be termed,) *which could not resolve to become an Accuser;* which how odious a thing it is, all the World knoweth; *especially in respect of the Person, whom I must have accused;* who I desire may be considered, *not as he hath been found since, but as he was reputed.* Although I confess, *that my Duty to the Publick, should have prevailed above all respect of my own private Disgrace which I apprehended in it. And that I did not consent to it upon any evil Ground,* let my frank, simple, and plaine Declaration, which I made upon my first calling to some, be Witness for me; wherein I have set down my whole Knowledge freely and directly, and presumed so much of my own Innocency, as touching any Consent or Participation in the Action, as I have omitted diverse Circumstances therein, which might most have justifyed my Intention. But the more really and plainly I have dealt therein, the more graciously I trust her Majesty will interpret my former Errour, which (the Lord is my Judge) was without Conceit of any traiterous or disloyall Thought against her Majestie. And desire God to deal in Mercy with my Soul, that I was going now into *France* with a full Purpose, Desire, and Resolution to serve her Majestie with all, that *Faith, Zeal,* and *Councell can witness I had done, in my former Imployment;* and will always do, whensoever it shall please her Majestie to call me to the like againe.

Neville's Vocabulary and Hamlet

In examining the text of this 1,379-word statement we have searched for words used in the play. These texts share not only single words, but pairs of words, and also phrases of three words (see addendum 1).

In Neville's statement there are 14 Shakespearean *hapax legomena,*[3] one of which occurs in *Hamlet.* This is in line with an average of one Shakespearean hapax for every 100 words in ten letters Neville wrote from 1599 to 1613 (amounting to 9,016 words with 89 hapaxes: 0.98 percent). We now list the hapaxes in Neville's trial statement in order of their occurrence in Shakespeare:

Uncharitably is unique to *Richard II.*

Objected is unique to *Henry IV* part 1. Neville used this word twice in the statement.

Inwardness is unique to *Much Ado About Nothing* (1598–99). Neville used this three times.

Opened is unique to *Twelfth Night* (1599–1600).

Formed is unique to *Twelfth Night.*

Really is unique to *Hamlet.*

Imbecility is unique to *Troilus and Cressida* (1602). Neville spells this **imbecilitie**, and this was the spelling used in the 1609 quarto of *Troilus and Cressida.* Neville used this word again in a letter dated 1603–4, spelling it then **imbecillyty**.

Proposition is unique to *Troilus and Cressida.*

Solicitation is unique to *Othello.* In the First Quarto, 1622, it is spelled with a double "l," just as in Neville's statement.

Treasurer is unique to *Antony and Cleopatra.*

Refusal is unique to *Coriolanus.* Neville spells this with a double "l." This same spelling is used in the First Folio.

Discourtesy is unique to *Cymbeline.*

Undoubtedly is unique to *Henry VIII.*

Secretary is unique to *Henry VIII.*

Of these, five were used by Shakespeare before Neville made this statement, while eight occur in later plays, Neville anticipating Shakespeare. The list contains two from the previous play, *Twelfth Night,* one from *Hamlet* and two from the next play, *Troilus and Cressida.* Such a pattern makes sense if Neville was the author of the works of Shakespeare.

Textual Parallels

In the statement there are a number of passages that may be seen to have parallels in *Hamlet*:

Neville wrote, "I have **set down** my whole knowledge."

In *Hamlet* Shakespeare used "set down" 5 times, including, "I set it down" and "I would set down."

Neville wrote, "partly upon an *Imbecillitie and* ***weakness*** *of my own Nature.*" Hamlet says, "perhaps out of my **weakness** and my melancholy" (2.2.597).

Neville wrote, "**deal** in Mercy with my Soul."
Hamlet says, "**deal** justly with me" (2.2.276).

Neville wrote, "it shall **please** her **Majesty**."
Hamlet says, "if **it please** his **majesty**" (5.2.170).

Neville ended with, "the **like again**."
Hamlet says, "I shall not look upon his **like again**" (1.2.188).

Neville wrote, "*abhorring* ***more then***[4] ***Death****, the Imputation of that fault, and loathsome Crime of Falshood and Treason.*"

Claudius says, "**more then** his Fathers **death**" (1604 quarto and First Folio spelling: 2.2.8). This death is a crime of treason. The words "abhorred" "imputation," "fault," "loathsome," "crimes," "falsehood" and "treason" also occur in the play, virtually every word in this passage.

Neville wrote of "**making** all the **hast** I could."
Bernardo, Hamlet and Claudius all say, "**make haste**" (1.1.13; 3.2.45; 4.3.59).
The phrase "**all the haste I** can" occurs in *Henry VI* part 1 (1.1.167).

Neville wrote of Essex, "when he was in his **highest** Fortune."
In *Hamlet,* Rosencrantz describes an image of the wheel of Fortune as "a massy wheel, Fix'd on the summit of the **highest** mount" (3.3.17).

Neville wrote that he "***could*** *not resolve to become an* ***Accuser;*** which how odious a thing it is, all the World knoweth; *especially in respect of the Person, whom I must have* ***accused***."

Hamlet says, "I **could** accuse" (3.1.124).

Richard II says, "ourselves will hear the **accuser** and the **accused** freely speak" (1.1.16). Neville used the two words in the same order. Shakespeare is said to have coined the term "the accused," changing an adjective into a noun (McQuain and Malless, 1998, 4).

Neville wrote, "I was going now **into France**."
Hamlet says, "since he went **into France**" (5.2.157).

Neville wrote, "After some ten Days **delay** on my part, and often **Sollicitation**." Hamlet delays acting, just as Neville deliberately did in the lead up to the Essex rebellion. Hamlet uses the word "solicited" (5.2.363) and Polonius speaks of "solicitings" (2.2.125). The word "delay" is used twice in the play. As ambassador and Essex supporter Neville indeed was in a situation similar to Hamlet's:

> like a man to **double business** bound
> I stand in pause where I shall first begin,
> And both neglect [*Hamlet,* 3.3.41].

Double Business: Hendiadys in Hamlet *and Neville's Trial Statement*

Hendiadys is a figure of speech in which two words are joined by a conjunction, usually "and." Shakespeare used hendiadys frequently in plays of the period 1600–1606 and most of all in *Hamlet,* e.g., "slings and arrows," where there are sixty-six examples (Wright, 1981, 173). James (2008, 255, and 2011, 30) found numerous hendiadyses in Neville's letters and especially in his 1614 treatise presented to Parliament. In his trial statement Neville used sixteen hendiadyses. This is a high number given the comparative length of the trial statement (there are sixteen hendiadyses in *Measure for Measure*). Many of these words occur singly in *Hamlet.*

freely and willingly	*Hamlet:* freely ×4; willingly ×2
loyall and faithfull	*Hamlet:* faithful ×3 ("faithful and honourable")
Falshood and Treason	*Hamlet:* falsehood ×1; treason ×5
the Nature and the Difficulties	*Hamlet:* nature ×25
bare and simple	*Hamlet:* bare ×1; simple ×1
Protestations and Assurances	
unkindness and discourtesy	
Friendship and Inwardness	*Hamlet:* friendship ×1
Pardon and Mercy	*Hamlet:* pardon ×6; mercy ×6
weak and unlikely	*Hamlet:* weak ×2
Imbecillitie and Weakness	*Hamlet:* weakness ×2
simple and plaine	*Hamlet:* simple ×1 ("simple and unschool'd") In *Julius Caesar* Brutus speaks of "plain and simple faith" (4.2.22).
freely and directly	*Hamlet:* freely ×4; directly ×2
really and plainly	*Hamlet:* really ×1

In the trial statement there are also two interrupted hendiadys:

Fault and loathsome Crime	*Hamlet:* fault ×5; loathsome ×1 ("vile and loathsome")
enticed, and in a manner enforced	*Hamlet:* manner ×1. Shakespeare never used "enticed" or "assurances," though he did use the singular "assurance" twice in *Hamlet.*

Edward de Vere used thirteen hendiadyses in his four letters, but these use much simpler vocabulary and are repetitive, using "friendly" three times and "brotherly" twice, neither of which occur in *Hamlet* (see addendum 2 below).

Neville also used pairs of words separated by "or" (or "nor"):

barely or nakedly	Shakespeare never used "nakedly" though the word "naked" occurs twice in *Hamlet.*
any hand or felowship in it	*Hamlet:* hand ×15; fellowship ×2
Malice or Discontent	
Consent or Participation	*Hamlet:* consent ×4
traiterous or disloyall	*Hamlet:* traitorous ×1
nor any Dependency on him, nor any Obligation	*Hamlet:* obligation ×2
formed nor resolved	

In *Hamlet* we find similar uses of "or" and "nor":

a frock or livery
we are pictures or mere beasts
to drown or hang themselves
he is the card or calendar of gentry
That are but mutes or audience to this act
If by direct or by collateral hand
If aught of woe or wonder
no soil nor cautel
neither a borrower nor a lender

There were no similar pairings with the word "or" in the four letters of Edward de Vere: indeed he only used "or" once, in letter 2: "ther ys nothinge in the world that I esteme more **or** accept more kindle [kindly]."

He did not use the word "nor."

Rare Words Used by Neville Before Shakespeare

All these words are used by Neville in the trial statement before the bard used them. Neville thus anticipated Shakespeare:

Abhorring only occurs in *Antony and Cleopatra* and *Coriolanus.*

Acknowledged only occurs in *Antony and Cleopatra, King Lear* and *Winter's Tale.*

Difficulties only occurs in *Troilus and Cressida* and *Measure for Measure.*

Requested only occurs in *Othello, Antony and Cleopatra, Coriolanus.*

Settle only occurs in *Antony and Cleopatra,* and *Winter's Tale.*

Dependency only occurs in *Measure for Measure, Antony and Cleopatra,* and *Cymbeline.*

Avow only occurs in *Troilus and Cressida* and *Henry VIII.*

Pertinent only occurs in *Coriolanus* and *Winter's Tale.*

Imbecility is unique to *Troilus and Cressida.*

Justified only occurs in *All's Well That Ends Well, Winter's Tale* and *Henry VIII.*

The only time Shakespeare used the words "little Comfort" in this order was in *Pericles:* again Neville anticipated Shakespeare.

Employment (spelled "Imployment" by Neville) was used in *Look About You,* a play Casson (2010, 119) has previously identified as an early work by Neville, before he took the pseudonym of Shakespeare. (The word is spelled "imployment" in the 1600 quarto of *Look About You* and in the 1599 quarto of *Romeo and Juliet.* In the 1604 quarto and 1623 First Folio editions of *Hamlet* it is spelled "imploiment." Shakespeare is believed to have coined the word "employer": "in some Shakespearean texts, the noun is spelled 'imploier'" (McQuain and Malless, 1998, 57). Neville used "imployed," "imploy," and "imployment" in his letter dated May 26, 1599 (Sawyer, 1725, vol. 1, 34).

Words Used by Neville but Not by Shakespeare

Nakedly, Intentions, Consultation, Candlemas, originally, enticed, Assurances, Secondly, October, signed, Dispatches, undigested, imparted, Fourthly, argueth, knoweth, testified, unequally, Revealer, disliked, Discontentment, Declaration, presumed.

Some words found in *Hamlet* are close to Neville's: naked, mass, assurance, second, dispatch, digested, impart, argues, knows, reveal, dislike. In other plays Shakespeare used words that are related to this vocabulary: intention, consult, candle, original, entice, sign, fourth, testify, discontent, declare, presume. This leaves only "October" used by Neville but never by Shakespeare.

Interestingly, given Shakespeare's predilection for words beginning with "un," Neville wrote "undigested" and "unequally," neither of which occur in the canon. "Unequal" occurs in *Hamlet* (2.2.462).

Neville's Letters 1600–1602 and Hamlet

The occurrence of vocabulary from *Hamlet* in Neville's trial statement might be dismissed as coincidence. We therefore look now at Neville's letters written during this period. In a letter dated April 24, 1600, Neville used the word "inhibition," which Shakespeare only used once, in *Hamlet.* In the same letter he also reported the recruitment of "Suissers" as mercenaries. The only time Shakespeare used this word is when Claudius calls for his Switzers (4.5.94). In this letter Neville also used the word "postscript," which Shakespeare only used twice: in *Hamlet* and *Titus Andronicus.* Furthermore, Neville used the words "ministers," "study," "conversation," "conference," "employment," "speedier," "devise," "choler," "conscience," "dangerous," "globe" and "petty," all of which occur in *Hamlet.* Just three days later, on April 27, 1600, Neville wrote another letter, in which he used the following words that occur in the play: "pastime," "audience," "innovation," "distinguish," "satisfaction," "commission," "marble," "chamber," "prize," "troubles," "remedy," "pangs," "passionate," "partial." Perhaps the most remarkable of these words is "innovation," used just three days after he had used the unique word "inhibition." In the play Rosencrantz says, "I think their **inhibition** comes by the means of the late **innovation**" (2.2.328). The word "innovation" here means a political insurrection and is believed to refer to the Essex rebellion (Crystal and Crystal, 2002, 240). Two weeks later, on May 9, 1600, Neville again referred to "Suissers": the French king had paid one and a half million to the "Suissers" while failing to pay any of his debt to Elizabeth I: "she might as **well look** to be regarded in her so just **demaunds** as the Suissers" (Sawyer, 1725, vol. 1, 181). Neville was writing from Paris and in this letter mentioned Denmark. In *Hamlet* Polonius refers to Danskers (Danish) in Paris and uses the words "well," "look," "demands" while talking about his son's expenses (2.1.6–12). Neville wrote "stepp first **into England**." Hamlet is "sent **into England**." Neville also used the words "warning," "patience," "signify," "surprised," "discourse," "speedy," "frankly," "dislike," "furnish," "ordnance," "necessaries," "pleasure," "contrary," "yesternight," "certainty," "afternoon," "dalliance," "proceeding," and "bonds," which are in the play.

Concerning Denmark, where Shakespeare set *Hamlet* (the only time he ever named that country), Neville wrote: "The Ambassador of Wirttenberg told me lately, that he had received Advertisement from a Friend of his in Hambourg, that the King of Denmark makes very great Preparation by Sea" (Sawyer, 1725, vol. 1, 183). The word "preparation" is also used by an ambassador in *Hamlet,* about war (Fortinbras's intended invasion of Poland, 2.2.63).

In the first scene Horatio and Marcellus discuss Denmark's "preparations" for a war, including ships and cannon, against Norway (1.1.108). In 1574 and 1578 Sir Thomas Gresham received licenses to export cannons to Denmark. One of his ships, containing cannons, sank in the Thames and was rediscovered in 2003 (James, 2008, 213). Neville inherited Gresham's iron foundry and exported cannons during the 1590s.

Five days after this last letter, on May 14, 1600, Neville used another word that occurs uniquely in *Hamlet,* "questionable." He also used "indifferently," "jealousy," "controversy," "consequence" and "infinite," which occur in the play. Furthermore, in *Hamlet* "questionable" occurs just seven lines before the word "marble," which Neville had used in a letter written just two weeks earlier (April 27, 1600).

The stage direction of *Hamlet,* act 1, scene 2, in the 1604 second, "good quarto," has Claudius entering with "Counsaile." In his letter of February 19, 1601, Neville used this very same spelling.[5]

In Chapter 1 we noted that Neville used words in two 1602 letters, written in the Tower, that occur in *Hamlet.* These include "blot," the queen's "eye," "soiled," "wipe away," "liberty," "occasion," "serve," "ugly" and "crimes." The words "serve" and "crime" also occur in Neville's trial statement.

Furthermore, James (2011, 302) noticed that Neville used the word "clemency" in a letter of July 1601 to Cecil, in which he hoped the queen would not ruin him. "Clemency" is unique to *Hamlet* (3.2.140).

Ten Words Used by Neville in His Letters and by Shakespeare

Jealousy, uncharitably, inwardness, inhibition, dependency, objected, solicitation, imbecility, ordnance, Denmark. None of these words were used by Edward de Vere, Earl of Oxford, in his letters (see below). All of them were used by Neville and Shakespeare between 1600 and 1601.

Four Letters Written by Edward de Vere, Earl of Oxford in 1601

Oxford's status as a leading authorship candidate suggests he is an ideal figure to use as a control in this study. We have treated these four letters in the same way as Neville's trial statement, counting only the first occurrence of a word, and so have used the four letters as if they were one piece of writing: the total number of words in the letters is 1,321, nearly equivalent to the 1,379 in Neville's statement. Oxford used 247 words that are to be found in *Hamlet*, whereas Neville's trial statement contains 426 words from the play. Thus Neville's use of *Hamlet* words is almost double that of Oxford. His vocabulary is also richer. There are far more instances of two words occurring together in Neville's deposition than in Oxford's letters (see addendums 1 and 2 below). However, they use virtually the same number of hapaxes, Oxford using 15. Of these, 7 were from plays written before 1601; 2 are from *Hamlet* ("backed" and "really," curiously, the second is the same word Neville used); 6 were used by Shakespeare after 1601. Neville used 14 hapaxes. Neville's use of unique words falls into a pattern that shows a contemporary fit with Shakespeare's writing, whereas Oxford's usage seems a random distribution and nearly half occur in plays written by Shakespeare (according to generally accepted chronology) after Oxford had died (1604). Oxford's letters are essentially courteous begging letters, asking Cecil for favors. Neville's letters show him as an ambassador reporting the king of Denmark's preparations for war and other material relevant to the themes of *Hamlet*.

An Early Reference to Hamlet

In 1605 Thomas Smith referred to *Hamlet* in his *Voyage and Entertainment in Russia,* comparing the government of Boris Godunov to "the *Poeticall Furie in a Stage-action,* complete yet with horrid and wofull Tragedies: a first, but no second to any *Hamlet;* and that now Revenge, just Revenge was coming with his Sworde drawne" (italics in the original). Smith would have known Neville, as they were both ambassadors and supporters of Essex, had both been imprisoned in the Tower after the Essex rebellion, and were both MPs and members of the second London Virginia Company. Indeed Neville named Thomas Smith in three letters from 1604 to 1608,[6] telling Winwood, in a letter dated March 11, 1605,[7] "I chanced to meet Sir *Thomas Smith* in *Westminster-Hall* in good leisure and fell into some Speech with him" (Sawyer, 1725, vol. 2, 198). Neville's son married Sir John Smith's daughter (John was Sir Thomas Smith's brother) in 1609. Despite referring by name to several English poets in his writing on Russia, Smith did not name Shakespeare.

Conclusion

The evidence in this study supports Neville being the hidden author of the works of Shakespeare. He was an ambassador, a prisoner, a man betrayed by friends in a political situation of great danger; these roles and themes occur in *Hamlet.* His trial statement shows him using all his powers of persuasion to survive. With Neville revealed as the playwright we can understand why Shakespeare wrote *Hamlet.*

Addendum 1

Analysis of Neville's Trial Statement

We have only counted the first occurrence of any word and only listed it once if it occurs in a phrase. We have put in brackets the number of times a word is used by Shakespeare unless it is so frequent as to be tedious to count. We have counted 421 words used in both play and trial statement (which contains 1,379), 30.5 percent. This is an underestimate, as we have not counted small words such as "you" or "the." The pattern of these may be significant but needs computer analysis. Thus about a third of the words in the statement are to be found in the play.

Single Words in Both Neville's Statement and Hamlet

Myself, altogether, blame, freely (×4), willingly, offence (×8), mercy (×5), soul (×29), faithful (×3), majesty (×16), death, imputation, fault (×4), loathsome, falsehood, treason (×5), desire (×8), only (×6), actions, privy, entreated, Sir, project, touching, good, assurance (×2), nothing (×27), hear, due, respect (×2), allegiance, messenger, ten (×4), days (×7), delay (×2), often (×2), house (×4), met, where, their, both, nature (×23), promise, only, advise, spake, heard, came, soon, after, unto, any, part, hand (×16), himself, because, indeed, finding, working, mind (×12), bare, simple, truth (×6), case, first (×16), manner, abused, rather (×5), opposition (×2), afterwards, evidence, circumstances, obligation (×), highest, fortunes (×2), times (×8), last (×12), begin (×6), friendship, besides, general (×2), consider, like, seeing (×3), four (×3), months (×4), after, lying, likewise, meeting (×2), seal, least (×2), money, forced (×2), length, purposed, set, forward (×2), ready (×4), making (×3), haste (×12), within (×13), few (×3), likelihood, build, likely (×2), especially (×2), noted, delivered, conception, resolution, articles, whereof (×2), deliberate, conference, broken, found (×4), little, comfort, hands, small, account, desperate

(×6), whatsoever, plain, argument, confession (×3), wherein (×8), delivered, matters, charge (×8), known (×8), some, things (×11), purpose (×12), seems (×5), think (×41), humbly (×5), pardon (×6), therein, personal, particular, weak, whensoever, passion, resolve, how, person (×4), since, confess, public, private, evil (×2), ground (×9), witness (×2), whole (×7), knowledge, directly (×2), most (×6), really, trust, interpret, judge (×3), conceit (×4), traiterous, thought (×12), God (×25), deal, faith, counsel (×3), employment (×2), always, please (×11), again (×29).

Pairs of Words in Neville's Statement and *Hamlet*

I mean (×5), the circumstance (×2), the best (×3), means to (×2), to try, the action (×2), as far, possible to, have already, the late, by them (×2), to understand, his own (×9), the state, my advice (×2), should be (×9), I might (×3), the words, my part, went to, with them (×2), against the (×8), I never, the matter (×13), speak with (×5), the third (×3), my thoughts (×3), have been (×7), fellowship in, I hope (×5), that neither, the better, that these (×2), be considered, went to, cause of (×5), between us (×2), kind of (×7), not till, to signify (and "signify to"), be considered, it appears, the Sunday, to gather, he hath (×8), and perhaps, but howsoever, my heart (×10), affection to, my lord, I hoped, have proved, a thing (×5), the world (×14), above all, consent to, set down (×5), much of (×2), which might, into France, to serve, my former, call me (×2), the like.

Some of these are not significant, though the sheer number is evidence of a link. One particular pair does point to shared authorship: "set down" (see first example under "Textual Parallels").

Phrases of Three Words

Together with all, as well as, so much as, the issue of, dealt with me, my duty to.

Addendum 2

Four Letters from Edward de Vere, Earl of Oxford, to Robert Cecil, 1601[8]

1. Cecil Papers 76/34, Oxford to Cecil, February 2, 1601

> At thys tyme, I am to trye my friendes: amonge whiche consideringe owre owlde aquayntance, familiarite heertofore, & alliance of houses, (then whiche can be noo streyghter) as of my Broother, I presume especiallye. Whearfore at

thys tyme, whearas sume good fortune (yf yt be backed by friendes) doothe in a manner presente yt selfe. I moost ernestlye crave yowre furtherance soo fare as the place and fauoure yow howlde may admite. And that ys as I conceyve: that yf her Magestie be willinge, to confer the Praecidentcie of Waales to me, that I may assure my selfe of yowre voice in Councell rather then a stranger. Not that I desyre yow showlde bee a mover, but a furtherer. for as the tyme ys yt weare nott reasone. But yf yt shall pleas her Magestie in regard of my yowthe tyme & fortune spent in her Courte, addinge therto her magesties fauours, & promises, whiche drue me one [= on] wythe ought any mistruste, the moore to praesume in myne owne expences, to confer soo good a turne to me. that then wythe yowre good woorde, and brotherlye friendshipe, yow will incorage her forwarde, and further yt as yow may. for I know her Magestie ys of that princlye dispositione that they shall nott be deceyved whiche put there truste in her. Whiche good office in yow, I will never forgett; and alwayes to my powre acknowlege in loue & kyndnes. hoopinge that as wee bee knytt neare in alliance: so hearafter moore nearer by good and friendly offices. Thus most ernestlye desyringe yow to haue me in friendlye remembrance, when tyme servethe: I take my leaue. thys 2d of Februarie.

Yowre assured and louinge Brother.
Edward Oxenford

2. Cecil Papers 182/23, May 11, 1601

I receyved this morninge yowre message by H[enry] Loke, wherby I see yow have not forgotten me to her Magestie, and so as yt ys muche to my contentment, I protest to god not so muche in that sumwhat her Magestie doothe satisfise my desyre, but that I finde that assurednes in yowre kindnes to me, wyth whome as we are streyghly [= straightly, closely] alyed, ther ys no reasone but I showld make especiall account of before all others, so am I glad mooreover to find an especiall friend constant and assured in yowre woorde. whiche thinge I vov [= vow] to god to acknowlege to yow in all faythe kindnes and loue, and in whatsoever I may stand yow in sted w[hi]ch accordinge to myn estate now ys littell, but in good will very great I will [acknowleg] wythe all alacrite and well wishinge performe, and this I boothe speake and wright vnto yow from my hart. Wherfore as yow have begone, so I most ernestly desyre yow to styke to me in this cause, for yt ys a thinge wherof I make great account, and yt ys a friendship whiche yow have done me aboue thankes, whiche I will frely impart to yow at my cominge to the Court, w[hi]ch I thinke shalbe to morow by the grace of God. tyll whiche tyme as a hater of ceremonies I will refer all other thankes and obseruationes whiche in me are as far from ordinarie accomplishments, as my thankfull accepetance of thys yowre frendly and brotherly office ys nere my harte simple and vnfayned. I sent my man as H. Loke informed me vnto yow that he myght open sumwhat moore playner the cause, the moore yow shall countnance him the more bouldly and frely he will certefie yow. I will only now end wholy recommendinge my cause to yowre friendship, assuringe yow that ther ys nothinge in the world that I esteme more or accept more kindle [= kindly] then yowre brotherly and frendly office which yow at thy [= this?] present vndertake in my behalfe. to morrowe I hoope to se yow my selfe at the court where I will more

francly and frely declare my self. for to day, althowghe I thowght to have come to yow yet consideringe yowre manyfold causes I thinke yt best to forbeare. In the meane seasone I rest yowre most thankfull brother and assured friende
Edward Oxenford

3. Cecil Papers 88/101, October 7, 1601

My very good Brother, yf my helthe hadd beene to my mynde I wowlde have beene before this att the Coorte, aswell to haue giuen yow thankes for yowre presence, at the hearinge of my cause debated as to haue moued her Magestye for her resolutione. As for the matter, how muche I am behouldinge to yow I neede not repeate, but in all thankfulnes acknowlege, for yow haue beene the moover & onlye follower therofe for mee, & by yowre onlye meanes, I have hetherto passed the pykes of so many adversaries. Now my desyre ys, sythe them selues whoo have opposed to her Magestyes ryghte seeme satisfisde [= satisfied], that yow will make the ende ansuerable, to the rest of yowre moste friendlye procedinge, for I am aduised, that I may passe my Booke from her Magestie, yf a warrant may be procured to my cosen Bacon and Seriant [= Sergeant] Harris to perfet [= perfect] yt. Whiche beinge doone, I know to whome formallye to thanke, but reallye they shalbe, and are from me, and myne, to be sealed vp in an aeternall remembrance to yowre selfe. And thus wishinge all happines to yow, and sume fortunat meanes to me, wherby I myght recognise soo diepe merites, I take my leaue this 7th of October from my House at Hakney. 1601.
Yowre most assured and louinge Broother.
Edward Oxenford

4. Cecil Papers 89/124, November 22, 1601

My good Brother, in that I haue not sent an answer to yowre laste letter, as yow myght expect, I shall desyre yow too [= to] hould me for exscused, sythe ever sythence the receyt therof by reason of my syknes I have not been able to wryght. And whearas yow doo conceyve that I haue bene carried to [= too] muche by the conceytes of Cauley, I doo asssure yow ther ys no suche thinge. I haue vsed hym and soo doo styll as a follower of my busines, wherin I doo not finde any cause to blame but rather recommend hys diligence. for Councell I haue suche lavers [= lawyers], and the best that I can gett as are to be had in London, whoo have aduised me for my best course, to desyre that her Magestye wowld graunt me her warrant signed, for the dravinge [= drawing] of a booke mentioninge what her plesure ys to graunt me concerninge the Escheete of Sir Charles Davers (de bene esse, quantum in Regina est) wherby shall ensue no preiudice vnto any of the pretenders whiche subieste [= suggest, pretend?] to be interessed [= interested] in any of the sayd landes, in regard, that yf the Quiene haue no titell, there passethe nothinge to mee. It ys a common course notwythstandinge any office founde agaynste the Quiene, that her Magestye grauntethe concealed landes in this course, whearof there are many yearly precidentes. So yat her Magestye grauntinge this to me, grauntethe but her owne interest, whiche in effect had bene nothinge, consideringe how this cause hathe bene caried, and so lekly to haue bene obscured for ever, yf yt had not bene my hap to have styrred therin.

for the rest of yowre letter, whatsoever yow have written, although yt be sum discoragment vnto me, yet I cannot alter the opinion whiche I have conceyved of yowre vertu and constancie, neyther can I suffer yt to enter my thought that a vayne fable can brandel the clearnes of yowre guyltles conscience sythe all the world doothe know that the crymes of Sir Charles Dauers were so byfolde, that Iustice could not dispence any farther; wherfore I cannot leue [= leave, abandon] that hoope and trust whiche I have hadd in yowre promises, but as I have done styll I doo wholy rely my self on yowre only friendship, and thus desyring yow to beare with the weaknes of my lame hand, I take my leaue from Hakney this 22th of November 1601.

Yowre louinge and assured Brother to his powre
Edward Oxenford

Single Words Found in Oxford's Four Letters and *Hamlet*

Letter 1: friends, among, acquaintance, houses, than, especially, wherefore, some, fortune, backed, doth, manner, present, itself, most, place, admit, conceive, majesty, regard, willing, assure, myself, reason, please, youth, spent, court, thereto, favours, without, turn, word, friendship, forward, further, disposition, deceived, trust, office, forget, always, power, love, near, hereafter, more, nearer, remembrance,

Letter 2: message, god, somewhat, especial, account, before, others, glad, moreover, friend, constant, assured, vow, faith, whatsoever, stand, estate, little, great, perform, speak, begun, stick, cause, above, thanks, freely, impart, coming, grace, till, simple, sent, open, countenance, only, nothing, world, undertake, frankly, forbear.

Letter 3: health, given, presence, hearing, moved, resolution, thereof, sith, themselves, opposed, right, seem, satisfied, proceeding, pass, book, warrant, sergeant, perfect, really, eternal, happiness, deep, house, hackney, loving.

Letter 4: answer, last, letter, sickness, able, used, still, wherein, rather, diligence, course, grant, pleasure, said, lands, Queen, passeth, common, found, against, granteth, effect, hap, cannot, opinion, virtue, neither, suffer, enter, vain, guiltless, conscience, crimes, justice, whereof, hope, bear, weakness, hand.

Two Words

Letter 1: this time, to try, our old, my brother, so far, and favour, your voice, a stranger, mine own.

Letter 2: I received, this morning, see you, not forgotten, is much, my desire, I find, to find, according to, my heart.

Letter 3: very good, had been, would have, as well, the matter, need not, have hitherto, so many, the end, the rest, my cousin, which being, to whom, to thank, means to.

Letter 4: hold me, to write, my business, to blame, the best, for ever, my thought.

Three or Four Words

Letter 1: I take my leave.
Letter 3: To my mind.
Letter 4: No such thing.

Hapaxes

LETTER 1

Serveth occurs in *Henry VI* part 1;
February in *Much Ado About Nothing;*
Backed in *Hamlet;*
Heretofore in *King Lear;*
Furtherer in *The Tempest.*

LETTER 2

Certify in *Henry VI* part 1;
Observations in *Much Ado;*
Hater in *All's Well;*
Secretary in *Henry VIII.*

LETTER 3

Hackney in *Love's Labour's Lost*, but this is of a horse, not a place;
Really in *Hamlet.*

LETTER 4

Bene in *Love's Labour's Lost;*
Granteth in *The Rape of Lucrece;*
Recommend in *Coriolanus;*
Regina in *Henry VIII.*

Thirteen Hendiadys in Oxford's Letters

place and fauoure	*Hamlet:* place (×8); favour (×4)
good and friendly	*Hamlet:* good (×89);
assured and louinge	*Hamlet:* assured (×2); loving (×3)
constant and assured	*Hamlet:* constant (×1); assured (×2)
kindnes and loue	*Hamlet:* love (×49)

thankes and obseruationes	*Hamlet:* thanks (×10)
frendly and brotherly	
simple and vnfayned	*Hamlet:* simple (×1); Shakespeare never used "unfained."
bouldly and freely	*Hamlet:* freely (×4)
brotherly and friendly	
francly and freely	*Hamlet:* frankly (×2); freely (×4)
vertu and constancie	*Hamlet:* virtue (×11);
hoope and trust	*Hamlet:* hope (×8); trust (×2).

Chapter 11

Poets, Politicians, Vicars and History in 1603

Illa quidem maioribus attolenda cothurnis quis negat?
[Who would deny that these should not be
further exalted on stage in Tragedy?]
—George Carleton, 1603

We have offered evidence that Henry Neville was a secret writer who used the name "William Shakespeare" as a pseudonym. Neville was accustomed to keeping secrets. He was a member of a family involved in secret government business. He was a diplomat, using spies and codes in his letters. Neville kept his part in the Essex rebellion secret until he was betrayed by Essex and Southampton. He kept his negotiations with King James secret until forced to admit in Parliament that he was the author of a paper about the relationship between the king and House of Commons (James, 2011). Many of the best kept secrets tend to leak, and we now present some of the leaks that reveal Henry Neville's identity as a poet.

On April 12, 1603, John Chamberlain, in a letter to Dudley Carleton, wrote, "The 10th of this month, the Earl of Southampton and Sir Henry Neville was delivered out of the Tower by warrant of the king. These bountiful beginnings raise all men's spirits and put them in great hopes, insomuch that not only Protestants, but Papists and Puritans, and the very Poets, with their idle pamphlets, promise themselves great part in his favour."

Chamberlain's alliteration of Protestants, Papists, Puritans, Poets, pamphlets, promise and part emphasizes the associations he was making between Southampton, whose family had Catholic sympathies; Neville, who was labelled a Puritan when he was ambassador to France; Poets and pamphlets.

Henry Wriothesley, the Earl of Southampton in his 1603 *Encomium* on Richard III, which he dedicated to Neville, referred to "pamphletts and playes" about the king (see Chapter 7 and Appendix A). Shakespeare, in dedicating his *Rape of Lucrece* to Southampton, referred to it as a "pamphlet."

Shakespeare/Neville, in Sonnet 107, was perhaps referring to the death of Elizabeth when he wrote, "the mortal moon hath her eclipse endured," their release from the Tower, when he mentioned "a confined doom"; and their hopes for the future with the phrase "peace proclaims olives of endless age." In the sonnet, death "subscribes" to the poet as his rhyme will outlast the brass tombs of tyrants. As a covert attack on Elizabeth I as a tyrant, this sonnet suggests that Neville feared he might die in the Tower. He was in danger of execution and was ill during his incarceration, as he stated in one of his letters to Cecil. Shakespeare subtly downgrades the tyrant's tomb to brass. The Shakespeare canon contains no expression of grief for Elizabeth's death. In 1603 Henry Chettle called on the bard to eulogize the queen (see Chapter 9), but he did not oblige. Henry Neville had no reason to regret her passing when it meant that he was released from the Tower and her unforgiving persecution.

John Davies' Microcosmos

In 1603 John Davies published his poetry anthology, *Microcosmos.* One poem was about Neville and contrasts brass and gold:

To the Noble, discreete, and wellbeloved

Knight Sir Henry Nevill.

There was a *Time* when, ah that so there *was,*
Whie not there *is?* There *is* and *was* a Time,
Whẽ *Men* might cal *Gold, Gold;* & *Brasse,* but *Brasse,*
And saie *it,* without *check,* in P*rose* or *Rime.*
Yet should I cal thee *Gold* some (*Brasse* perchance)
VVould saie I err'd because I nere *toucht* thee,
And so did cal *thee* through meere ignorance,
Or (which is worse) through abiect *Flatterie.*
I am too ignorant (I doe confesse)
To iudge thy *woorth,* which worthiest *Men* cõmend,
Yet may I say (I hope) and not transgresse,
Th'art *Vertue, Valour, Truth,* and *Honors* friend;
All *which* presume thou art not gilt by guile
Because thy noble *name* denies the *vile* [Ne-vile] [Davies, 1603, 143].

Immediately we can see that Davies is suggesting Neville is a fine man and indeed "the real thing": i.e., gold, not brass. Intriguingly, he uses the word "***toucht.***" Is it a reference to a touchstone? (A touchstone was a piece of basalt used to tell the difference between gold and base metals.) As long ago as 1592–3 Shakespeare had used this image in two plays, *Edward III* and *Richard III.* In the first, the French king John says, "your intended force must abide the **touch**" (3.3.141), meaning "stand the trial," as metal is tested by a touchstone. In *Richard III* the king says:

> O Buckingham, now do I play the **touch**,
> To try if thou be current **gold** indeed [4.2.8].

James and Rubinstein (2005, 131) revealed that Neville's land agent Richard Beaumont informed him in March 1600 that he had found a touchstone on his land. James linked this with Touchstone in *As You Like It,* which was written at that time and sees Touchstone, the clown courtier, as standing for Neville himself. Shakespeare used this image again in *Measure for Measure* when the Duke says to Angelo, "Spirits are not finely **touch'd** But to fine issues" (1.1.36). Kermode (2001, 147) commented, "The idea of touching leads back to the goldsmith." This last use of the image is contemporary with Davies' poem and is in a play that has scenes in prison and includes Claudio who, like Neville, survived the threat of execution. It is believed to have been written 1603–4.

Davies is concerned to remove any suggestion of guilt from Neville as a newly released prisoner by referring to gilt (gold) rather than guilt. He stresses the meaning of Neville's name as if rehabilitating him after his time in the Tower. The poem furthermore opens with contrasting a past time and a present time as if suggesting a period before the imprisonment and a new time now, when Neville is free to receive such a poem. Neville is described as "discreete." Davies is saying that Neville could keep a secret, as he had done during the Essex rebellion to his great cost; this adjective would also suit a man who was hiding his authorship of the Shakespeare plays. Later in *Microcosmos* Davies commented on actors and may have referred to William Shakspere.

> *Players,* I love yee, and your *Qualitie,*
> As ye are Men, that pass time not abus'd:
> And[c] some I loue for[d] *painting, poesie,*
> And say fell *Fortune* cannot be excus'd,
> That hath for better *uses* you refus'd:
> *Wit, Courage, good shape, good partes,* and all *good,*
> As long as these *goods* are no *worse* vi'd,
> And though the *stage* doth staine pure gent'e bloud,
> Yet[e] generous yee are in *mind* and *moode.*

Davies' marginal annotations are as follows:

[c]**W. S. R. B.**

[d]Simonides saith that painting is a dumb Poesy & Poesy a speaking painting.

[e]Roscias was said for his excellēcy in his qualay, to be only werthie to come on the stage, and for his horse-fly to be more worthy thē to come theron [Davies, 1603, 116].

We know that Richard Burbage (R. B.) was a painter because on March 31, 1613, the Earl of Rutland's steward paid 44s "to Mr. Shakspeare in gold about my Lord's *impresa*" and another 44s "to Richard Burbage for painting and making it" (Schoenbaum, 1987, 272). What we do not know for sure is whether this Shakspeare, who it seems devised the impresa (a shield with a symbolic design and motto), was William Shakspere from Stratford or someone else with the initials W. S. Davies introduces W. S. and R. B. as players. As well as painting he mentions poetry but does not identify W. S. directly as a poet: all we can tell is that Davies loves some players for poesie (which could mean writing or speaking poetry). James and Rubinstein (2005, 57, 204–5) pointed out that Davies later (in the *Scourge of Folly,* 1610–11) wrote another poem about Shakespeare that might suggest he knew the identity of the hidden author. The title of this poem is "To Our English Terence." Educated Elizabethans knew that Terence was a Roman actor who was accused of having given his name to plays written by other authors. They also revealed that Davies was a member of the Mitre Club and so would have met Neville (James and Rubinstein, 2005, 57, 204–5).

Davies' final line in his epigram to Neville, "Because thy noble *name* denies the *vile.*" recalls Shakespeare's Sonnet 121: "'Tis better to be vile th**en vile** esteem'd," which, as James (2008, 106) has shown, includes the name "**n vile**" or indeed the whole name, with the initial "Ne" reversed as "en" from "th**en**" [=than], the original spelling in the 1609 first printing of the sonnets. Similar puns are found in the First Folio version of *Henry V*'s St. Crispin's Day speech (see Chapter 5) and the Latin poem, *Mr. Hoskins, His Convivium Philosophicum* (see Chapter 8).

George Carleton's Heroici Characteres

Also in 1603, George Carleton (1559–1628) published a book, *Heroici Characteres,* written in Latin verse (James and Rubinstein, 2005, 202). This title may be translated as *Epic Figures.*[1] He dedicated it *Ad Illustrissimum Equitem, Henricum Nevillum* (To the Most Distinguished Knight, Henry Neville). In his dedication Carleton, like Davies, also likened Neville to gold, noting,

"Just as the noble quality of gold emerges from the refiner's fire freer of alloy; so blameless character, wrestling against critical adversity, in like manner shines back, embellished by the very stress it has undergone" (Deas, 2013).

Carleton went to Oxford in 1576 and in 1580 was elected a fellow of Merton College. Neville matriculated at Merton in 1577 and is therefore likely to have known Carleton, who had already gained a reputation as a poet and orator. Carleton maintained a long association with Oxford, gaining an MA in 1585 and a BD in 1594; he became a Doctor of Divinity in 1613. Carleton was also a supporter of Essex. Neville sponsored Carleton to become his vicar at Mayfield, Sussex, in 1589 when Neville was living there. Neville started shifting his family back to Billingbear after his father died in 1593, and he sold his Mayfield property in 1597/8. Carleton left Mayfield in 1605, became bishop of Llandaff in 1618 and bishop of Chichester from 1619 to 1628. Carleton eventually married Neville's widow, Anne, in 1619.

Carleton's book *Heroici Characteres* begins with an extended dedication to Neville and then has sections eulogizing Elizabeth I; James I; Robert Devereux, Earl of Essex; and Philip Sydney. By far the longest section is on Essex. Carleton is putting Neville into a context of royal, political and poetic figures. Neville knew all these personally. In the book's dedication, Carleton likens Neville to the biblical Joseph, falsely imprisoned by the pharaoh and now released. He also exhorts Neville to "grasp firmly the rewards of your achievements, **you who will have the Muses to bear witness to you**, and your unspotted excellence to guide you" (our emphasis; Deas, 2013).

By evoking the muses, Carleton seems to be suggesting Neville was a poet. He then proceeds to praise Neville's talents specifically in the last intriguing 12 lines of the 89-line dedication.

Iam quia te virtus albo signavit in isto,
Silicet, o nostris qui feceris otia musis,
Nominis umbra tui magnorum emblemata parva
Protegat Heroum: solito haec quoque suscipe vultu.
Illa quidem maioribus attolenda cothurnis
Quis negat? ultro etiam tenuis tentamina musae
Agnosco, nec in hac quicquam me gloria laude
Sollicitat: nec me vatis pro crimine nomen
Obiectum fallit. Quin contra murmura vatem
Tu clypeo defende tuum. Cantata per orbem
Et sine vate sibi per se celeberrima gesta
Heroum, sat erit nostram tentasse Camanam.

Translation:

Now since your fortitude[2] has sealed your place in this record,
You will have provided the leisure for my/our Muses,
May your reputation shelter these little pictures
Of epic figures; support this work, too, with your accustomed favour.
Who would deny that these should not be further exalted on stage in Tragedy?
I freely acknowledge these experiments of the slighter Muse.
In this matter, fame does not concern me at all;
Nor does the description "poet," when thrown at me as a charge, betray[3] me.
How could it, when against such muttering you protect your poet with your shield?
Even without a poet, the feats, so famous in themselves, of these epic figures
Will go on being sung throughout the world; and it will be enough that I have been able to put my/our Muse to the test!

The second line may be interpreted to mean, "You who have spent your leisure in literature and made time for poetry." "Otia" has a further meaning of private time, free of public responsibilities. Carleton is acknowledging Neville's long support for his poetry in giving him the time for his creativity, but by using "nostris" he could mean "our," their shared creativity. The Latin "nostris/nostrum," which most readers of the time would read as "my," could also mean "our" Muse, so Carleton may be saying they shared an interest in, and practice of, writing poetry. The last line, "I have been able to put my/our Muse to the test," means "I have been able to put my poetic talent to the test," but throughout there is an ambiguity about Neville's own poetic talent.

The fourth line makes the suggestion that Carleton's epic figures may be put on stage in tragedy: he signifies this by using the word "cothurnis," the raised boots classical tragic actors wore to make them larger than life. Ben Jonson used the same image in his opening tribute to Shakespeare in the First Folio, "to hear thy Buskin tread, and shake a Stage." Is Carleton suggesting here that Neville write tragedy? Shakespeare had already written *Romeo and Juliet, Hamlet* and *Othello.* Carleton's exhortation comes as the bard was about to embark on his other great tragedies, *Macbeth* and *King Lear.*

The "slighter Muse," (or slender Muse), is a reference to Callimachus, who claimed that Apollo visited him and admonished him to "fatten his flocks, but to keep his muse slender."[4] In Sonnet 38, Shakespeare wrote, "If my **slight Muse** do please these curious days, / The pain be mine, but thine shall be the praise."

Carleton's disclaimer that he does not fear being called a poet may be a suggestion to Neville that he need not be ashamed to be called a poet himself. Carleton writes of "the description [nomen = name] 'poet,' when thrown at me as a charge [accusation or crime]." He might be suggesting that this had happened to Neville, or that he had been in some danger of this, or feared it.

Taken at face value it may simply be Carleton stating boldly he has no fears, yet to write a poem about Essex would have led to a charge against him had he published in the reign of Elizabeth I. Only the arrival of James I made the publication possible, when James rehabilitated the Essex supporters and released Southampton and Neville as one of his first acts even before he arrived in London.

Just as Beaumont and Fletcher gave their manuscript of *A King and No King*[5] to Neville, so Carleton offered his Latin poem. Both bear witness to Neville's interest in poetry and theater. Even if we may be accused of over-interpreting this Latin poetry, Carleton is associating Neville with the Muses, with tragedy, and with poets, and celebrating his position as a senior player in the cultural and political life of the nation.

However, Neville was not too pleased with the dedication. Soon after Henry Neville died in 1615, George Carleton tried to bring out a second printing of his book. He wrote to his kinsman, Sir Dudley Carleton, seeking to have the book printed in the Netherlands, because stock had run out in England. According to his letter, dated 1617:

> Sir Henry Neville in his life tyme wished that the dedication had been altered, and the verses written to hym placed in som other part of the book, which may be done with little alteration. It is looked for that all should be removed and the dedication don to the Prince. Som of place willed me so to do. Of these things I make small reckoning, but youe se I am bould with you to write any thing to youe, and will be herein directed as yourself shall think fittest [Milton, 2005, 59].

In 1603, Neville's caution is perhaps understandable in light of his recent release from two years imprisonment in the Tower of London. It is curious that even after Henry Neville's death, some unnamed people in high places were keen to replace the dedication with one to the king or prince. The letter is testimony to Neville's preference for secrecy. Carleton in this letter and in his dedication asserted his boldness in speaking out, being unashamed to be a poet and to praise Neville. Who might these people in high places be?

A possible clue is the fact that the final section of Carleton's *Heroici Characteres* is a panegyric to Philip Sydney. This eulogy was first published in 1587 in an anthology of Latin poetry written by Oxford fellows and students and dedicated to Philip Sidney, called *Exsequiae Illustrissimi Equitis.* It was edited by William Gager (see Chapter 6). Neville knew Sidney and his brother Robert, as their fathers were close friends. Mary Sidney (1561–1621) was the sister of Philip and Robert. She published Philip's *Arcadia.* She was a friend of Neville's mother and mother-in-law. Her children, William and Philip

Herbert, became patron and mentors of Henry Neville's oldest son Henry and grandson Richard. William Herbert, Earl of Pembroke, "was stoutly Protestant, and in December 1628 his brother, the Earl of Montgomery (Sir Philip Herbert), appointed Neville a gentleman of the privy chamber in extraordinary. Moreover, following Neville's death, Pembroke purchased the wardship of Neville's son, and his secretary, Sir John Thoroughgood, subsequently married Neville's widow and acquired the wardship himself."[6] William and Philip, the earls of Pembroke and Montgomery, were the patrons of Shakespeare's First Folio. Thus, Neville's friends, political supporters and patrons were Shakespeare's dedicatees, Southampton, Montgomery and Pembroke. However, as George Carleton wrote in his letter to Dudley that the dedication to Neville "should be removed and the dedication don to the Prince. Som of place willed me so to do," we can presume "the Prince" here would mean King James I or his son Charles. When Robert Cecil had died and Neville was expected to be his replacement as secretary of state, we know that the king declined to appoint him because he was too popular. Therefore, we suggest the pressure to change the dedication in 1617 had come from high up in the court.

Carleton Connections

George Carleton[7] referred to Dudley Carleton as his "cosin" in his correspondence with him. Dudley Carleton (1574–1632) became an M.P. in 1604. He married Anne, the stepdaughter of Sir Henry Savile, Henry Neville's friend and former tutor. George was close friends with Henry Savile's younger brother, Thomas. Dudley appointed Henry Neville the "sponsor," or godfather, of his newborn child in 1609 (Brown, 2010, 51). Dudley also had an uncle called George Carleton (1529–90), who was arrested during the Marprelate controversy. He died awaiting trial. Job Throckmorton was also suspected of the authorship of the Marprelate pamphlets. These witty pamphlets ridiculed the pompous and corrupt Church of England bishops and were authored by Martin Marprelate, an obvious nom de plume. Job narrowly escaped prosecution, denying the authorship. He was a cousin of Henry Neville. Neville had met Arthur Throckmorton when travelling through Europe in the early 1580s. Job and Arthur were first cousins. Shakespeare may have been referring to the Marprelate controversy in *As You Like It*, in which a vicar is called Sir Oliver Martext in act 3, scene 3. Job died in 1601, just over a year after *As You Like It* was written. This is a decade after the Marprelate controversy, which is itself an example of authors keeping their identity secret in order to write material that challenged the establishment. The danger, which George Carleton, the elder, and other writers including Ben Jonson, Thomas Nashe, Thomas Kyd and John Stubbe[8] faced, was imprisonment, torture and destruction of their work. That George Carleton, the younger, hinted at Neville's interest in poetry and the stage in his dedication, and that Neville did not want it printed—indeed people in high places later asked for it to be reallocated—suggests Neville was a secret author.

As bishop, Carleton employed a theological assistant, Thomas Vicars, who married Henry Neville's daughter Anne (and Carleton's stepdaughter). In 1628, the year Carleton died, Vicars published the third edition of his book, written in Latin, on rhetoric. In this edition he added to the text where he named English poets (particularly praising John Davies; see above) and referred to Shakespeare indirectly: "to these I believe should be added the famous poet who takes his name from **shaking and spear**." In Latin the words are "quassatione & hasta"[9] (Schurink, 2006, 73). This phrase is highly suggestive of inside knowledge that the name "Shakespeare" was a pseudonym. Vicars, having married Neville's daughter, would perhaps have been told the family secret but sworn not to reveal it.

In his dedication Carleton predicted that Neville's "blameless good character, staying constant in the midst of crisis through which you pass, keeps its gracious self control and awaits the renown that will not die." Perhaps only now is his true undying fame dawning.

Chapter 12

The Writer Revealed

Henry Neville in His Political Context

Truth's authentic author to be cited...—*Troilus and Cressida* (3.2.179)

With Henry Neville revealed as the hidden writer of the works of Shakespeare, many puzzles are solved. One such puzzle is how and why an unknown man from Warwickshire could suddenly write a four-part political epic on English history and get this on stage as his first work. The tetralogy is full of members of the Neville family, yet there is not a single Shakspere and no mention of Stratford-upon-Avon. The county of Warwickshire[1] is named only twice in the entire canon: first by Richard Neville in *Henry VI* part 3 (4.8.9); then by Falstaff in *Henry IV* part 1 when he is speaking to Ralph Neville (4.2.51). We might more reasonably have expected the first work of a writer from a country town to be about the picaresque adventures of a poor tradesman daring to venture into the exciting world of the city of London. It might comment on the city–country contrasts of his experience. Yet Shakespeare never wrote such a play. His earliest comedies were set in Italy (*The Taming of the Shrew* in Padua and *The Two Gentlemen of Verona* in Verona and Milan). We know Neville travelled in Italy in 1581 and left Padua travelling in the direction of Vicenza and so towards Verona (according to Arthur Throckmorton's diary: Rowse, 1962, 90). We know also that before the *Henry VI* trilogy was written, Neville was annotating *Leicester's Commonwealth* with notes specific to the content of the history plays (Casson, 2010). Neville's authorship explains the genesis of Shakespeare's works, whereas William from Stratford presents us with an enigma: a towering genius appearing without any foundation. The real author must have been a well-educated man with regular access to rare and expensive source works (some of which were in foreign languages and not available in translation) and a background of broad, international experience from which to draw as he created the plays: just such a man was Henry Neville.

With Neville as the writer it is possible to investigate early anonymous works that were his juvenilia. Co-writing with others who also chose to be anonymous might further disguise Neville's part authorship of works such as *Locrine* and *Arden of Faversham* (Casson, 2009). We can understand why Shakespeare's plays were on stage when their writer was anonymous and why Shakspere did not appear until after they had been written. The earliest possible reference to William from Stratford in London was in 1592, namely the notoriously cryptic, satirical attack on "the upstart crow" by Greene/Chettle. Shakspere does not appear in the cast lists of Pembroke's or Strange's Men, yet these were the companies that performed the early Shakespeare plays. The earliest use of Shakespeare as the author's name was in 1593 with the publication of *Venus and Adonis.* The only record of "Willm Shakespeare" being paid for a theater performance (whether as actor or company manager/sharer is not clear) was in 1595. No play was attributed to him until *Love's Labour's Lost* was published as by "W. Shakespere" and *Richard II* and *Richard III* by "William Shake-speare" in 1598. Henry Neville listed the latter two and identified them as by William Shakespeare (spelled thus) on the Northumberland Manuscript in 1596–7. He was apparently the first person to know these works were by Shakespeare, up to two years before they were printed.

Above all it is the history plays themselves that demonstrate that Henry Neville was the author, for they are political plays showing the pre-eminent role of members of the Neville family in the succession crises of the realm. Identifying Neville as the playwright also explains why Shakespeare's perspective is that of the aristocratic governing class, why he focuses on the elite, on "kings and their aristocratic rivals," whereas other contemporary playwrights wrote "from a commoner's point of view" (Helgerson, 1992, 237–9, in Price, 2012, 258).

Henry Neville was politically ambitious and sought high office. His first pseudonym was Phaeton, which he used when he offered the Phaeton sonnet for publication in 1591. In effect he knew ambition was dangerous, and he not only used the Phaeton myth in the history plays but linked it to Falconbridge, a hidden Neville (Casson, 2009, 20). For Neville the Phaeton myth was prophetic because he himself fell during the Essex rebellion, but only after the secrecy he had so carefully practiced was betrayed by Essex and Southampton. Neville had multiple reasons for keeping his authorship secret. Above all, the politics of the situation demanded discretion. John Davies described

Neville as "discrete" in his 1603 poem *Microcosmos,* written, like George Carleton's *Heroici Characteres,* to welcome Neville's release from the Tower and praise him for his support for Essex (see Chapter 11).

Speculating on the Genesis of the History Plays

Throughout this book we have presented evidence backed up by primary sources: contemporary manuscript documents, letters, books, annotations. We have sought to present evidence and deliberately avoided speculating. We have done this because we know that many studies of Shakespeare use words such as "must have," "probably," and "is very likely to have." Now, however, we allow ourselves space to reflect and speculate, basing our ideas on the historical record in the hope that this may lead, through further research, to the discovery of new evidence.

The politics of Elizabeth I's reign were dominated by five men: Robert Dudley, Earl of Leicester; Francis Walsingham; William Cecil; his son Robert Cecil; and Robert Devereux, Earl of Essex. Henry Neville knew all these men. William Cecil, Lord Burghley, was secretary of state for fourteen years (1558–1572), then was made lord treasurer in 1572 until he died in 1598, when his son Robert took over his role. Francis Walsingham was secretary of state from 1573 until his death in 1590. Walsingham's sympathies were set early on as a Marian exile, escaping Queen Mary I's persecution of Protestants. He lived in Italy and Switzerland, developing skills in languages and friendships with other Marian exiles who included Henry Neville's father. Already experienced in foreign affairs, Walsingham became a diplomat for Elizabeth. He was in Paris with Henry Killigrew, Neville's father-in-law, during the St. Bartholomew's Day Massacre in 1572. Although he escaped unharmed, his anti–Catholic politics were, no doubt, confirmed by this experience. He became secretary of state soon after.

In 1583, Walsingham conducted a diplomatic mission to Scotland, accompanied by his friend, the diplomat Henry Killigrew.[2] They were also accompanied by two young men. These were Robert Devereux, Earl of Essex, and Henry Neville, who would marry Killigrew's daughter, Anne, that same year. While on this mission Neville was described by the Oxford academic, Dr. Richard Eedes, as "distinguished for his book-learning" (James and Rubinstein, 2005, 83). Neville had recently returned from four years travelling through Europe with his Oxford tutor, Henry Savile, and Robert Sidney, the brother of Philip Sidney. At this time, Philip Sidney, the poet who was to be a major influence on Shakespeare, had just married Walsingham's daughter, Frances, but within three years, she was widowed and married Robert Devereux, Earl of Essex, who, like Philip, was a soldier for Protestant causes and heir to Walsingham's spy network gathering intelligence in Europe.

The very year that Neville travelled to Scotland with him, Sir Francis Walsingham set up the theater company named Queen Elizabeth's Men. "The Queen's Men were a deliberately political company in origin, and their repertory appears to have followed the path no doubt pointed out for them by Sir Francis Walsingham." In the plays they acted, "one finds no conflict or disturbance that is not settled in the interests of Tudor conservatism"[3] (McMillin, 1987, 59). Shakespeare rewrote some of the Queen's Men's plays (including *King John, Richard III, Henry V* and *King Lear*). Pitcher (1962) showed there was evidence for Shakespeare's authorship of *The Famous Victories of Henry V,* the early play that was a source for *Henry IV* and *Henry V. The Famous Victories* introduced Sir John Oldcastle, the original Falstaff, and it features many incidents that we see developed in the Shakespeare plays. It also uses the same method of inserting unhistorical figures into the story to represent contemporary, politically powerful, courtiers. However, Pitcher (1962, 192, note 92) pointed out that there was also

> negative evidence to prove the topicality of such references. Ralph Neville (1364–1425), 1st Earl of Westmoreland, who, by testimony of the chronicles, had played a part in the deliberations prior to the declaration of war against France, is excluded in Scene 9 of *The Famous Victories,* almost certainly because his Elizabethan descendant, Charles Neville, 6th Earl of Westmoreland, was in exile abroad after his notorious attempt in 1569 to release Mary Stuart from captivity.

This is another example of the negative Neville bias we have found in the history plays when a Neville is removed from the story to protect the family name. When Shakespeare wrote *Henry IV* and *Henry V* he included Ralph Neville in the plays, but this may have been because Charles Neville was dying in poverty abroad and effectively forgotten by that time. Neville, however, did not forget Charles, because he corrected pages 730 and 987 of his copy of *A Catalogue of Honor*, which referred to his conspiracy with Henry Percy and escape abroad from execution. *The Famous Victories* was written in 1586. Pitcher (1962, 231) also showed that the annotations in the copy of Hall's *Chronicle* discovered by Alan and Lubbock (1954) were by the author of *The Famous Victories,* and these have been shown to be by Neville (James and Rubinstein, 2005). Casson (2010, 73) dated the annotation to 1586–96, so it is likely that the earliest use of these notes was during the writing of *The*

Famous Victories. Scoufos (1979, 179) proposed that Henry Evans wrote the play and Shakespeare later satirized him in *The Merry Wives of Windsor.* Evans was head of the Earl of Oxford's Boys theater company, and *The Famous Victories* includes a pro–Oxford bias. It is possible that the play was co-written, with Neville devising the plot and Evans writing the text.

One of the playwrights who wrote for the Queen's Men was George Peele, and *The Troublesome Raigne of John King* was one of their plays. There is evidence that Neville co-wrote this play (see Chapter 1) and later revised it after Peele's death. This leads us to speculate that Walsingham may have recruited the young Neville to write plays and ensured his secrecy. The company went into decline from 1588 and were replaced by the Admiral's Men and Lord Strange's Men, who then evolved into the Earl of Derby's Men. The latter worked with Pembroke's and Sussex's men to perform *Titus Andronicus* (as is stated on the title page of the 1594 quarto). Peele is believed to have had a hand in *Titus Andronicus.* Shakespeare was certainly associated with Lord Strange's Men, who performed *Henry VI* part 1 (see Chapter 6). When Lord Strange became Earl of Derby, Derby's Men may have performed *Edward III* (see Appendix B). Pembroke's Men performed the early version of *Henry VI* part 3 and *The Taming of A Shrew* (again according to the frontispiece of the 1595 and 1594 quartos). We may therefore trace a development of Neville's writing through these companies and his preference in these early plays for anonymity. We have evidence that Neville was associated with Walsingham and the Pembrokes. Furthermore, we have seen that the writers of *The Troublesome Raigne of John* foregrounded members of the Neville family and an Earl of Essex (see Chapter 1). Neville was a writer who knew all the major figures and was close to the heart of government, able to observe these powerful men and, like the bastard Falconbridge, sardonically reflect on their struggles.

We have also presented evidence that Neville knew Henry Wriothesley (see Appendix A). Shakespeare is believed to have been commissioned to write the early sonnets to persuade Henry Wriothesley, the young Earl of Southampton, to marry and procreate. These poems were probably commissioned by William Cecil, Lord Burghley, who wanted Wriothesley to marry his own granddaughter. In 1591 Burghley had commissioned John Clapham to write a Latin poem, *Narcissus,* for the same purpose (Duncan-Jones and Woudhuysen, 2007, 27). Shakespeare's sonnets refer to Narcissus and use the image of a rose, suggestive of Wriothesley, which can be pronounced "Rosely." Neville acknowledged at his trial that he had met Henry Wriothesley when he was a boy. Indeed, according to his Parliamentary biography,[4] Neville went to school at Burghley's, where later Wriothesley was also educated. In questioning where

Shakespeare gained his considerable medical and alchemical knowledge, Showerman (2013, 108) pointed out that Burghley "had a magnificent library with nearly 200 editions on alchemy and medical topics from all over Europe." Having experience of Burghley's school would also explain Shakespeare's ability to parody Burghley's advice to his son in Polonius's precepts for Laertes (Price, 2001, 276). On May 17, 1590, Neville wrote a letter to Lord Burghley about his ordnance manufacture and a conflict with the Earl of Warwick (Lansdowne MSS 25 in the British Library). All this serves to demonstrate that Neville was in the right social network, at the right time, to cooperate with Walsingham and Burghley. Neville's father and father-in-law knew and worked with both.

Shakespeare's collaboration with other authors is increasingly being recognized in mainstream academia. As a way of confusing the question of authorship, co-writing may have been a successful strategy to help conceal Neville's identity. When we see Neville as the senior member of a team, possibly initiated by Walsingham, his protection as a writer makes sense. It is possible that the use of the pseudonym "William Shakespeare" for the team as a whole, or for the team leader, was intended to disguise the identities of these writers. With Walsingham's death this team changed their allegiance to Essex. Neville, Peele, Gager and Carleton all supported Essex, as did Neville's tutor Henry Savile. With Essex's death, Neville became dangerously exposed, which may be one reason why Shakespeare stopped writing history plays and turned to tragedy at that time.

This book does not exhaust the evidence supporting Neville's authorship. Further research with computer-aided analysis could build on the work of James (2008) and Casson (2010), who have shown that Neville used rare vocabulary in his letters and notebooks, vocabulary that occurs too frequently in the Shakespeare plays to be dismissed as coincidence (see Chapters 5 and 10). We are confident that there will be more books on this subject providing more evidence of a previously concealed truth that we believe has now been finally revealed. Understanding the "discreete" life and "wellbeloved" character of Henry Neville (John Davies, 1603; see Chapter 11) will reveal new insights into the whole Shakespeare canon. In the year 2015, the four hundredth anniversary of Henry Neville's death, it is at last possible to say that "truth makes all things plain" (*A Midsummer Night's Dream,* 5.1.127).

Appendix A

The Earl of Southampton, *Richard III*, Shakespeare and Henry Neville

This appendix is a study written before we wrote the book. It repeats some material in Chapter 7. We have included it because it contains important evidence of Neville's authorship. Shakespeare dedicated two poems to the Earl of Southampton, and yet there is no extant evidence of any relationship between the Earl and William Shakspere from Stratford. This appendix shows that there was a long and intimate relationship between Henry Neville and Southampton over thirty years.

The Third Earl of Southampton and Henry Neville

From 1601 to 1603 the third Earl of Southampton, Henry Wriothesley, was incarcerated in the Tower of London as a result of his part in the Earl of Essex's rebellion. Also imprisoned there was Sir Henry Neville. He had been implicated by Essex at his trial on February 21, 1601. "It was Southampton whose testimony ... provided confirmation for Essex's original, highly unexpected claim that Neville, the respected Ambassador to France, was involved in treasonable conspiracy" (James and Rubinstein, 2005, 145, 159; James, 2008, 359; Stopes, 1922, 229).

Neville had originally met Southampton when he was a child, at Burghley's house, at some time during 1583–5. According to his parliamentary biography, Neville had been educated in Burghley's household in the 1570s.[1] Years later he told his secretary of an assault on Southampton in a letter dated January 29, 1601 (Sawyer, 1725, vol. 1, 292). He certainly met Southampton on February 2, 1601, during the lead-up to the Essex rebellion. In 1613 John Chamberlain wrote that Southampton was Neville's "great patron" because he was the foremost supporter in the latter's bid to become the secretary of state (McClure, 1939, vol. 1, 401). In a letter dated August 6, 1613, Southampton expressed his confidence that Sir Henry Neville would become secretary (Stopes, 1922, 363). Their close friendship was acknowledged by Henry Howard, Earl of Northampton, who, in a letter dated November 1613, wrote to Rochester describing Neville as Southampton's "Dear Damon."[2] The earl appeared to be referring to the play *Damon and Pythias* by Richard Edwards, which had been published in 1571 (James and Rubinstein, 2005, 246). Hamlet calls Horatio "O Damon dear" (3.2.275), in what is believed to be a reference to this play (Thompson and Taylor, 2006, 318). Since the Greek legend tells of two friends, both of whom were imprisoned and under threat of execution, and were later pardoned, this reference in *Hamlet* resembles Neville and Southampton's situation in 1601–3.

"Neville and Southampton were related because both of them sprang from a common Neville ancestor—Ralph Neville, Earl of Westmoreland" (James, 2008, 124). Westmoreland appears on stage in Shakespeare's *Henry IV* parts 1 and 2 and *Henry V.* Southampton was also descended from John Neville, a younger brother of Richard Neville, the Kingmaker. John appears on stage as the Marques of Montague in *Henry VI* part 3. (For more genealogical information showing Southampton's descent from the Nevilles see Stopes, 1922, 18, 488.)

The Encomium of Richard III

Henry Wriothesley, the Earl of Southampton, dedicated a document about Richard III to "Sr Henry Nevill" (James and Rubinstein, 2005, 320). He signed it, "Your Honoures most affectionat Servante" (see addendum 1, below). This is to be found in the British Library (Additional MS 29307). It has been dated to circa 1600 by previous scholars. However, having examined it carefully, Casson found it was written on paper watermarked 1603: the date is very clear on the last sheet, but the same watermark can be seen on the dedication page and folios 3 and 15. The date is just visible on the first two. This watermark, of two columns surmounted by a bunch of grapes (the grapes are visible on folios 7, 8, 11 and 14), is listed in two books the British Library holds on watermarks (Heawood, 1950, and Churchill, 1935). The earliest dates for examples of this watermark are 1615 and 1625. Therefore the watermarks of Additional MS 29307 predate these by at least twelve years. Dr. Arnold Hunt of the British Library Manuscripts Department, commenting on the paper used in this manuscript, wrote: "Most of the paper used in England at this period came from France, where the new year officially began on 1 January, so this paper could have been made at any time after 1 January 1603" (e-mail to author, September 13, 2010).

Henry Wriothesley, Earl of Southampton, and Henry Neville were released from the Tower of London by James I on April 9, 1603 (Stopes, 1922, 260). The document could therefore have been written in the Tower of London before their release; indeed this is more likely, for after their release Southampton would not have had so much time on his hands to write such a long document. That Wriothesley signed the dedication to Neville as plain "Hen: W": in small letters, without any title, when he signed letters after his release with a large "H. Southampton," suggests that it was written during his incarceration, when he had been stripped of his titles and reduced to plain Mr. Henry Wriothesley. Two documents written by Southampton while in prison were signed "H. Wriothesley" (Salisbury, 1906, vol. 11, 72–3).

The document is actually based on an *Encomium* in support of Richard III written by Sir William Cornwallis. Zeeland (1940, 949) established that the document must have been written during 1583–1603. As Cornwallis was born circa 1579, it is likely he wrote it at the end of this period. He published essays in 1600 and 1601, but these did not include his defense of Richard III, so it is possible that the *Encomium* was written as late as 1601. This late dating could suggest a possible political motive for the essay: if Richard III was not all bad, perhaps the disgraced Essex, who was executed in 1601, might also be rehabilitated. While not apparently involved in the Essex rebellion, Cornwallis "lived quietly for the rest of Queen Elizabeth's reign and was for a time in Edinburgh[3] where he introduced Sir Thomas Overbury to Robert Carr" (Kincaid, 2004; ODNB, 2004, vol. 13, 488). Overbury became a friend of Henry Neville.

Kincaid (1977), who undertook a major study of the *Encomium,* was unsure of the date but suggested it was written in the late 1590s and that the earliest extant copy was at Chatsworth House. This is the Hardwick MSS 44, which is undated. Casson examined it and found a previously unnoticed watermark.

This discovery offers the possibility that we can tentatively date the document. Though visible, the watermark is obscured on the pages that are written over on both sides, but on the final sheet, where there is no writing, it is clear enough to identify it as one of the pot motifs illustrated by Heawood (1950).

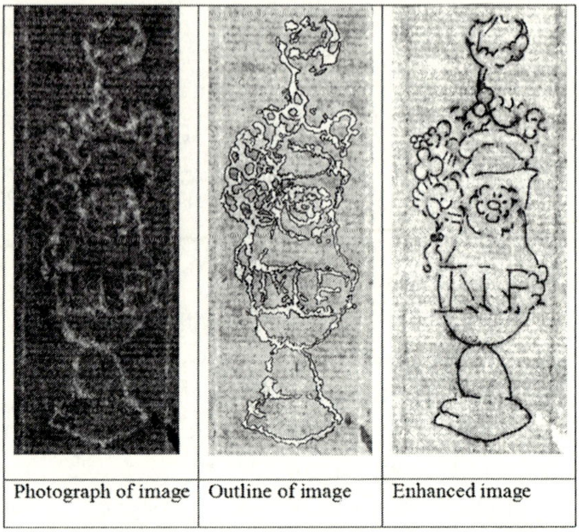

Hardwick MSS 44, Devonshire Collection, Chatsworth (by permission of the Chatsworth Settlement Trustees).

This one-handled pot is a synthesis of six examples of the pot motif illustrated in Heawood's plate 480, numbers 3549–3554. All these watermarks have capital letters running across the center of the pot: the Hardwick MSS 44 watermark seems to have the letters NF (or possibly NP) in this place. Heawood's watermarks are dated from 1589 to 1598. It seems reasonable to see the Hardwick MSS 44 version as a development of the simpler versions in Heawood: the crown in Hardwick MSS 44 seems more elaborate and there appear to be roses above the pot and below the rim. It would therefore be possible to suggest a date in the second half of the 1590s: from 1595 to 1600. Heawood locates all these watermarks in London. The paper is brown, and English paper was coarser than the whiter papers made in France.

Another document with a very similar pot watermark is a letter from Sir Henry Neville to a noble lord written 1603–4.[4] This watermark is also to be found in the paper of the Hand D section of *Sir Thomas More*, believed to have been written by Shakespeare himself. The revisions of *Sir Thomas More* that include Hand D have recently been dated to 1603–4 (Jowett, 2011, 432).

The watermark on Southampton's version of the *Encomium* is of columns enclosing the date 1603, surmounted by grapes. The grapes watermark (without columns or date) is to be found on a letter from Henry Neville to Robert Cecil, written, partly in cipher, from Paris, on January 14, 1600

The pot motif watermark (Vian Smith).

(National Archives at Kew, PRO 30/50/70/8). The Bodleian Library copy of the Richard III *Encomium* (Rawlinson D 718) likewise has the grapes watermark. Heawood (1950) has a watermark (2090) from a letter dated 1604 that is very close in design to the Rawlinson D718 mark. This manuscript predates Southampton's version but depends on the Chatsworth manuscript; indeed Kincaid (1977, v) thought it might have been a revision by Cornwallis himself. The grapes watermark may therefore suggest Rawlinson D 718 could be dated circa 1600. It seems likely that this, or some other lost copy of the manuscript, was the original that Southampton copied in his version.

Shakespeare's play *Richard III* was written c. 1592 but may not have been seen in London until the theaters reopened after the plague in 1594. The *Encomium* could therefore have been a response to the play: so dark a portrait of a king who had reigned just one hundred years earlier was bound to provoke a reaction. This matches the possible dating of the Chatsworth watermark, suggesting the *Encomium* was written during 1595–1601. The fact that Shakespeare is not named in the *Encomium* might point to its having been written before 1598, when the second quarto of *Richard III* first identified the author as "William Shake-speare." Indeed the fact that the *Encomium* does not depend on the text of Shakespeare's play would suggest the writer might have seen the play but did not have the text to hand: this would suggest a dating for the *Encomium* before the play was first printed in 1597. Cornwallis did enjoy the theater. In a verse epistle to John Donne he wrote (circa 1598–1600):

> If then for change, of howers you seem careless
> Agree wth me to lose them at the playes [Whitt, 1932, 161].

A sequence can therefore be suggested:

1592–4	Shakespeare's *Richard III* written and first performed.
1595–1601	Cornwallis composed the *Encomium:* Hardwick MSS 44, Chatsworth.
c. 1600–1	Second copy of the *Encomium:* Rawlinson D 718, Bodleian, Oxford.
1603	Southampton's *Encomium:* Additional MS 29307, British Library, London.

John Chamberlain wrote, in a letter dated December 18, 1604, "Here is speech that ... Sir *Henry Neville*" was a possible ambassador "for *Spaine.*" Neville did not become ambassador. It was Cornwallis's father, Sir Charles, who instead went as ambassador to Spain in 1605. It is likely therefore that Neville would have known Cornwallis, father and son.

Southampton and the Encomium

Morton, the Bishop of Ely, appears on stage in *Richard III.* He is a supporter of Richard, indeed abjectly fawns on him, immediately rushing off to satisfy him when Richard asks for some strawberries. This incident was reported by Sir Thomas More in his *History of King Richard III.* More had been a page in Morton's household (Hammond, 1985, 338). A possible lost source for the *Encomium* was a manuscript by John Morton, Bishop of Ely, said by Sir George Buck to have been in the possession of "Mr. Roper of Eltham." According to another note by Buck, Sir Edward Hoby saw the book, and this is thought to have been at some time before 1596 (Kincaid, 1977, iii). In 1596 Sir John Harrington said he had heard that Sir Thomas More's *History of King Richard III* was based on Morton's manuscript. The Ropers were More's relatives: More's daughter married William Roper. The Ropers of Eltham leased a house in Holborn from the Earl of Southampton. "The Ropers had substantial legal connections with Southampton" (Kincaid, 1977, iv). Cornwallis also lived in Holborn. This evidence would seem to confirm the *Encomium* was written during 1596–1601.

In dedicating the earliest manuscript of the *Encomium* to the poet John Donne, Cornwallis stated that he wanted to restore "this defamed Prince, whose life lately **reading**": this suggests he had been reading a biography, most probably works by Morton and/or More. John Donne's mother was related to Sir Thomas More. In the late 1590s Donne emerged in London society, becoming secretary to Sir Thomas Egerton in 1597–8. From 1597 Cornwallis was the member of Parliament for Lostwithiel. Donne, Cornwallis and Henry Neville were, with Southampton, supporters of the Earl of Essex. Cornwallis was knighted in 1599 for his part in Essex's Irish campaign (Kincaid, 2004; ODNB, 2004, vol. 13, 488). In James I's reign Cornwallis and Neville were both especially involved in the parliamentary work to establish the Union with Scotland. Donne and Neville were members of the Mitre Club 1608–11 (Gayley, 1914, 147–8). Katherine, Southampton's aunt (his father's sister) married Sir Thomas Cornwallis (Stopes, 1922, 5, 46, 311).

We know Southampton was keen on the theater. In 1599 Rowland White wrote to Sir Robert Sydney, "My Lord Southampton and Lord Rutland come not to the court ... they pass away the time in London merely in going to plaies every day" (Collins, 1746, ii. 132). In January 1605 Southampton staged *Love's Labour's Lost* for Queen Anne (Stopes, 1922, 173, 289).

Southampton changed the text of Cornwallis's *Encomium* in two places that show his interest in theater. Halfway through (on folio 8) he altered the text from "the partiall writings of an vndiscreete Cronicler a fauorer of the Lancastrian familye." To "the partiall writings of undiscreete Croniclers and **witty Play-makers**." On the penultimate page (f 16v) Southampton added: "but that wee must still make him more Cruelle infamous **in pamphletts and playes**." These additions suggest Southampton was referring to Shakespeare's plays *Richard III* and *Henry VI* parts 2 and 3 (in which Richard also appears). *The First Part of the Contention* (*Henry VI* part 2) had appeared in quarto in 1594; *The True Tragedy of Richard Duke of York* (*Henry VI* part 3) was published in 1595 and the First Quarto of *Richard III* appeared in 1597. All three were published anonymously. It was in the following year, 1598, that the Second Quarto of *Richard III* appeared as by "William Shake-speare"[5]: this was the very earliest that any play had been attributed to this name. The name "Nevil" occurs eight times in *Henry VI* part 2, which is the first play in which Richard appears (see Chapter 6).

In 1594 *Rape of Lucrece* had been published as by William Shakespeare. In the dedication to Henry Wriothesley, the Earl of Southampton, the bard refers to this work as a "pamphlet." Roe (1998, 140) stated that "in Shakespeare's day "pamphlet" could mean any form of publication including all literary genres." Therefore we might infer that by stating that Richard III's infamy was broadcast "**in pamphletts and playes**," Southampton could be referring to the printed quartos and the performances of the plays.

Southampton added more passages to Cornwallis's original, quite changing the nature of the document. Whereas Cornwallis had written a historical study and was attempting to redress the balance in Richard's favor, Southampton distorted this document for a political purpose: he was using the history as a metaphor for the present. Kincaid (1977, v–vi) analyzed these changes and concluded that the document had been sent to Neville to persuade him to join the Essex rebellion in 1600. However, the watermark dating of 1603 means that we must now see it as a belated self-justification with Southampton offering arguments to support taking action: he wrote, "New necessities require new remedies" and the ancient nobility should challenge "new Statistes" (which Kincaid took to be a reference to the Cecils). Hamlet refers to "our statists" (5.2.33), Shakespeare using this word just once, before Southampton used it in his *Encomium* (though the singular, "statist," is in *Cymbeline:* 2.4.16). Southampton is cautiously cryptic and ends his attempt to rehabilitate the last Plantagenet king, who had Neville blood in his veins, playfully writing, "I hold this but as a Paradox."

This use of history as metaphor for the present is to be seen in Shakespeare's history plays and in Henry Neville's own manuscript copy of *Leicester's*

Commonwealth (Worsley MSS 47; Casson, 2010). Richard III is referred to several times in the latter and Henry Wriothesley's father, the Second Earl of Southampton, also figures.

Southampton's great, great-grandfather, John Writhe, as the Garter King of Arms, officiated at the coronation of Richard III. Neville corrected his copy of *A Catalogue of Honor*, naming "John" as "Garter, Principall King at Armes" on page 1029. His younger son Thomas's "last public work was to superintend the gorgeous ceremonial of the coronation of Anne Boleyn" (Stopes, 1922, 485). This scene is represented in Shakespeare's *Henry VIII* with the Garter King of Arms "wearing his coat of arms and a gilt copper crown" (4.1.36.13). Sir Thomas changed the family name to Wriothesley. His brother's son, another Thomas, became the first Earl of Southampton and was an executor of Henry VIII's will (Stopes, 1922, 486). Henry Neville's father was also a signatory of that testament.

Shakespeare, Neville and Southampton

Rychard the third is listed on the Northumberland Manuscript, just below the name William Shakespeare. This manuscript was owned by Henry Neville (the name "Nevill" is visible, with the family motto, at the top left of the page) and it has been dated to 1596–7.

In dedicating his version of the *Encomium* to Henry Neville, Southampton seems to point to his authorship of *Richard III.* We can compare his dedication to Neville of the *Encomium* with Shakespeare's dedications to Southampton in *Venus and Adonis* and *The Rape of Lucrece.* Both writers are self-depreciatory: Shakespeare in *Venus and Adonis* writes of his "unpolished lines" and in *The Rape of Lucrece* "untutored lines." Southampton regrets his work is "not trickt up with elegancie of phrase" and describes it as "this small porcion of my privat Laboures." Shakespeare in *Venus and Adonis* writes, "**But if** the first heir of my invention prove deformed, **I shall** be sorry..."; "**if your** honour seem but **pleased**"; and promises "some graver **labour**." Southampton states, "**But** howsoever **yf you please** to accept **I shall** think my **Laboures** well bestowed." Both use the words "your honour." Both begin with the words:

SHAKESPEARE: "To the Right Honourable..."
SOUTHAMPTON: "To the Honourable..."

Both end their dedications similarly:

SHAKESPEARE (*Venus & Adonis*): "Your Honour's in all duty."
SOUTHAMPTON: "Your Honoures most affectionat Servante."

While these similarities may be due simply to convention, it is nevertheless possible that Southampton was recalling Shakespeare's dedications. (See addendum 1 below for Southampton's dedication to Neville.) James (2008, 239) found the rough draft of a letter written by Neville in the Berkshire Records Office Archives (D/EN/F6/2/3), which she identified as due to be sent to Southampton c. 1604, asking for help in recouping his financial losses.[6] She showed how the language of this letter matched that in the dedication to *The Rape of Lucrece* and *Hamlet.*

Shakespeare certainly loved Wriothesley, as is evident in his sonnets and the dedications of *Venus and Adonis* (1593) and *The Rape of Lucrece* (1594). Southampton returned that love to Neville: in his dedication he describes the *Encomium* as "an ernest peny of my love." No evidence has ever been found that shows any connection whatsoever between the earl and William Shakspere from Stratford.

A further link is apparent between Southampton's *Encomium* and Shakespeare's sonnets. The final sentence of Southampton's manuscript includes these words: "This Paradoxe of myne as a Charytable **well wisheinge** to a scandalyzed and defamed kinge; Yett for all this knowe, I holde this but as a Paradoxe" (folio 17r). This is different from the earlier manuscript versions at Chatsworth and the Bodleian, which have the words "well wisher" (Kincaid, 1977, 32).

The *Encomium* was eventually printed in 1616 by Thomas Thorpe, who had published Shakespeare's Sonnets in 1609. In the dedication to those Sonnets the words "**well-wishing** adventurer" occur. "Well-wishing," with a hyphen, is the usage in the printed *Encomium* of 1616, providing further evidence that Thorpe took Southampton's version as the basis for this printed text. According to the LION and EEBO databases no other writer used "well-wishing," with a hyphen, during 1603–9 (except John Norden who wrote "wel-wishing" with one "l" in *The surueyors dialogue* in 1607). The dedication to the Sonnets is another document that ties Southampton together with Shakespeare and Neville (James, 2008). The sequence therefore is this:

1603: Southampton, "well-wishing";
1607: Norden, "wel-wishing";
1609: Shakespeare, "WELL-WISHING";
1616: Anon, the printed *Encomium on Richard III*, "well-wishing."

Both the title pages of the 1598 quarto of *Richard III* and the 1609 Sonnets spell "Shake-speare" with a hyphen.

Neville and the Encomium

Kincaid (1977, i) traced the history of the *Encomium* to Sir Thomas More's *History of King Richard III,* which was published by John Rastell. More's *History* was the most important source for Shakespeare's *Richard III* (Jowett, 2000, 1; Hammond, 1985, 75–78). Neville was aware of John Rastell's three-volume legal encyclopaedia, the *Graunde Abridgement,* referring to it in his copy of *Leicester's Commonwealth* (Casson, 2010, 98, 167). John Rastell was Sir Thomas More's brother-in-law, a lawyer, playwright and publisher. More, Rastell and Neville's grandfather, Edward, were all present at the Field of the Cloth of Gold in 1520. Southampton's great-uncle Sir Thomas Wriothesley was also there. In Shakespeare's *Henry VIII,* the Duke of Norfolk describes the "earthly glory" of this splendid diplomatic extravaganza to Lord Abergavenny, George Neville, brother of Edward. George Neville was son-in-law to the Duke of Buckingham, who is also present in this scene. Later we witness Buckingham's fall (see Chapter 8). Thomas More's father, John, who had been Buckingham's solicitor, was one of the judges at his treason trial (Guy, 2009, 71).

Neville's great-uncle, Thomas Neville, was elected speaker of the House of Commons in 1515, knighted and became a royal counsellor (Guy, 2009, 56, 165). More and Thomas Neville were friends: Neville's servants were mentioned in a comic Christmas entertainment at More's house in 1525 (Guy, 2009, 165). Thomas Neville had a successful career, unaffected by the disgrace of one brother (George) and the execution of another (Edward). He became wealthy, and Charles Brandon, the Duke of Suffolk, pawned jewels worth £700 with him. Henry Neville specifically named Charles Brandon in his annotations to his copy of *Leicester's Commonwealth.* Brandon appears on stage in *Henry VIII.* His father William appears as Henry VII's standard-bearer at Bosworth in *Richard III* (5.4.4.) and is killed at the battle of Bosworth (5.7.14). The *Encomium* recounts that it was Richard III himself who slew Sir William Brandon. Southampton added the detail that he was "stout" (f 16). This suggests some personal knowledge: Charles Brandon was godfather to Southampton's father.

One unique annotation in Neville's copy of *Leicester's Commonwealth* is "Doct Shawe." Shakespeare mentions Doctor Shaw in *Richard III* (3.5.97). Shaw is also mentioned in the *Encomium.*

Neville was conducting historical research while imprisoned in the Tower: indeed his notebook, Worsley MSS 40, dated 1602, is in the Lincoln Archives. This contains Neville's annotations about laws, coronation ceremonial, noble families' pedigrees and the history of Parliament. In the latter he refers to Grafton, who was one of Shakespeare's sources for *Henry VI* part 2. He lists statutes dating from Edward I through many reigns including Richard II, Henry IV and V. He briefly refers to Richard III when he was "d. Glouster in nominee Rex."

We may therefore reasonably infer that Neville and Wriothesley discussed history during their sojourn in the Tower. This period in the Tower would have been full of ominous meaning for Neville; many of his ancestors had been imprisoned there and his grandfather Edward was buried in the chapel.

Neville himself mentioned Richard III in a speech he made to the House of Lords in 1607. He had been chosen to represent the Commons in discussions about the Union of England and Scotland. He warned the Lords that if the Scots continued their special relationship with the French this could endanger the union: "How dangerous this may be we may guess by the example of Richard III," he said (Duncan, 1974, 209).

The Neville and Cornwallis families eventually intermarried. Richard Neville, third Baron Braybrooke (1783–1858), published anonymously in 1842 *The Private Correspondence of Jane, Lady Cornwallis, 1613–1644.* In 1608 Jane (Bacon, née Meautys) had married Sir William Cornwallis (the elder, William Cornwallis's uncle, who died in 1611). Richard Cornwallis Neville was the fourth Baron Braybrooke, 1820–1861. Henry Neville's portrait still hangs in the Braybrookes' Audley End House.

Publication of Southampton's Version of the Encomium

The *Encomium* was eventually printed in a collection of *Essays of Certain Paradoxes* in 1616 by Thomas Thorpe, who had published Shakespeare's Sonnets in 1609. The date of publication of the *Encomium,* 1616, is one year after Neville died, two years after Cornwallis had died. It must have been popular, as it was reprinted in 1617. A copy of the 1616 edition is to be found in the library at Audley End House.

The printed version is based on the Earl of Southampton's copy: it includes virtually all the additions he made to the text, including "witty Playmakers" and "but that we must still make him more cruelly infamous in Pamphlets and Playes." It does not have any dedication. It was also anonymous. "The author hateth nothing more than coming in publick," wrote Henry Olney in his dedication to Cornwallis's *Essays.* However, the fact that the version printed by Thomas Thorpe is that given by Southampton to Neville is evidence of a connection between Neville and Thorpe, who had published Shakespeare's sonnets. Given that Southampton's unique hand-written copy of the *Encomium* was given to Neville, this copy must have been the source document for Thorpe's printing, though he must have been told not to include the dedication to Neville. This is similar to Neville's express preference that Carleton's dedication to him of the *Heroici Characteres* be removed in a second printing (see Chapter 10). Cornwallis himself wrote in a letter to Sir John Hobart, who had commended the Paradoxes, that "in keeping them secret, he had shown some little discretion" (Whitt, 1932, 161). He was not the only one who preferred to keep his writing secret, though such secrecy resulted in the authorship being attributed to another man.

Why Did Southampton Choose to Dedicate This Document to Henry Neville?

Southampton and Neville were both in the Tower of London 1601–3, the scene of Richard III's crimes, so vividly portrayed in Shakespeare's play. Perhaps they discussed the historical events in which members of their families had taken part. It is possible that Southampton was attempting, albeit playfully, to justify himself in Neville's eyes: if a bad king was not so bad then maybe Southampton himself was not so bad. He himself had betrayed Neville. Is Neville referring to Southampton's betrayal in Sonnet 34?

> For no man well of such a salve can speak
> That heals the wound and cures not the disgrace:
> Nor can thy shame give physic to my grief;
> Though thou repent, yet I have still the loss:
> The offender's sorrow lends but weak relief
> To him that bears the strong offence's cross.
> Ah! but those tears are pearl which thy love sheds,
> And they are rich and ransom all ill deeds.

The very next sonnet follows on with:

> No more be grieved at that which thou hast done:
> **Roses** have thorns, and silver fountains mud;
> Clouds and eclipses stain both moon and sun,
> And loathsome canker lives in sweetest bud.

The choice of the rose imagery points to Wriothesley, which was spelled "W**rose**ly" in the baptismal register for his son in 1607 (Stopes, 1922, 313).

Green (1993) provided compelling evidence to support the view that the rose imagery in the sonnets refers to Wriotheseley. The very first sonnet, encouraging the young Southampton to breed, refers to him as "beauty's rose." The above sonnets of betrayal make sense when we are able to identify Shakespeare as Neville in the Tower, with Southampton. The poems show Neville working through his friend's betrayal and triumphing over the circumstances: however wounded, the friendship survived, and we can see Southampton's work on Richard III as a peace offering.

Conclusion

There is documentary evidence associating Henry Neville with the Earl of Southampton over thirty years. A pattern of interweaving themes appears, of Southampton, Neville, Shakespeare and Richard III. There is no evidence whatsoever linking William Shakspere from Stratford with the Earl of Southampton.

Addendum 1:
The Dedication to Henry Neville in MS Additional 29307

To the honourable Sir Henry Neuill knighte.

I am bold to adventure to your hono^{rs} viewe this small porcion of my privat labo^{rs}, as an earnest peny of my loue, beinge a mere Paradoxe in prayse of a mostt blame worthie, and Condemned prince kinge Richard ye third; who albeit I shold guilde with farr better termes of eloquence then I have don, and sweate myself to deathe in pursuite of his Commendacions, yet his disgrace beinge soe publicke, and the worlde soe opinionate of his misdoings as I shold not be able soe farr to iustifie him, as they to condemne him yett that they may see what may be saide and shewe how farr they haue mispraysed his virtues, this followinge Treatise shall make manyfest. Your Hono^{r} may pervse and censure yt at your best leisure, and though yt be not trickt vp with elegancye of phrase yet may it satisfie a right curious Iudgemente, yf the reasons be Considered as they oughte: But howsoever yf you please to accepte it I shall think my Labo^{rs} well bestowed; who bothe in this and what elles I may devote myself to Your Hono^{r}, and rest

Your Hono^{rs} most affectionat Servante,
Hen: W:

APPENDIX B

What's a Pelican Doing in *Edward III*?

A Tudor Interpretation of a Plantagenet History Play

Edward III is a history play about aspects of the reign of King Edward III (1327–77; see Chapter 2). The play has been accepted as at least in part by Shakespeare and therefore it has been included in the Shakespeare canon[1] (Sams, 1996; Blakemore, 1997; Melchiori, 1998). Acts 1 and 2 are identified as most strongly Shakespearean, while the collaborator largely responsible for acts 3–5 has yet to be conclusively identified (Watt, 2009). This appendix is based principally on Giorgio Melchiori's edition of *Edward III.*

Historically, King Edward III and his oldest son, Prince Edward, the Black Prince, have been lauded in England as leaders who achieved significant military victories. Unlike most of the dramatis personae, the king and the prince feature in every act of the play *Edward III.* As such, their characters and relationship appear to be a principal unifying theme.

English victories against the French at Crecy (1346) and Poitiers (1556) and the siege and surrender of Calais (1347) are dramatized in acts 3, 4 and 5 respectively. Acts 1 and 2 describe sieges of a different kind. In act 1, the king relieves a Scottish siege of Roxburgh, where the Countess of Salisbury is ensconced (1341). In act 2, it is the king who is besieging the countess in his desire to bed her. The king fails in his siege of the countess, but, in the process, demonstrates dishonorable behavior in his contempt for his own wife and son, as well as for the countess, her husband and her father.

The theme of honor is flagged early in the play by Prince Edward, who says, "Within this school of honour I shall learn" (1.1.165). Honor, or lack of it, is spectacularly demonstrated with eloquence and drama in act 2. We will now explore this theme for the whole play.

Melchiori identified Bandello's 1554 story about King Edward III and the Countess of Salisbury as a source for acts 1 and 2, noting that this novella was "written in 1547 upon hearing of the death of Rome's arch enemy, Henry VIII, who spilled so much blood" (Melchiori, 1998, 36). Despite this, few commentators have considered that this theme might have been continued in the play *Edward III.*

Melchiori identified numerous interpretive difficulties and anomalies with the historical narrative in this play. For example, the father–daughter relationship between principal characters in acts 1 and 2, the countess and Warwick, is at odds with history. So is the presence of Audley and Derby at Crecy in act 3. For an English monarch, King Edward appears particularly dishonorable compared to Bandello's story as translated by William Painter. In contrast to the earlier Bandello/Painter version, which had a bachelor King Edward marrying a widowed countess (Painter, 1566, 334), the play's story is more historically correct, with the married king considering adultery with the married countess. Furthermore, in the play, the king's relationship with his son at times appears very fraught (2.2.107–8, 3.4.36–7, 3.4.121–126).

These are resolved if they are considered as metaphors for Tudor royal behavior. The play acquires an emotional integrity if this covert critique of the reign of King Henry VIII (1509–47) is recognized.

The Picture of the Bonny Bullen

There are two word-pictures portrayed in act 3 (3.1.175–9 and 3.4.121–126), the meanings of which have been considered problematic. These pictures appear to be the creation of the author without any source from either Froissart's or Holinshed's *Chronicles.*

In the first scene of act 3, a mariner describes to the French king a battle between the French and English navies. This naval battle bears some resemblance to the Battle of Sluys in 1340, with one fleet described as "a grove of withered pines" (3.1.66), similar to Froissart's description of the French fleet by Sluys, as "so great a nombre of shippes that their mastes semed to be lyke a gret wood" (Melchiori, 1998, 108). But there are obvious anachronisms in this scene, such as the use of cannon fire (3.1.121–3), and the Spanish term "armado" (3.1.64). The term "armado" was not in wide English use before the attack of the Spanish Armada in 1588. Cannons were first placed on warships in Henry VIII's reign, not two hundred years before. Within his description of this naval battle, the mariner pictured two specific warships that sank.

> We liuely pictured, how the one for fame;
> The other by compulſion laid abont;
> Much did the *Nom per illa*, that braue ſhip;
> So did the blacke ſnake of Bullen, then which
> *A* bonnier veſſel neuer yet ſpred ſayle,

***Edward III* 1596 quarto (3.1.175–9) (Thomas Fisher Rare Book Library, University of Toronto).**

It is generally accepted that the letters italicized in the quarto[2] refer to the warship called the *Nonpareille*, which was a leading warship that fought the Spanish Armada in 1588—not a French navy at Sluys in 1340. Neither Melchiori (1998, 113) nor Sams (1996, 116) considered that the "Bullen" may also be an anachronism or metaphor.

Melchiori interpreted the "Bullen" in this passage of text to refer to a ship from Boulogne, even though there is no historical record of this ship and this French port does not feature in the play. It would be odd for the French to name a ship the "Snake of Boulogne" as suggested by Melchiori. Furthermore, it is also peculiar that the dramatist should extravagantly describe a French ship, saying that "a bonnier vessel never yet spread sail" (3.1.179). Such unusual praise would surely be only reserved for an English warship, and it is very unlikely for the English to name one of their own ships after a French port.

"Bullen" is the spelling of Anne Boleyn's surname in Shakespeare's *Henry VIII* and in Holinshed's *Chronicles.* There is record of a warship called the *Anne Boleyn*, named after Elizabeth I's mother and seemingly commissioned by Henry VIII in 1526 (Weir, 2012, 215). Unfortunately, records of this ship are poor.

Before Henry VIII's infatuation with Anne Bullen, Mary Bullen was Henry VIII's mistress for three to five years, beginning in 1522 (Loades, 2011, 51). Also in 1522, a captured French warship was commissioned into the English navy and renamed the *Bark of Bullen* (Derrick, 1806, 17, 19, 20, 23, 25).[3] The *Bark of Bullen* was part of the English navy during the reigns of Henry VIII, Edward VI and Elizabeth I, but not during the reign of Mary I.[4] Presumably, the Catholic queen Mary understood that this ship was named after one of the Bullen sisters, and decommissioned it. There is also a record in 1523 of the king's ship called the *Mary Boleyn* (Loades, 2011, 52), which may or may not be the same ship.

Much as the *Nonpareille* was misspelled, it is proposed that the ship (or "bark," as in 3.1.90) called the *Bark of Bullen*, has been misspelled. Perhaps the "snake of Bullen" is a flawed reference to the historical English warship, the *Bark of Bullen*.

The first quarto of *Edward III* appears to have been printed by Cuthbert Burby from the author's own manuscript (Sams, 1996, 214). Burby's compositors are not renowned for accuracy (Evans, 1984, 208), and it seems that they were not aware of the sixty-ton *Bark of Bullen*, one of twenty-four warships in the Royal Navy, just ten years before the attack by the Spanish Armada (Derrick, 1806, 25). One of the most famous ships to battle the Spanish Armada in 1588, the *Nonpareille*, appears to have been treated as a Latin quotation.

The compositors of the First Quarto have italicized the name of one ship and not the other. They generally only italicized stage directions and Latin quotations, such as "*Ave Casar*" (sic) in 1.1.164. It appears as though the italicization of "*Nom per illa,*" as well as its misspelling and its division into three separate words, was thus probably due to the misapprehension that it was a Latin quotation. In contrast, French quotations in the First Quarto, such as "Vive el Roy" (sic) for "Vive le roi" (3.3.165) and "Mordiu" (sic) for "Mort Dieu" (4.6.40), were not italicized.

Just as the compositors appear to treat one of the most famous ships to battle the Spanish Armada in 1588 as a Latin quotation, the compositors may not have been aware of the sixty-ton *Bark of Bullen*, one of twenty-four warships in the Royal Navy in 1578 (Derrick, 1806, 25).

Melchiori interpreted this text as a reference to a ship called the "Black Snake of Boulogne," presuming that three initial letters should be capitalized. In the First Quarto though, only "Bullen" has an initial capital letter. As apparent in the facsimile of the First Quarto above, the initial letter of "snake" was printed with the long Elizabethan "s" shape. The compositor may have interpreted the initial letter of the hand-written "Bark" of the original manuscript as a long "s." We have already suggested that the compositor did not anticipate a proper name of a warship when compositing "Nonpareille."

It is proposed therefore that the compositor, not wise to the ships of the English navy, misread the original manuscript in which *Bark of Bullen* was hand-written, and consequently set his type to resemble "ſnake of Bullen." This requires fewer compositor errors than appear in "*Nom per illa*" from "Nonpareille." Understanding this warship to be the *Bark of Bullen*, a known Tudor warship as recorded in Samuel Pepys's notes (Derrick, 1806, 25), like the *Nonpareille*, resolves its otherwise contrary meaning and makes sense with respect to naval history, albeit Tudor.

As the adjective "black" does not originally begin with a capital, it does not necessarily form part of the warship's name. Rather, "black" has a specific emotional resonance that connects it with other elements in this play, which will become evident when these are discussed.

The ship called "the black Bark of Bullen" requires fewer compositing errors to arrive at the text of the first quarto, and has much greater explanatory power, than does Melchiori's "Black Snake of Boulogne."

The Lord Chamberlain's Mother

When Mary Bullen died in 1543, her young son and the future lord chamberlain, Henry Carey, "was taken into the royal household" (Loades, 2011, 177–8). As a novice soldier, he accompanied Lord Admiral John Dudley at Portsmouth in 1545, where the English army was stationed and English navy was anchored (Bindoff, 1982). His uncle, John Carey, was vice admiral of the navy. John Carey was also the stepfather of the fifteen-year-old Francis Walsingham, the future spymaster, advisor to Queen Elizabeth I and founder of the theater company the Queen's Men in 1583.

This suggests a tantalizing possibility. When at Portsmouth, Henry Carey may have seen the warship named after his mother, and watched the Battle of the Solent that same year. In that year, with cannons blazing, the French navy attacked the English navy at anchor in Portsmouth harbor. It is intriguing to consider that this may have been a moment of great emotional resonance to a young Henry Carey in the wake of his mother's death two years before, and which the dramatist transformed into metaphor.

Furthermore, less than fifty years later, in July and August 1591, Henry Carey, now lord chamberlain as well as governor of the English army, organized the itinerary and accommodation at Cowdray House for his cousin, Queen Elizabeth I, when she visited during her progress through Sussex (Cole, 1999, 31; Heale, 2007). At an inspection of Cowdray House, Henry Carey would have seen the large painting of the Battle of the Solent (Davies, 2002, 60–4). This picture illustrated the naval battle and the Portsmouth army encampment where he was stationed as a novice soldier, forty-six years previously. In addition, it documents two ships sinking. Neither ship was the *Nonpareille*, or the *Bark of Bullen*, but this oblique reference to his mother in the "Bark of Bullen" metaphor may have also been born from a painting.

The Picture of the Pelican in Its Piety

At the end of act 3, there is another puzzling word-picture. After the victory at Crecy, Prince Edward presents a picture of a "pelican-in-its-piety" to the king, with the provocative declaration, "and so should you" (3.4.121–126).

> KING EDWARD: What picture's this?
> PRINCE: A pelican, my lord,
> Wounding her bosom with her crooked beak,
> That so her nest of young ones might be fed
> With drops of blood that issue from her heart.
> Motto Sic et vos: "And so should you" [3.4.121–126].

Melchiori claims this scene is a mistake and should be relocated elsewhere (1998, 133–4). Royal Shakespeare Company director Anthony Clarke suggested it is satirical of the self-sacrificing values of weaker kings (Massai, 2004). Neither Melchiori nor Clarke recognized that this self-sacrificing pelican was a heraldic symbol of Shakespeare's reigning monarch, Queen Elizabeth I (Montrose, 2006, 53).[5] The pelican was believed to feed its chicks by piercing its own breast and letting drops of blood drip to feed its young ones.

Tromly (2010, 274) suggested that we look beyond the obsequious and courtly language of the text and see the context in which Prince Edward is rebuking his father for selfishness, suggesting that the wanton king of acts 1 and 2 is not so reformed. Furthermore, the dramatist exaggerated the historical record of Froissart's *Chronicle* to suggest a more selfish king and to set the scene for the pelican confrontation that ends act 3. The king calls a retreat at Crecy, deserting his son in battle, saying, "We have more sons than one, to comfort our declining age" (3.4.36–7). Despite the odds, his son Prince Edward is victorious, after which the king claims the glory, declaring, "Thou knowest King Edward for no wantonness, no love-sick cockney" (3.4.113–4). He then orders his son into a new battle at Poitiers, while the king lays siege to civilians at Calais. It is in this context that Prince Edward suggests that his father should be selfless, like Queen Elizabeth I's pelican.

The Pelican could also be a reference to an earlier pelican emblem prior to Elizabeth's becoming queen. In 1544, Henry VIII launched his own invasion of France. He personally attended the siege of Boulogne, about 100 kilometers south of Calais. In the same year, Henry VIII ordered Thomas Cranmer, Archbishop of Canterbury and godfather of Princess Elizabeth, to adopt the selfless "pelican-in-its-piety" on his coat-of-arms, for his "young ones" (Wordsworth, 1810, 359, footnote).

The Lord Chamberlain's Father

Having emotionally neglected his "young ones," himself, for years, Henry VIII appears to have ordered his archbishop to selflessly care for the king's children. This delegation of parental self-sacrificial love appears perverse, and the prince declaring to the king in *Edward III,* "And so should you!" may represent outrage at such behavior. Presumably, the king's children included Prince Edward, Princess Mary, Princess Elizabeth and possibly Henry VIII's illegitimate offspring. Whereas Henry VIII had made both Mary and Elizabeth bastards by decree when it suited him, he never acknowledged his bastard daughter Etheldreda Malte. There is evidence suggesting that Henry VIII's other illegitimate offspring included Katherine and Henry Carey, children of Anne Bullen's sister, Mary Carey, née Bullen (Varlow, 2007; Hoskins, 1997; Weir, 2012,[6] 201).

Roger Prior (1993/4) provided evidence that the dramatist of *Edward III* used as a source the lord chamberlain's highly prized and personal copy of Froissart's *Chronicle.* The lord chamberlain, of course, was Henry Carey (1525?–1596), the son of Mary Carey, née Bullen.

Models for the Characters in Acts 1–2 and Acts 3–5

There are further anomalies in *Edward III,* relating to its dramatis personae. In particular, there are anomalies regarding the play's two exemplars of honor and self-sacrifice, the countess (2.2.196) and Audley (4.7.34–6). These two serve to further highlight the dishonorable behavior of the king.

Audley, Derby, Percy and Carey in Acts 3 to 5

The lord chamberlain would have been aware of the liberties that the playwright took with this history play (Prior, 1993/4). For example, Melchiori noted that it is historically wrong to suggest that Audley was an "aged impotent" at Crecy (3.3.124) or an "old man" at Poitiers (4.4.150), or that he mustered soldiers with Prince Edward (1.1.140–1). Indeed, historically, Audley was not at the Battle of Crecy, nor is there record of him fighting Chatillon at Poitiers (4.4.32–39) (Melchiori, 1998, 118, 183, 128, and 144–5). Were there reasons for this artistic license on the playwright's part, before his future patron?

During Henry VIII's reign, there was a famous aged soldier (of similar age to Henry VIII), called Thomas Audley (1492–1554), about whom Henry Carey, the lord chamberlain, would have known. Both Audley and Carey are recorded in Holinshed's *Chronicles* as officers in the English army during the conflict with Scotland in 1547.[7] Audley was aged fifty-five years, while Carey was about twenty-two years. They stayed at Berwick and pitched camp at the ruined castle at Roxburgh, reminiscent of the conflict with Scotland in act 1 of *Edward III* (quarto spelling):

> Barwicke is won, Newcastle spoyled and lost,
> And now the tyrant hath beguirt with seege
> The Castle of Rocksborough, where inclosd
> The Countess Salsbury is like to perish [1.1. 128–131].

This conflict with Scotland is called the "Rough Wooing" war (1543–1550). Indeed, the countess may be discreetly referring to the Rough Wooing when she says, "To be **wooed** with broad untuned oaths / Or forced by **rough** insulting barbarism" (1.2.8–9). The lord chamberlain eventually became governor of Berwick from 1568 to 1588.

Carey may have heard of Audley in the previous year during Henry VIII's fraught invasion of France. In 1546, Audley was appointed by Henry VIII to be lieutenant of "The Old Man" bulwark at the second siege of Boulogne and fought the French army led by Monsieur de Chatillon, Capteine of Montplaisier, based at the Fort de Chatillon, near Boulogne. That same year, the young Henry Carey accompanied the Lord Admiral John Dudley when he went to France to negotiate a peace treaty at Boulogne[8] (Loades, 2011, 177–8).

After Henry VIII died in 1547, Audley personally presented, to the newly crowned Edward, his *Booke of Orders for the Warre both by Sea and Land*.[9] This treatise had been commissioned by Henry VIII for Prince Edward's benefit. In it, Audley advised Edward to "chose your captaynes and Souldiers by their worthynes and not by favour" (Davies, 2002, 18) and thus Audley did, at the very least, have an advisory role in mustering troops with Edward, as suggested in the play. Thomas Audley was also appointed gentleman usher of the king's privy chamber, for both King Henry VIII and King Edward VI.

In addition to being a model of self-sacrifice (4 .4 and 4.7), the Audley of *Edward III* is distinguished for his fatherly care for Prince Edward (3.4).

Indeed, Prince Edward's otherwise perplexing comment, "Audley, sound those silver wings of thine" (4.4.125), may be a direct allusion to this paternal embodiment of the pelican-in-its-piety with its characteristic outstretched and protective wings. Likewise, the aged Tudor soldier Thomas Audley was a man "who was so wise, so valiaunte and so sufficient a man of warre as that in king Edward the sixthe's time Sir James Wilford, Sir James Crofts and Sir Thomas Wiatt, Coronell Randall and all the rest of our best soldiore of that time termed him 'father' and father of the English soldiorie" (Hale, 1983, 263).

It is therefore highly likely that the twenty-two-year-old soldier Henry Carey knew of the fifty-five-year-old soldier Thomas Audley, either directly during the Rough Wooing campaign, or through his general military reputation, his defense of Boulogne, his military treatise or in his mentoring capacity as the "father of English soldiery." While neither Sir James Audley (c. 1318–1369) nor the aged Thomas Audley (1492–1554) were at the famous Battle of Crecy, the latter Tudor Audley resembles the personal characteristics portrayed in this play, at least as much as the Plantagenet Audley, if not more.

These Tudor conflicts were part of the Renaissance Wars in which England was allied with the emperor and the Netherlands, and France was allied with Scotland and Turkey, very similar to those alliances portrayed in the play (2.2.8–9, 3.1.24, 5.1.232–3).

Melchiori also noted the anomaly that Derby, who appears in every act of the play, was, according to Froissart's *Chronicles,* not at Crecy or Calais (Melchiori, 1998, 206, 209). He suggested the possibility that *Edward III* was first performed by Derby's Men between September 1593 and April 1594 (Melchiori, 1998, 179), such that the namesake of their patron, Ferdinando Stanley, Lord Strange, the Earl of Derby (1559–94), was deliberately and prominently featured at the great English victories portrayed in the play. Likewise, the historically anomalous visit of Percy to Calais (4.2.36–59) in the play may be acknowledgement of his friendship with Derby and George Carey, the son of Henry.

The close affinity between these three is illustrated by George Chapman's contemporaneous comment that "most ingenious Darbie [Derby], deepe searching Northumberland [Henry Percy, 1564–1632], and skill-embracing heire of Hunsdon [George Carey, son of Lord Chamberlain, 1547–1603] had most profitably entertained learning in themselves, to the vitall warmth of freezing science."[10] George Carey and Ferdinando Stanley (Derby) were also brothers-in-law, as they were married to the Spencer sisters, Alice (1559–1637) and Elizabeth (1552–1618), who were also patrons of the arts.

The Countess, Warwick and Lodowick in Acts 1 and 2

While Froissart's *Chronicle* and Bandello's novella 37 are major sources for the descriptions of the Countess of Salisbury in acts 1 and 2, Shakespeare's countess is a more outstanding exemplar of bravery and honor compared to these earlier portrayals of the countess (2.2.196). This is particularly so when she is up against a king more bereft of honor, who is contemptuous of his own wife and child (2.2.107) as well as the countess's husband and his loyal soldier (2.1.272–5), and who considers using his powers of state to murder his wife and queen (2.2.150 and 159–62).

The identity of Shakespeare's Countess of Salisbury is vague (see Tables 1 and 2 in Chapter 2), although she is related to the Montacute family. Both Bandello and Shakespeare identify her father as Warwick, despite this being unhistorical to Edward III's reign (Melchiori, 1998, 57). Was there another woman of unimpeachable virtue and courage who Bandello and Shakespeare may have considered as a model for the Countess of Salisbury in *Edward III?*

Melchiori (1998, 186) did not consider the Countess of Salisbury from Henry VIII's reign. Margaret Pole (1473–1541) was one of the few countesses of Salisbury who held her title independent of her husband. She was descended from Alice Montacute and her son was Lord Montagu/Montacute. Her brother became the seventeenth Earl of Warwick. While her father was George Plantagenet (Duke of Clarence), her grandfather was the sixteenth Earl of Warwick. Indeed, Melchiori (1998, 184) noted that Bandello called her father "Ricciardo conte di Varuccia." Melchiori acknowledged that this was a direct reference to Richard Neville, sixteenth Earl of Warwick, the Kingmaker (*2 Henry VI*, 2.2.80).

This Warwick was mentioned in three previous plays recently completed by Shakespeare at the time of this play. Those plays are parts 2 and 3 of *Henry VI,* performed in 1590, and *Richard III*, performed in 1592. Ignoring the anachronism, Warwick, the Kingmaker, was one of the few people who could get away with condemning the king, such as in act 2, saying "Deck an ape in tissue, / and the beauty of his robe adds / but greater scorn unto the beast" (2.1.445–7).

Margaret Pole, née Plantagenet, herself features as the innocent "girl" in the dramatis personae of *Richard III.* In Henry VIII's reign, Margaret Pole was too mature a woman to be of amorous interest to the king. Indeed in 1515, Henry VIII described her as the "saintliest woman in England and whom he greatly delighted to honour."[11] In 1522, she was appointed governess to Princess

Mary, the same year Mary Carey, née Bullen, became the king's concubine. By 1526/7, Henry VIII's interest in Mary had faded, only to be replaced by his passion for her sister, Anne Bullen.

The countess's continued support for Henry VIII's wife, Katherine of Aragon, and their daughter, despite Henry's inconstancy, led to her estrangement from the king. When her son, Reginald Pole, denounced Henry VIII for his lust, cruelty and corruption years later, the countess was sacrificed by Henry VIII in 1541 (five years after Anne Bullen's execution), in lieu of his being unable to murder Reginald Pole. The eleven blows of the axe required to hack off the sixty-seven-year-old countess's head may have established her as a self-sacrificing martyr for her own "young ones," Princess Mary and Reginald Pole. Lord Montacute and Edward Neville (Henry Neville's grandfather), were also executed "for devising to maintain, promote, and advance one Reginald Pole, late Dean of Exeter, enemy of the king, beyond the sea, and to deprive the king" (Turner, 1827, 483).

While it may be argued that Bandello saw Margaret Pole is a Catholic saint and perhaps, therefore, anathema to the Protestant Bullens, there is cause to consider that during this period, things were less black and white. A Protestant contemporary of both Henry VIII and Shakespeare, Anthony Gilby, wrote of Henry VIII and his reign, "Thus there was no reformation, but a deformation, in the tyme of that tyrant and lecherous monster.... This monstrous bore for al this, must nedes be called the Head of the Churche in paine of treason, displacing Christ, our onlie Head, who oght alone to have this title" (McIlwain, 1918, xviii).[12] Reginald Pole was maligned as a heretic by Pope Julius III, and furthermore, Queen Elizabeth I's close confidante for the last forty years of her reign, Dorothy Stafford, was Margaret Pole's granddaughter. Both women had numerous family members who had suffered under Henry VIII's executioner.

The character of Lodowick, the king's secretary in acts 1 and 2, further supports this Tudor metaphor. As Melchiori (1998, 189) indicated, "Lodowick, in the traditional role of confidante, is a creation of the dramatist," rather than a character derived from Edward III's reign. He is also a comic character who, despite being "well read in poetry" (2.1.53) and being able to "turn thy ink to gold" (2.1.126), fails miserably in the writing of "love-lays" (2.1.97) to the countess on the king's behalf. He was no Cyrano de Bergerac.

At the same time that Margaret Pole was Princess Mary's governess, Ludovicus Vives (1493–1540) was appointed Mary's tutor from 1524. He was friends with the Countess's son, Reginald Pole.[13] Vives was one of the most erudite men of his age and also wrote numerous books. In his *Education of a*

Christian Woman (1524), he advocated an extensive reading list for the education of women but condemned the reading and writing of romantic poetry (Watson, 1912, 23). The play's comic Lodowick becomes all the more amusing if considered to be modelled on Ludovicus. It was Vives who wisely advised Queen Katherine not to mount a formal defense at the potentially humiliating divorce court at Blackfriar's, but to appeal directly to the king for justice and pity, as dramatically portrayed in *Henry VIII*, act 2, scene 4 (Fantazzi, 2008, 132).

Henry VIII "never spared man in his anger, nor woman in his lust,"[14] but he attempted to keep his extramarital relationships discreet. In 1536, Reginald Pole provided an example of the king's "rough wooing," saying to Henry VIII about Anne Bullen, "Is she not the sister of her whom first you violated [that is, Mary Carey taken by force] and for a long time after kept as your concubine? She certainly is."[15]

The line "Lilies that fester smell far worse than weeds" (2.1.452) suggests that the abuse of authority and corruption of the nobility, demonstrated in act 2, was the inspiration for Shakespeare's Sonnet 94. The theme of rape, in particular, preoccupied Shakespeare, and soon after completing this play in 1593, he published the play *Titus Andronicus* (1594) and his poem *The Rape of Lucrece* (1594), suggesting ongoing outrage at the abuse of women by tyrants. Indeed, the play's countess is likened to Lucrece (2.2.193–4). All three works also allude to the classical myth of Philomel, who was raped by her sister's husband, King Tereus (*Titus Andronicus*, 2.4.1–2; *The Rape of Lucrece*, 1079; *Edward III*, 1.1.111 and 2.1.107–112).

Unlike the sisters Philomel and Procne, Mary and Anne Bullen never exacted revenge on their abuser. The historical Countess of Salisbury from Edward III's reign was possibly raped by Edward III and so provided another metaphor for describing Henry VIII's excesses (Melchiori, 1998, 23; Trigg, 2012, 57–8). (See Chapters 6 and 9 for further material on this concern with tyrannical rapes.)

The countess's situation in the play resembles the predicament in which Anne and Mary Bullen were placed by Henry VIII. But the conclusion of the countess episode in the play is less bloody and degrading, because the king's "adulterate wrong" (2.1.111) was only in thought and word, rather than deed. But the similarity of Bandello/Shakespeare's countess with the virtuous Tudor countess, Margaret Pole, herself with no record of "adulterate wrong," yet beheaded just fifty-two years previously by Henry VIII, provided a heroine to give voice to the muted and much-maligned Bullen sisters, against their abuser.

Henry VIII, the Lord Chamberlain and Bullen Sisters, Anne and Mary

Fear continued after Henry VIII's death in 1547, and may have contributed to the playwright/s devising ambiguous and "oblique contemporary allusions" (Neill, 2000, 1). Shakespeare's *Henry VIII,* dating from 1612, stops abruptly with Anne Bullen giving birth to Elizabeth, avoiding mention of her later beheading. In *Edward III,* the dramatist appears to have chosen metaphor as his disguise. A difficulty with metaphor is to know when the metaphor ends and the history play resumes. But as the Bullen picture metaphor is limited to about 4 lines, it is worth speculating on the meaning of these few lines.

In act 2, the king contemplated his wife's murder (2.2.2.159–161), perhaps like the sinking of warships at sea (3.1.169–171). The *Bark of Bullen* is described as "black," much as the king's wife (2.2.107–8) is called "black." The scorned wife of the king and mother of his child also bears a resemblance to the experiences of the Bullen sisters, who both may have had children by Henry VIII. Both Henry VIII and his Catholic enemies had blackened the name of Bullen, the maternal name of Shakespeare's ruling monarch, as inherently associated with whores, concubines and incestuous fornicators. It is little wonder that the reference to the blackened Bullen name is so oblique.

In light of Reginald Pole's report that the married Mary Bullen was taken by force, or "violated" (Bridgett, 1888, 148),[16] one may speculate that the warship, the "bonny" *Bark of Bullen*, represents Mary Bullen, who "by compulsion laid about" (3.1.176).

Perhaps therefore, the "brave" *Nonpareille*, a vessel characterizing the highpoint of Elizabeth's reign, represents Elizabeth's mother, Anne Bullen (3.1.165). Drawing the analogy of the play's picture further, this would suggest that it was Anne Bullen, as the "brave" *Nonpareille*, who "laid about" "for fame" (3.1.175–6). This characterization is apt, considering that Anne Bullen had ample warning from her family of Henry VIII's voracious sexual appetite, and that she demanded to be the king's married wife and queen before sleeping with him. As Reginald Pole noted to Henry VIII, Anne "would not give you your will unless you rejected your wife, whose place she longed to take. The modest woman would not be your mistress; no, but she would be your wife" (Bridgett, 1888, 148).

In the midst of describing sinking warships, the mariner reports, "Here flew a head dissevered from the trunk" (3.1.165). Anne Bullen, and her brother and his wife, George and Jane Bullen, were beheaded just over fifty years prior to this play's premier. Just as the passage about the *Nonpareille* and *Bark of*

Bullen (3.1.178) is preceded by stage directions for "echoing cannon shot" (3.1.123), Shakespeare, twenty years later, would have similar stage directions (*Henry VIII,* 1.4.50) heralding our introduction to Anne Bullen in the play *Henry VIII* (1.4.92).

The discreet Queen Elizabeth I "never spoke of her mother" (Loades, 2011, 201), but she did wear jewellery to remind her of her mother, such as her locket ring containing a miniature picture of Anne Bullen (Weir, 2010, opposite p. 203). Having a discreet picture of her mother in a history play may not be so far-fetched.

Edward III also seems to address the neglect of the king's legitimate and illegitimate children. The play highlights a king prepared to "counterfeit his stamp" (2.1.256). In the pelican scene, his son, the prince, challenges him to be a real father, prepared for self-sacrifice. And when the prince comes of age, he vows "to patronage the fatherless and poor" (3.3.214). The fatherly mentoring of the prince by Audley in *Edward III* may also have similarities with the association between the orphaned young captain, Henry Carey, and the respected veteran soldier, Thomas Audley of Henry VIII's reign. While Prior (1993/4) suggested that King "Edward resembles Hunsdon both in his situation and his personality," this paper contends that the analogy is between the play's Prince Edward and Lord Hunsdon (i.e., Henry Carey).

In contrast, King Edward resembles Henry VIII. When King Edward asks the countess to "lend [your body] me to sport withal" (2.1.235) and the countess responds, saying, "My body is her [my soul's] bower, her court, her abbey" (2.1.240), one is reminded of Henry VIII's dissolution of monasteries and abbeys beginning in 1536. Furthermore, one could not have a better example of the ripple effect of a king's lust, cruelty and corruption into international affairs, as portrayed in this play (e.g., 2.2, 3.3.53–65 and 3.3.155–7), than Henry VIII and his reign.

If Henry Carey was the unacknowledged bastard son of Henry VIII, as some suspect, his comparison with the Black Prince is all the stronger. Nowhere in the play is the prince referred to as the Black Prince; rather, he is pejoratively described as "black" by his father and enemies (2.2.107 and 4.5.111) like his mother (2.2.107) and the Bullen (3.1.178). This equates well with the lord chamberlain, commonly described as a choleric and disappointed man.[17] The reason for this is unknown, but one might speculate from this play that it was because he was never acknowledged by his real father, Henry VIII. In light of this, the vehement challenge against the king's neglect of his children in the pelican scene acquires added poignancy.

Despite his characteristic choleric personality, the Lord Chamberlain may have forgiven the numerous historical anomalies in *Edward III.* One might suspect that he experienced a moment of exhilaration as he witnessed family truths revealed in this play, albeit by allusion and metaphor. This play dealt with issues close to his heart and perhaps that of his close relative, Queen Elizabeth I, namely, those terrorized lives of their mothers, Anne and Mary Boleyn.

Soon after this play was performed, the lord chamberlain became the patron of the Chamberlain's Men, Shakespeare's theater company. A sympathetic performance of *Edward III,* in expression, costume and gesture, may have highlighted the metaphorical aspects of the play and encouraged his adoption of the actors and playwrights of Derby's Men, after the untimely death of Derby in April 1594. The source documents, the "picture" metaphors and the Tudor models for many of the dramatis personae, further support Professor Roger Prior's thesis that *Edward III* was a compliment to Henry Carey. Indeed, the knowledge of Carey's personal life revealed in this play may suggest it was commissioned by him.

In conclusion, we suggest that the tender description of the "Bullen ... a bonnier vessel never yet spread sail," and the prince's impertinent demand of the king, "And so should you" be like the self-sacrificing pelican, are not accidental but are critical to understanding the deep emotional meaning resonating in this play. The alternative to this thesis is to accept as inexplicable numerous historical and emotional anomalies in this play. This risks underestimating the intelligence and skills of the dramatist/s.

This paper was first presented by Mark Bradbeer at the conference Shakespeare and Emotions, the Eleventh International Conference of the Australia and New Zealand Shakespeare Association, November 2012, at the University of Western Australia.

Chapter Notes

Foreword

1. Neville's birth date is uncertain. This matter is discussed in James and Rubinstein (2005, 69). When Neville matriculated at Merton College, Oxford on Dec. 20, 1577, his age was given as 15, meaning that he was born from Dec. 1561 to Dec. 1562. Neville was first elected to Parliament in 1584. If he was born in 1564, he would have been aged 19 or 20 when first elected. While there are precedents for election younger than 21, it was obviously more likely that he was 22 or 23 when first elected. Also, if he was only 13 in 1577, he was arguably too young to go on the European tour with Savile. He was baptized in May 1564. The portrait of Neville at Audley End House, dated 1599, which states "Age 36," may help in dating his birth, for if he was born in June 1562 he would have been 36 in Apr. 1599, when the portrait may have been completed before he left for France.

Introduction

1. Henry Neville himself made the following marginal notation in his manuscript copy of *Leicester's Commonwealth*: "Howe y[e] Kingdome was first brought into the howse of Lancaster. Henr: 4.5 & 6 of the howse of Lan: Edw: 4th & Rich 3 of the howse of Yorke Hen: the firste Sonne of John of Gaunte" (Casson, 2010, 214).

Chapter 1

1. For lineation, the Arden edition of *King John* (Honigmann, 2006) has been used.
2. Faulconbridge is variously spelled: Falconbridge, Fauconbridge, and so on. We have chosen the spelling used in the first edition of the play.
3. Chatillon also appears in *TR*, where the name is spelled *Shattilion* and *Chattilion*. The First Folio spelling is *Chattyllion* (Stokes, 1993, 63). All these names end in "ion," as does Neville's version, *Castalion*. All are printed in italic, just as names are in italic in Neville's handwritten copy of *Leicester's Commmonwealth* (Worsley MSS 47).
4. They may have read the biography *The Lyfe of the Most Godly, Valiant and Noble Captaine ... Shatilion* (Serres and Hotman, 1576).
5. Page numbers refer first to the printed edition then to the web download (in italics).
6. Holinshed Project, 1587, vol. 6, 161, http://www.english.ox.ac.uk/Holinshed/texts.php?text1=1587_2724, accessed May 2012.
7. Ibid.
8. The Lord Abergavenny in *Henry VIII* was George Neville (1469–1535), who was the older brother of Edward Neville (1471–1538): see Chapter 8.
9. Wikipedia, "William Longespée, 3rd Earl of Salisbury," http://en.wikipedia.org/wiki/William_de_Longespee,_3rd_Earl_of_Salisbury, accessed May 2012.
10. Wikipedia, "Queen Elizabeth's Men," http://en.wikipedia.org/wiki/Queen_Elizabeth's_Men, accessed May 2012.
11. In his copy of *A Catalogue of Honor*, on p. 365, Neville made a correction about the death of Hubert's wife Isabell, who was the divorced wife of King John.
12. The second, italic number refers to the internet download: see Peck in the references.
13. James (2008, 247) pointed out that Shakespeare and Neville (in his letters) both use the word "**clean**" in this sense of "absolutely."

14. Eleanor's grandmother, Margaret Echingham Blount, wife of William Blount, was a descendant of John's son, Henry III, through her mother, Margaret West, wife of Thomas Echingham, and daughter of Reynold West, sixth Lord la Warre, third Lord West (descendant of King Henry III). The Blounts feature in Chapter 4. Douglas Richardson, *Plantaganet Ancestry* (Salt Lake City, Utah: Douglas Richardson), 677, http://books.google.co.uk/books?id=kjme027UeagC&pg=PA677&lpg=PA677&dq=MARGARET&redir_esc=y#v=onepage&q=MARGARET&f=false, accessed Feb. 4, 2014.

Chapter 2

1. "Reign" is spelled "Raigne," as Neville spells it in Worsley MSS 74, 7 and as it is spelled on the title page of *TR*.

2. Audley later suggests to Prince Edward that he use a lance as a pen (3.3.192–6). The Duke of York uses this very image in *Henry VI* part 2: "Achilles' spear is able with the change to kill or cure" (5.1.100).

3. He shared this responsibility with Henry Lord Percy.

4. Edward "stablysshed the lorde Persy and the lorde Neuyll [Neville] to be wardyns of the realme" (Froissart, ch. 121).

5. Sir Edward Hoby (1560–1617) married Henry Carey's daughter, Margaret. His mother was Elizabeth Cooke, sister of Catherine Killigrew, née Cooke, Henry Neville's mother-in-law. Henry Neville knew Hoby, who was a fellow MP, representing Berkshire at different times and both had been to Scotland on diplomatic missions (www.historyofparliamentonline.org/volume/1558-1603/member/neville-henry-1562-1615 and http://www.historyofparliamentonline.org/volume/1558-1603/member/hoby-edward-1560-1617).

6. Lansdowne MSS: Number 65, item 64, British Library.

7. Thomas Hoby, *The Travels and Life of Sir Thomas Hoby, Kt. of Bisham Abbey, Written by Himself, 1547–1564,* http://archive.org/stream/travelslifeofsir00hobyrich/travelslifeofsir00hobyrich_djvu.txt, accessed Jan. 12, 2014.

8. For Bisham burials see Find a Grave, "Richard 'Kingmaker' Neville," http://www.findagrave.com/cgi-bin/fg.cgi?page=gr&GRid=62624506; Wikipedia, "Richard Neville, 16th Earl of Warwick," http://en.wikipedia.org/wiki/Richard_Neville,_16th_Earl_of_Warwick, accessed Jan. 12, 2014; Packrat Productions, "Genealogical and Historical Database," http://www.packrat-pro.com/stevens/gr.htm, accessed Jan 12. 2014; Wikipedia, "William Montagu, 1st Earl of Salisbury," http://en.wikipedia.org/wiki/William_Montagu,_1st_Earl_of_Salisbury, Jan 12. 2014.

9. At the time, the names Montague and Montacute were interchangeable. Spelling was not standardized.

10. Everything2, personal Web page by "aneurin," "Salisbury and Longespee," http://everything2.com/index.pl?node=Earl%20of%20Salisbury, accessed Feb. 1, 2012.

11. The Earl of Southampton, Shakespeare's patron for *The Rape of Lucrece*, was a Montague on the mother's side, she being Mary, daughter of Anthony Browne, first Viscount Montague. His grandmother was Lucy Neville (Ewald, 2012).

12. The emblem of the bear chained to the ragged staff came from the Beauchamps, who had been earls of Warwick before Richard Neville gained the title though his wife. The Neville crest was a bull's head (Stokes, 1993, 227).

13. George is drowned in a butt of Malmsey wine in *Richard III.*

14. See Casson, 2010, 225.

15. These underlined words are scored through as deleted.

16. See Table 2 for her family tree.

17. The word "ordinance" occurs in the play (5.1.135) in a passage that also refers to "cannons" (5.1.157). Ordinance has a double meaning in the text, both of the "battle array" (Melchiori, 1998, 166 note) and as cannon, as is clear when it is described as "brazen ordinance."

18. Extant letters in British Museum (1819), *Catalogue of the Lansdowne Manuscripts in the British Museum*, London: His Majesty King George III and House of Commons, 9, 139, 146, 148.

19. The Thracian poet is Orpheus.

20. "Rhodope's pyramis" is mentioned in *Henry VI* part 1 (1.6.22); this pyramid is in Bulgaria, the ancient area of Thrace from whence Orpheus came.

Chapter 3

1. Preserved in the Lincoln Archives as Worsley MSS 40 and discovered by Brenda James (James and Rubinstein, 2005).

2. Shakespeare only used the word "misgovernment" once: in *Much Ado About Nothing* (c. 1598; i.e., before Neville used it in the Tower

notebook). According to LION, no other writer used this word from 1597 to 1602.

3. LION: The Literature On Line database. EEBO: Early English Books On Line.

4. Henry IV qualified the legitimation by stopping the descendants from inheriting the crown (Minchin, personal communication to the author, Apr. 25, 2013).

5. Answers.com, "John of Gaunt, 1st Duke of Lancaster," http://www.answers.com/topic/john-of-gaunt-1st-duke-of-lancaster, accessed Mar. 2, 2013.

6. This is Worsley MSS 47 housed in the Lincoln Archive and the subject of Casson's 2010 *Much Ado About Noting.*

7. It is possible to date these annotations, as they must postdate publication, 1610, and one refers to Prince Henry as still alive. He died in Nov. 1612.

8. Also spelled "Montagu" (Dawson and Yachnin, 2011, 133).

9. Hoby's mother, Elizabeth (née Cooke) was a sister of Neville's mother-in-law, Catherine (Killigrew, née Cooke).

10. In his Tower notebook, Neville refers to these parliamentary records, which were then kept as "Ancient Records" in the Tower of London.

Chapter 4

1. Wikipedia, "Ralph Neville, 1st Earl of Westmorland," http://en.wikipedia.org/wiki/Ralph_Neville,_1st_Earl_of_Westmorland, accessed Feb. 15, 2013.

2. Wikipedia, "House of Neville," http://en.wikipedia.org/wiki/House_of_Neville, accessed Feb. 15, 2013.

3. Ibid.

4. Shakespeare, William, *Henry IV, Part 2*, quarto 1600, act 1, scene 3, from "Treasures in Full: Shakespeare in Quarto, British Museum," 14, http://special-1.bl.uk/treasures/SiqDiscovery/ui/PageMax.aspx?strResize=no&strCopy=96&page=14, accessed Jan. 5, 2014.

5. Wikipedia, "Umfraville," http://en.wikipedia.org/wiki/Umfraville, accessed Feb. 15, 2013.

6. Sir John died in battle at Rouen, and the inheritance fell to Thomas. Thomas married, and in 1420 Neville's great, great, great-grandfather Walter, first Baron Mountjoy, was born.

7. This Blunt may be yet another Blunt (Weis, 2008, 120, footnote).

8. Richard II was childless and there were several possible heirs.

9. "Ne" is used by Henslowe in his famous diary to signify a "new" play. Price (2001, 282), however, suggested it might mean a higher admission charge for that particular performance.

10. William from Stratford's father, John Shakspere, did not die until 1601.

11. Anonymous personal Web page, "Henry Percy—Did He Write Shakespeare?" http://henry-percy-did-he-write-shakespeare.blogspot.co.uk/2007/05/charles-percy-henrys-brother-and-play.html, accessed May 30, 2013.

Chapter 5

1. In a letter dated July 21, 1570, when Neville was about eight years old, his father wrote, "I heard a bird sing this..." (Salisbury Papers, 9th Report, 1883, Appendix, Hatfield MSS, Part 1, 476, British Library).

2. His heir to the Salisbury title was Richard Neville. In 1415, when the battle of Agincourt was fought, Richard Neville was only fifteen, and it was not until 1428 when his father-in-law died that Richard became Salisbury.

3. After Henry's death her second marriage was to Owen Tudor, and so she became grandmother to the founder of the Tudor dynasty, Henry VII.

4. Hands = handwriting. At the time there were different styles taught: court hand, secretary script and italic.

5. Hamlet, the Undiscovered Country, "Burghley's Precepts to His Son," http://www.princehamlet.com/burghley.html, accessed Jan. 18, 2014.

6. Robert Sidney was present at the battle, and Neville had known Robert since at least 1578. Robert was William Herbert's uncle (James and Rubinstein, 2005, 199).

7. Orwin was the printer of *The Troublesome Raigne of John King of England*, 1591.

8. WikiSource, "Williams, Roger (1540?-1595) (DNB00)," http://en.wikisource.org/wiki/Williams,_Roger_(1540%3F-1595)_(DNB00), accessed June 1, 2013.

9. Though James I is not named as such, there is an allusion to him in *Henry VIII* (5.4.41–54).

10. History of Parliament, "Neville, Sir Henry I (1564–1615), of Billingbear, Waltham St. Lawrence, Berks. and Tothill Street, Westminster; formerly of Mayfield, Suss.," http://www.historyofparl iamentonline.org/volume/1604-1629/member/neville-sir-henry-i-1564-1615, accessed Jan. 18, 2014.

11. In 1613 John Chamberlain wrote that

Southampton was Neville's "great patron" because he was the foremost supporter in the latter's bid to become the secretary of state (McClure, 1939, vol. 1, 401).

12. Moschee = mosque.

13. James I, king of England, *The Political Works of James I,* 1616 (Cambridge, Mass.: Harvard University Press, 1918), https://archive.org/details/politicalworksj00igoog, accessed Jan. 20, 2014.

14. Shakespeare used "bruit" four times, in *HVI* part 3, *Hamlet, Troilus and Cressida,* and *Timon of Athens.*

15. It is spelled "Salicke" in the 1600 quarto.

16. Shakespeare never used the word "occult." He did use the word "occulted" in *Hamlet* (3.2.75), which was written within two years of *Henry V.*

17. Such as *KL* 3.2.71, 3.4.138; *1H4* 3.2.87; *1H6* 5.3.112, 5.4.16; *AW* 2.1.174; *AC* 5.2.313; *LLL* 4.3.272; *KJ* 3.4.138; and *JC* 1.3.111.

Chapter 6

1. In his copy of *Leicester's Commonwealth* and his letters, Neville italicized names.

2. Thomas Neville was the son of John Neville, third Baron de Raby, who fought at the Battle of Neville's Cross, which we see at the start of the play *Edward III* (see Chapter 2).

3. Known as Derby's Men after Ferdinando's father's death. They also performed *Titus Andronicus.*

4. In the Bodleian Library, written mostly in Greek.

5. E. M. Bell-Irving, *Mayfield: The Story of an Old Wealden Village* (London: William Clowes and Sons, 1903), 50, http://archive.org/stream/mayfieldstoryan00irvgoog#page/n68/mode/2up, accessed Oct. 20, 2013.

6. History of Parliament, "Neville, Henry (1562–1615), of Billingbear, Berks. and Mayfield, Suss.," http://www.historyofparliamentonline.org/volume/1558–1603/member/neville-henry-1562–1615, accessed Feb. 9, 2014.

7. See KIR/3/4 for Sept. 1594 and KIR3/6 for Apr. 1597 at the East Sussex Record Office, http://apps.nationalarchives.gov.uk/a2a/records.aspx?cat=179-kir&cid=-1#-1,accessed Feb. 9, 2014.

8. The Tereus/Philomel story from Ovid is also referred to in *The Rape of Lucrece* and *Cymbeline.*

9. Browning, 2012.

Chapter 7

1. Richard III Society, "Bosworth Fielde," http://www.r3.org/richard-iii/the-battle-of-bosworth/the-ballad-of-bosworth-field/bosworth-fielde/, accessed Feb. 17, 2014.

2. Wikipedia, "Sir Richard Pole," http://en.wikipedia.org/wiki/Sir_Richard_Pole, accessed July 13, 2013.

3. History of Parliament, "Neville, Sir Henry I (1564–1615), of Billingbear, Waltham St. Lawrence, Berks. and Tothill Street, Westminster; formerly of Mayfield, Suss.," http://www.historyofparliamentonline.org/volume/1604–1629/member/neville-sir-henry-i-1564–1615, accessed Feb. 16, 2014.

4. http://en.wikipedia.org/wiki/Henry_Wriothesley,_3rd_Earl_of_Southampton, accessed Oct. 28, 2014.

Chapter 8

1. The scenes that show most Shakespeare influence are 1.1–4, 2.1–2, 3.1–2 (lines 1–203), and 5.1.

2. Oxford Dictionary of National Biography, "Participants in the Field of Cloth of Gold," http://www.oxforddnb.com/templates/theme-print.jsp?articleid=98210, accessed 12/11/13.

3. Catherine is spelled Katherine in the First Folio version of the play, and we have retained this spelling.

4. Sonnet 125 seems to refer to the Earl of Essex (the words "compound sweet" seem to suggest Essex's monopoly on sweet wines, which he lost in 1600; this was a factor in his downfall) and possibly to the Earl of Southampton as "thou suborn'd informer" (Southampton implicated Neville at his trial).

5. Neville invested in the East India Company (Duncan, 1974, 199).

6. Despite his own and his allies' efforts Neville was unsuccessful; however, Winwood did become secretary in Mar. 1614, so Neville's secretary during his time as ambassador in France became secretary of state. Neville may have felt disappointed when all his attempts to become secretary failed, but he may also have been relieved and shared Wolsey's sentiments about "the blessedness of being little" (4.2.64).

7. Duetsch-Britishe Gesellschaft Rhein-Necker, "Elizabeth and Frederick: the 400th Anniversary," https://www.sites.google.com/site/dbgrheinneckar/elizabeth-frederick-the-400th-anniversary, accessed Nov. 4, 2013.

8. See: http://www.heidelbergmarketing.de/content/culture_events/events/festivals/heidelberg_castle_festival/index_eng.html accessed 4/11/13.

9. She-philosopher.com, personal Web site, "Don Pedro de Zuñiga, the Spanish Ambassador to England (fl. 1605–1612)," http://www.she-philosopher.com/ib/bios/zuniga.html, accessed 5/11/13.

10. David Herber, "Robert Cecil: 1st Earl of Salisbury," Brittania Biographies, www.britannia.com/history/r-cecil.html, accessed Nov. 5, 2013.

11. "A Declaration of the Practises and Treasons Attempted and Committed by Robert Late Earle of Essex and His Complices..." (London: Robert Barker, 1601), https://archive.org/stream/declarationofpra00esse#page/n5/mode/2up, accessed Nov. 7, 2013.

12. C.M. Gayley, "Francis Beaumont: Dramatist" (London: Duckworth & Co.,1914), Chapter 10, "An Intersecting Circle of Jovial Sort with poem translated by John Reynolds," *Mr Hoskins, His Convivium Philosophicum*, http://www.gutenberg.org/files/34214/34214-h/34214-h.htm, accessed Nov. 6, 2013.

Chapter 9

1. *Troublesome Raigne* line numbers are from Forker, 2011.

2. Their full names being Lucius Junius Brutus and Marcus Junius Brutus.

3. The second italic number refers to the internet download; see Peck in references.

4. History of Parliament, "Neville, Sir Henry I (1564–1615), of Billingbear, Waltham St. Lawrence, Berks. and Tothill Street, Westminster; formerly of Mayfield, Suss.," http://www.historyofparliamentonline.org/volume/1604–1629/member/neville-sir-henry-i-1564–1615#footnote40_1ezy0qa, accessed March 30, 2014.

5. Neville had a habit of displacing "n" and "i" (Casson, 2010, 65).

6. Partially lost down inside the binding, this is hard to photograph but can be clearly seen by eye.

Chapter 10

1. "At the Lord Admiral's house in Chelsea" (James and Rubinstein, 2005, 146).

2. Lettice Knollys was the granddaughter of Mary Boleyn and so was related to Elizabeth I. She was mother of Robert Devereux and Lady Penelope Rich. Her second marriage to Robert Dudley, Earl of Leicester, offended the queen, so she was banished from court. Her third husband was Christopher Blount, who was executed after the Essex rebellion (Chapter 4). A woman whose remarriage after her first husband's death was tinged with scandal, she is a possible model for Gertrude.

3. A hapax legomenon is a word used only once by an author.

4. "Then" is an old spelling for "than."

5. Two copies of this letter exist: A draft is in the National Archives, Kew, PRO 30/50/2 folio 104; the copy that was posted to Cecil is in the Cotton Manuscripts, Caligula EX folio 21V, at the British Library, but was damaged by fire. Being able to compare the two versions has enabled Casson to reconstruct the burned sections of the latter.

6. The three letters are in Sawyer, 1725, vol. 2, pp. 35, 198, and 399; the letters are dated Nov. 1, 1604; Mar. 11, 1605; and May 12, 1608.

7. This letter would now be dated 1606, as under the Julian calendar the year started on Mar. 25.

8. Oxford's letters of 1601, transcriptions at http://socrates.berkeley.edu/~ahnelson/llperson.html, personal Web site, accessed Sept. 2012.

Chapter 11

1. "Heroici Characteres" may also be translated as demi-gods: the semi-divine figures of classical mythology, such as Hercules. For a modern readership I have chosen "epic figures," though "iconic superheroes" or "mega-celebrities" might be more contemporary translations.

2. "Virtus," here translated as fortitude, has a rich meaning. Carleton has chosen a word that includes classical ideas of manliness, courage, heroicism. Carleton was clearly referring to Neville's fortitude in surviving two years in the Tower. John Davies also refers to Neville's "virtue." Ben Jonson's epigram praising Neville, "Who now calls on thee, Neville, is a Muse" reinforces such an image of a man whose qualities include "virtue."

3. "Fallit" may be translated "catch me out," deceive, beguile; "me fallit" may be "I am mistaken, I do not know."

4. Wikipedia, "Callimachus," http://en.wikipedia.org/wiki/Callimachus, accessed Feb. 21, 2014.

5. *A King and No King* is a political play concerned with the contemporary issue of

absolute monarchy. It was on stage in 1611, just as Fletcher started working with Shakespeare on the last three plays.

6. History of Parliament, "Neville, Sir Henry III (1588–1629), of Billingbear, Waltham St. Lawrence, Berks.," http://www.historyofparliamentonline.org/volume/1604-1629/member/neville-sir-henry-iii-1588-1629, accessed Dec. 27, 2013.

7. Coincidentally, it was Dudley Carleton's brother-in-law Hercules Underhill who sold New Place, in Stratford-upon-Avon, to William Shakspere. Underhill married Dudley's sister Bridget. The sale of New Place to Shakspere was made in 1597 and confirmed in 1602. Soon after the sale in 1597, Underhill was poisoned by his son Fulke.

8. Stubbs had his hand chopped off for offending Elizabeth I in print (Casson, 2009, 161; 2010, 141).

9. Dana F. Sutton, Introduction to *Thomas Vicars, Extract from Χειραγωγία, Manuductio ad Artem Rhetoricam,* 1628, http://www.philological.bham.ac.uk/vicars/intro.html, accessed Feb. 21, 2014.

Chapter 12

1. Furthermore, Price (2012, 279) pointed out that characters from places in Warwickshire, such as Woncot/Wincot and Burton Heath, are drunken oafs. In *Henry IV* part 2 a man called William Visor (a Mask) from Woncot is described as an arrant knave.

2. Soon after 1583, Henry Killigrew became one of three government censors or editors examining the Holinshed *Chronicles* in preparation for the publication of the second edition in 1587. It is the second edition of these chronicles upon which most of Shakespeare's history plays are based. With his father-in-law working on Holinshed, it is possible that Henry Neville had early access to the volume.

3. Wikipedia, "Queen Elizabeth's Men," http://en.wikipedia.org/wiki/Queen_Elizabeth's_Men, accessed October 5, 2013.

4. History of Parliament, "NEVILLE, Sir Henry I (1564–1615), of Billingbear, Waltham St. Lawrence, Berks. and Tothill Street, Westminster; formerly of Mayfield, Suss.," http://www.historyofparliamentonline.org/volume/1604-1629/member/neville-sir-henry-i-1564-1615, accessed October 5, 2013.

Appendix A

1. History of Parliament, "NEVILLE, Sir Henry I (1564–1615), of Billingbear, Waltham St. Lawrence, Berks. and Tothill Street, Westminster; formerly of Mayfield, Suss.," http://www.historyofparliamentonline.org/volume/1604-1629/member/neville-sir-henry-i-1564-1615, accessed October 5, 2013.

2. MSS Dd. 3. 63, on folio 50 verso, Cambridge University Library.

3. Cornwallis' choice of Edinburgh for his temporary residence is suggestive of a strategic exile with possible political motives: Essex supported James I's claim to the throne, and Cornwallis, in becoming friendly with Overbury, who was to become an important figure in the early part of James' reign, might be seen as positioning himself for positive relations with the future monarch.

4. D/EN F6/2/3 at the Berkshire Records Office, Reading, UK.

5. The same spelling, with a hyphen, was used on the front page of the *Sonnets*.

6. Having examined the letter, Casson considered it more likely to have been written to Robert Cecil.

Appendix B

1. Melchiori, 1998. Unless otherwise stated, all text citations will be taken from this edition of *King Edward III* and cited in the text by act, scene, and line number.

2. *The Reign of King Edward III* first quarto facsimile, https://archive.org/details/reignofkingedwar00shakuoft, accessed Jan. 29, 2013.

3. Some of these records are based on Pepys's *Miscellanies,* vol. 8, 143, 153 and 175.

4. Wikipedia, "List of Early Warships of the English Navy," http://en.wikipedia.org/wiki/List_of_early_warships_of_the_English_navy#Henry_VIII_.28additions_1509-1547.29, accessed Dec. 2012, summarizes information about the Royal Navy at various times during the sixteenth century. These are largely based on Pepys' *Miscellanies*, vol. 8, 153 and 175.

5. Signature portraits of Queen Elizabeth I with the "pelican-in-its-piety" emblem are as follows:

(a) *The Pelican Portrait*, by Nicholas Hilliard (c. 1575) (http://www.elizabethanportraits.com/Elizabeth22.jpg, accessed Dec. 2012).

(b) Engraving by Crispin van de Passe I (1596), with a pelican emblem in upper left hand corner (see also http://www.luminarium.org/renlit/oceanintro.htm, accessed Dec. 2012).

(c) Engraving by William Rogers (c. 1595), with pelican emblem in lower left hand corner (see http://www.npg.org.uk/collections/search/portraitLarge/mw126583/Queen-Elizabeth-I%20accessed%20December%202012, accessed Dec. 2012, or Loades, 2011, 129).

6. This book also summarizes the current evidence for Henry VIII's paternity of Katherine Carey, while providing references and evidence for and against similar royal paternity for Henry Carey in Chapter 8, "Hiding Royal Blood."

7. Holinshed *Chronicles,* 1587 edition, 980, with Thomas Audley as harbinger in the English army; p. 986 with the future lord Chamberlain as captain in the English army, and p. 990 with the English army encamped at ruined castle of Roxburgh. See also the Holinshed Project (2008–10), http://www.english.ox.ac.uk/holinshed/texts.php?text1=1587_8053 http://www.english.ox.ac.uk/holinshed/texts.php?text1=1587_8095 http://www.english.ox.ac.uk/holinshed/texts.php?text1=1587_8122 respectively, accessed Dec. 2012.

8. Holinshed *Chronicles,* 1587 edition, 974. For Admiral John Dudley's peace negotiations in France, see the Holinshed Project (2008–10), 973, http://www.english.ox.ac.uk/holinshed/texts.php?text1=1587_8011, accessed Dec. 2012.

9. "Audley, Thomas II (by 1492–1554), of St. Ives, Hunts (Woodbridge, Suffolk, UK and Rochester, NY, USA: Boydell and Brewer)," in Bindoff, 1982; also History of Parliament, "Audley, Thomas II (by 1492–1554), of St. Ives, Hunts," www.historyofparliamentonline.org/volume/1509-1558/member/audley-thomas-ii-1492-1554, accessed Dec. 2012. For the conflicts over the Fort de Chatillon in 1546, see the Holinshed *Chronicles,* 1587 edition, 975–976, and the Holinshed Project (2008–10), http://www.english.ox.ac.uk/holinshed/texts.php?text1=1587_8023, through to http://www.english.ox.ac.uk/holinshed/texts.php?text1=1587_8029, accessed Dec. 2012.

10. G. Chapman, 1594, dedication of the poem "The Shadow of Night" in *The Works of George Chapman,* vol. 2, *The Poems* (Picadilly: Chatto and Windus, 1875), https://archive.org/details/worksofgeorgecha00chapuoft, accessed Dec. 2012.

11. M. Haile, *Life of Reginald Pole* (London: Sir Isaac Pitman and Sons, 1910), 12, https://archive.org/details/lifeofreginaldpo00hailuoft, accessed Dec. 2012.

12. James I, *The Political Works of James I,* ed. C. H. McIlwain (Cambridge: Harvard University Press, 1918), https://archive.org/stream/politicalworksj00igoog/politicalworksj00igoog_djvu.txt, accessed Oct. 24, 2014.

13. F. Watson, *Luis Vives: el gran Valenciano 1492–1540,* Hispanic Society and Monographs of America (London: Oxford University Press, 1922), 58, http://www.archive.org/stream/luisviveselgranv00watsuoft/luisviveselgranv00watsuoft_djvu.txt, accessed March, 2 2014.

14. R. Naunton, *Fragmenta Regalia* (1641; electronic publication, Jim Manis, 2000), 48, http://www2.hn.psu.edu/faculty/jmanis/hent_naun/hentzner_naunton.pdf, accessed March 2, 2014.

15. T. E. Bridgett, *The Life of St. John Fisher,* 4th ed. (London, 1922), 148. This book has a translation of Reginald Pole's *Pro ecclesiasticæ Unitatis defensione,* which dates from 1536.

16. T. E. Bridgett, *Life of Blessed John Fisher, Bishop of Rochester, Cardinal of the Holy Roman Church, and Martyr Under Henry VIII* (London: Burns and Oates, 1888), https://archive.org/details/blessedjohnfisher00briduoft, accessed March 2, 2014. This book has a translation of Reginald Pole's *Pro ecclesiasticæ Unitatis defensione,* which dates from 1536.

17. E. A. Mann, *Survey of London Monograph 5: Brooke House, Hackney* (London: English Heritage, 1904), 14–25; see also British History, "Brooke House Biographical Account," http://www.british-history.ac.uk/report.aspx?compid=117391, accessed March 2. 2010.

References

Archer, I., W. S. Adams, and G. W. Bernard, eds. 2003. *Religion, Politics and Society of 16th Century England.* Camden Fifth Series. Vol. 22. Cambridge, UK: Royal History Society.

Armitage, D., C. Condren, and A. Fitzmaurice. 2009. *Shakespeare and Early Modern Political Thought.* Cambridge: Cambridge University Press.

Armstrong, E. A. 1979. *Shakespeare's Imagination: A Study of the Psychology of Association and Inspiration.* Lincoln: University of Nebraska Press.

Bate, J. 2001. *Shakespeare and Ovid.* Oxford: Clarendon.

Bednarz, J. P. 2001. *Shakespeare and the Poets' War.* New York: Columbia University Press.

Bell-Irving, E. 1903. *Mayfield: The Story of an Old Wealdon Village.* London: William Clowes.

Bevington, D. 2008. *Henry IV Parts 1 and 2.* The Oxford Shakespeare. New York: Oxford University Press.

Bindoff, S. T. 1982. *The History of Parliament: The House of Commons (1509–1558).* Woodbridge, Suffolk, UK: Boydell & Brewer. Also available online at *The History of Parliament: British Political, Social and Local History,* http://www.historyofparliamentonline.org/volume/1509-1558/member/carey-henry-1526-96.

Bloom, H. 1999. *Shakespeare: The Invention of the Human.* London: Fourth Estate.

Boswell-Stone, W. G. 1907. *Shakespeare's Holinshed: The Chronicle and the Historical Plays Compared.* London: Chatto & Windus.

Braunmuller, A. R. 1989. *The Life and Death of King John.* Oxford: Oxford University Press.

Bridgett, T. E. 1888. *Life of Blessed John Fisher.* London: Burnes and Oates.

Brook, C. F. T. 1951. "The Life and Times of William Gager (1555–1622)." *Proceedings of the American Philosophical Society,* 95: 401–31.

Brown, A. 2010. *The Genesis of the United States: A Narrative of the Movement in England, 1605–1616, Which Resulted in the Plantation of North America by Englishmen....* Boston: Houghton Mifflin. E-book: Allen County Public Library Genealogy Center, available from http://www.ebooksread.com/authors-eng/alexander-brown/the-genesis-of-the-united-states-a-narrative-of-the-movement-in-england-1605-1-wor/page-51-the-genesis-of-the-united-states-a-narrative-of-the-movement-in-england-1605-1-wor.shtml.

Browning, K. 2012. *Shakespeare Re-Invented.* Chapter 13, "William Gager, Top of the Class in Latin." Personal web site, http://shakespearereinvented.wordpress.com/2012/12/17/shakespeare-re-invented-8-10/.

Bulwer-Lytton, E. 1891. *The Last of the Barons,* London: Routledge.

Burgoyne, F. J. 1904. *Collotype Facsimile and Type Transcript of an Elizabethan Manuscript Preserved at Alnwick Castle, Northumberland.* London: Longmans, Green.

Cairncross, A. S. 1964. *The Third Part of King Henry VI.* The Arden Shakespeare. London: Methuen.

Carleton, G. 1603. *Heroici Characteres ad Illustrissimum Equitem, Henricum Nevillum.* London. Reproduction from original in the Henry E. Huntington Library and Art Gallery. Early English Books Online.

Casson, J. 2009. *Enter Pursued by a Bear: The Unknown Plays of Shakespeare-Neville.* Bognor Regis: Music for Strings. Republished by Dolman Scott, 2010.

______. 2010. *Much Ado About Noting: Henry Neville and Shakespeare's Secret Source.* Thatcham, West Berkshire, UK: Dolman Scott.

Chambers, E. K. 1944. *Shakespearean Gleanings.* London: Oxford University Press.

Childs, J. 2006. *Henry VIII's Last Victim.* New York: St. Martin's.

Churchill, W. A. 1935. *Watermarks in Paper in Holland: England, France, Amsterdam, Etc., in the XVII and XVIII Centuries and Their Interconnection.* Amsterdam: Menno Hertzberge.

Churchyard, T. 1563. *Shore's Wife in The Mirror for Magistrates.* John Higgins, ed., Thomas Marsh, printer.

Churchyard, T., R. Robinson, and E. van Meteren. 1602. *A True Discourse Historical, of the Succeeding Governors in the Netherlands and the Civil Wars There Begun in the Year 1565 with the Memorable Services of Our Honourable English Generals, Captains and Soldiers Especially Under Sir John Norice, Knight, There Performed from the Year 1577 Until the Year 1589 and Afterwards in Portugal, France, Britaine and Ireland Until the Year 1598.* London: Imprinted by Felix Kingston for Matthew Lownes. Available on EEBO (Early English Books Online).

Clegg, C. 1997. "'By the choise and inuitation of al the realme': Richard II and the Elizabethan Press Censorship." *Shakespeare Quarterly* 48: 432–48. Baltimore: Johns Hopkins University Press.

Cole, M. H. 1999. *The Portable Queen: Elizabeth I and the Politics of Ceremony.* Amherst: University of Massachusetts Press.

Collins, A., ed. 1746. *Sydney Papers in Letters and Memorials of State, from the Reign of Queen Mary to That of Charles II.* London: T. Osbourne.

Corbin, P., and D. Sedge. 2002. *Thomas of Woodstock, or King Richard the Second, Part One. The Revels Plays.* Manchester: Manchester University Press.

Craig, H., and A. Kinney, eds. 2009. *Shakespeare, Computers and the Mystery of Authorship.* New York: Cambridge University Press.

Craik, T. W. 1995. *King Henry V. The Arden Shakespeare.* London: Routledge.

Crofts, P. 1991. "The Reputation of Robert Cecil: Libels, Political Opinion and Popular Awareness in the Early Seventeenth Century." *Transactions of the Royal Historical Society*, sixth series, 1: 43–69. Cambridge: Cambridge University Press.

Crystal, D., and B. Crystal. 2002. *Shakespeare's Words: A Glossary and Language Companion.* London: Penguin.

Cust, R. 1995. "Honour, Rhetoric and Political Culture: The Earl of Huntingdon and His Enemies." *Political Culture and Cultural Politics in Early Modern England.* S.D. Amussen, and M.A. Kishlansky, eds. Manchester: Manchester University Press. 297.

Davies, J. 1603. *Microcosmos.* Oxford: Printed by Ioseph Barnes. Early English Books Online.

Davies, J. 2002. *Thomas Audley and the Tudor "Art of Warre."* Farnham: Pike and Shot Society.

Davila, H. C. 1678. *The History of the Civil Wars in France.* Trans. W. Aylesbury and R. L'Estrange. London: Henry Herringman.

Dawkins, P. 2004. *The Shakespeare Enigma.* London: Polair.

Dawson, A. B., and P. Yachnin. 2011. *The Oxford Shakespeare: Richard II.* Oxford: Oxford University Press.

Deas, L. 2013. English Translation of Carleton's 1603 Latin *Heroici Characteres.* Unpublished personal communication with the authors.

Derrick, C. 1806. *Memoirs of the Rise and Progress of the Royal Navy.* London: Printed by H. Teape, Tower Hill.

Dorsch, T. S. 2004. *The Comedy of Errors. The New Cambridge Shakespeare.* Cambridge: Cambridge University Press.

Duncan, O. L. 1974. *The Political Career of Sir Henry Neville.* Unpublished PhD thesis, Ohio State University.

Duncan-Jones, K., and H. R. Woudhuysen. 2007. *Shakespeare's Poems.* 3rd series. *Arden Shakespeare.* London: Thompson Learning.

Edwards, R. 1582. *Damon and Pythias: A Play.*

Egan, M. 2006. *The Tragedy of Richard II, Part One: A Newly Authenticated Play by William Shakespeare.* 4 vols. Lewiston, NY: Edwin Mellen.

Evans, G. B., 1997. *William Shakespeare.* Riverside Shakespeare. Boston: Houghton Mifflin.

Evans, G. B., ed. 1984. *Romeo and Juliet.* Cambridge: Cambridge University Press.

Fantazzi, C. 2008. *A Companion to Juan Luis Vives.* Leiden, Netherlands: Koninklijk Brill NV.

Farmer, J. S., ed. *Early English Dramatists.* Vol. 10, *The Dramatic Writings of Richard Edwards, Thomas Norton and Thomas Sackville.* London: Early English Drama Society, 18. https://archive.org/stream/dramaticwritings00edwauoft#page/18/mode/2up, accessed Nov. 2, 2014.

Feingold, M. 1984. *The Mathematician's Apprenticeship.* Cambridge: Cambridge University Press.

Forker, C. R., ed. 2011. *The Troublesome Reign of John, King of England by George Peele.* Manchester: Manchester University Press.

Froissart, J. *The Chronicles of Froissart* (1337–1410); ed. G.C. Macaulay, trans. John Bourchier, Lord Berners (1523–25). Harvard Classics 1910. New York: P. F. Collier, http://www.fordham.edu/halsall/basis/froissart-full.asp, accessed October 2014.

Gajda, A. 2012. *The Earl of Essex and Late Elizabethan Political Culture.* Oxford Historical Monographs. Oxford: Oxford University Press.

Gayley, C. M. 1914. *Francis Beaumont, Dramatist.* London: Duckworth.

Given-Wilson, C., and A. Curteis. 1984. *The Royal Bastards of Medieval England.* London: Routledge and Kegan Paul.

Goddard, H. C. 1951. *The Meaning of Shakespeare.* Vol. 1. Chicago: University of Chicago Press.

Green, M. 1993. *Wriothesley's Roses in Shakespeare's Sonnets, Poems and Plays.* Baltimore: Clevedon.

Grummitt, D. 2013. *Participants at the Field of the Cloth of Gold.* Oxford Dictionary of National Biography. http://www.oxforddnb.com/templates/theme-print.jsp?articleid=98210.

Guy, J. 2009. *A Daughter's Love.* London: Harper Perennial.

Hale, J. R. 1983. *Renaissance War Studies.* London: Hambledon.

Halio, J. L. 1999. *King Henry VIII.* The Oxford Shakespeare. New York: Oxford University Press.

Hall, E. 1809. *The Union of the Two Noble and Illustre Families of Lancaster and York.* London: Johnson & Rivington. Originally published 1548. www.gutenberg,org/files/4860/4860-h/4860-h.htm, accessed Oct. 26, 2014.

Halliday, F. E. 1964. *A Shakespeare Companion.* Harmondsworth, UK: Penguin.

Hamilton, D. 1992. *Shakespeare and the Politics of Protestant England.* Lexington: University Press of Kentucky.

Hammond, A. 1985. *King Richard III. The Arden Shakespeare.* London: Methuen.

Hattaway, M. 1990. *The First Part of Henry VI.* The New Cambridge Shakespeare. Cambridge: Cambridge University Press.

_____. 1993. *The Third Part of Henry VI.* The New Cambridge Shakespeare. Cambridge: Cambridge University Press.

Hawkyard, A. 2004. "*Neville, Sir Edward (*b. *in or before 1482,* d. *1538).*" http://www.oxforddnb.com/index/19/101019930/, accessed March 30, 2014.

Head, D.M. 2004. "*Howard, Thomas, second duke of Norfolk (1443–1524).*" http://www.oxforddnb.com/index/13/101013939/, accessed March 30, 2014.
Heawood, E. 1950. *Watermarks Mainly of the 17th and 18th Centuries.* Hilversum, Netherlands: Paper Publications Society.
Helgerson, R. 1992. *Forms of Nationhood.* Chicago: University of Chicago Press.
Hicks, M. 2007. *Anne Neville: Queen to Richard III.* Stroud, Gloucestershire, UK: Tempus.
Holinshed, R. 1587. *Chronicles.* London: Iohn Harison, George Bishop, Rafe Newberie, Henrie Denham and Thomas Woodcocke. Also available from http://www.english.ox.ac.uk/holinshed/texts.php?text1=1587_2724.
Honigmann, E. 2006. *King John.* The Arden Shakespeare. London: Thomson Learning.
Hoskins, A. 1997. "Mary Boleyn's Carey Children: Offspring of King Henry VIII." *Genealogists' Magazine* 25, no. 9 (March 1997). http://archive.is/foSI7, http://www.genealogymagazine.com/boleyn2.html, and http://www.genealogymagazine.com/boleyn3.html.
Humfreys, A. R. 1966. *Henry IV Part II.* The Arden Shakespeare. London: Methuen.
James, B. 2008. *Henry Neville and the Shakespeare Code.* Bognor Regis: Music for Strings.
_____. 2011. *Understanding the Invisible Shakespeare.* Bognor Regis: Cranesmere.
James, B., and W. D. Rubinstein, 2005. *The Truth Will Out: Unmasking the Real Shakespeare.* Harlow: Pearson Longman.
Jardine, L., and A. Stewart. 1998. *Hostage to Fortune: The Troubled Life of Francis Bacon.* New York: Hill and Wang.
Jenkins, H. 1995. *Hamlet.* The Arden Shakespeare. London: Routledge.
Johnson, P. 1973. *The Life and Times of Edward III.* London: Book Club Associates.
Johnson, S., and G. Steevens. 1788. *The Dramatik Writings of Will Shakespeare.* Vol. 10, *Annotations Upon King John.* London: John Bell, British Library.
Jowett, J. 2000. *Richard III.* The Oxford Shakespeare. London: Oxford University Press.
_____. 2011. *Sir Thomas More. The Arden Shakespeare.* London: Methuen Drama.
Keen, A., and R. Lubbock, 1954. *The Annotator.* London: Putman.
Kermode, F. 2001. *Shakespeare's Language.* London: Penguin.
Kincaid, A. N. 1977. *The Encomium of Richard III by Sir William Cornwallis the Younger.* London: Turner and Devereux.
_____. 2004. "Cornwallis, Sir William, the younger (c.1579–1614)." *Oxford Dictionary of National Biography.* Vol. 13. Oxford University Press. http://www.oxforddnb.com/view/article/6345, accessed Nov. 3, 2014.
Lacey, R. 1971. *Robert, Earl of Essex: An Elizabethan Icarus.* London: Phoenix.
Levy, P. 1988. *New Verses by Shakespeare.* London: Macmillan.
Loades, D. 2011. *The Boleyns.* Stroud, UK: Amberley.
Lothian, J. M., and T. W. Craik. 2005. *Twelfth Night. The Arden Shakespeare.* London: Thomson Learning.
Mantell, H. 2010. *Wolf Hall.* London: Fourth Estate, Harper Collins.
Massai, S. 2004. "Redefining the Role of the Editor for the Electronic Medium: A New Internet Shakespeare Edition of Edward III." *Early Modern Literary Studies* 9.3 Special Issue 12, 5.1–10. http://extra.shu.ac.uk/emls/09-3/massrede.htm. London: King's College.
Mayer, T., and C. Walters. 2008. *The Correspondence of Reginald Pole: A Biographical Companion.* Vol. 4. *The St. Andrews Studies of Reformation History.* Farnham, Surrey, UK: Ashgate.
McClure, N. E., ed. 1939. *The Letters of John Chamberlain.* 2 vols. Philadelphia: American Philosophical Society.
McIlwain, C. H., ed. 1918. *James I: The Political Works of James I.* Cambridge: Harvard University Press.
McMillin, S. 1987. *The Elizabethan Theatre and the Book of Sir Thomas More.* Ithaca, NY: Cornell University Press.
McMillin, S., and S. MacLean. 1998. *The Queen's Men and Their Plays.* Cambridge: Cambridge University Press.

McQuain, J., and S. Malless. 1998. *Coined by Shakespeare: Words and Meanings First Penned by the Bard.* Springfield, MA: Merriam-Webster.

Melchiori, G. 1984. "Sir John Umfrevile in Henry IV Part 2." In *REAL: The Year Book of Research in English and American Literature,* vol. 2, eds. H. Grabes, H-J Diller, and H. Bungert. 1.1.169–79. New York: de Gruyter.

_____. 1998. *King Edward III.* The New Cambridge Shakespeare. Cambridge: Cambridge University Press.

_____. 2007. *Henry IV Part 2.* The New Cambridge Shakespeare. Cambridge: Cambridge University Press.

Michell, J. 2000. *Who Wrote Shakespeare?* London: Thames and Hudson.

Milles, T. 1610. *A Catalogue of Honor.* London: Jaggard. Volume at Audley End House Library, ID number: 88094471.

Milton, A. 2005. *The British Delegation and the Synod of Dort (1618–1619).* Woodbridge, Suffolk, UK: Boydell.

Montrose, M. 2006. *The Subject of Elizabeth: Authority, Gender and Representation.* Chicago: University of Chicago Press.

Mortimer, I. 2008. *The Fears of Henry IV.* London: Vintage.

_____. 2008. *The Perfect King: The Life of Edward III, Father of the English Nation.* London: Vintage.

Motley, J. L. 1867. *History of the Netherlands,* 1586–89, Volume 2, Chapter 18, 1588, Part 1, online www.gutenberg.org/files/4860/4860-h/4860-h.htm, accessed Oct. 26, 2014.

Muir, K. 1960. *Shakespeare as Collaborator.* London: Methuen.

Neill, M. 2000. *Putting History to the Question: Power, Politics and Society in English Renaissance Drama.* New York: Columbia University Press.

O'Callaghan, M. 1998. "Talking Politics: Tyranny, Parliament, and Christopher Brooke's the Ghost of Richard the Third (1614)." *The Historical Journal* 41: 97–120. Cambridge: Cambridge University Press.

ODNB. 2004. *Oxford Dictionary of National Biography.* ed. H. C. G. Matthew. Oxford: Oxford University Press.

Painter, W. 1566. "The Countess of Salisbury." Novel 46 in *The Palace of Pleasure, Vol. 1.* London: Henry Denham for Richard Tottel and William Jones. http://www.gutenberg.org/files/20241/20241-h/20241-h.htm.

Parker, R. B. 1998. *Coriolanus.* The Oxford Shakespeare. Oxford: Oxford University Press.

Parr, A. 1995. *Three Renaissance Plays.* The Revels Plays. Manchester: Manchester University Press.

Peck, D. C., ed. 2006. *Leicester's Commonwealth: The Copy of a Letter Written by a Master of Art of Cambridge* (1584) and Related Documents. Athens: Ohio University Press. Reprinted in PDF format, 2006. http://www.dpeck.info/write/leic-comm.pdf. In referencing this we have listed the page numbers in the printed edition first then the page in the PDF file in italics.

Pitcher, S. M. 1962. *The Case for Shakespeare's Authorship of "The Famous Victories."* London: Alvin Redman.

Pointon, A. J. 2011. *The Man Who Was Never Shakespeare.* Tunbridge Wells, Kent: Parapress.

Powell, E. 1902. *Travels and Life of Sir Thomas Hoby, Knight, of Bisham Abbey (1547–64).* Vol. 10. London: Royal Historical Society.

Price, D. 2012. *Shakespeare's Unorthodox Biography: New Evidence of an Authorship Problem.* Westport, CT: Greenwood, republished in paperback with revisions in 2012 by shakespeare-authorship.com.

Prior, R. 1993/4. "Was the Raigne of King Edward III a Compliment to Lord Hunsdon?" *Connotations, a Journal of Critical Debate* 3: 3. Germany: University of Tubingen.

Railton, M. 2006. *St Lawrence's Church Waltham St. Lawrence: A Short History and Guide.* Maidenhead, Berkshire, UK: Denwal.

Richardson, D. 2011. *Plantagenet Ancestry: A Study in Colonial and Medieval Families.* 2nd ed. Baltimore: Genealogical.

Rigg, A. G. 1967. "Two Poems on the Death of Sir Richard Gresham." *The Guildhall Miscellany* 2, no. 9: 389–91.

Roe, J. 1998. *The Poems: Venus and Adonis, Rape of Lucrece etc.* Cambridge: Cambridge University Press.

Rollett, J. 1999. "Secrets of the Dedication to Shakespeare's Sonnets." *The Oxfordian* 2.

Ross, C. 1981. *Richard III.* London: Eyre Methuen; Berkeley: University of California Press.

Rowse, A. L. 1962. *Raleigh and the Throckmortons.* London: Macmillan.

Rubinstein, W. D. 2012. *Who Wrote Shakespeare's Plays?* Stroud, Gloucestershire, UK: Amberley.

Saccio, P. 1977. *Shakespeare's English Kings: History, Chronicle, and Drama.* New York: Oxford University Press.

Salisbury, 1906. *Calendar of Manuscripts of the Marquis of Salisbury at Hatfield House.* Vol. 11. Dublin: HMSO.

Sampley, A. M. 1936. "Plot Structure in Peele's Plays as a Test of Authorship." Publication of the Modern Language Association of America (PMLA), 51: 689–701.

Sams, E. 1986. *Shakespeare's Edmund Ironside: The Lost Play.* Aldershot, Hants, UK: Wildwood House.

_____. 1996. *Shakespeare's Edward III: An Early Play Restored to the Canon.* London: Yale University Press.

Sawyer, E. 1725. *Memorials of State in the Reigns of Q. Elizabeth and K. James I Collected from the Original Papers of the Right Honourable Sir Ralph Winwood.* 3 vols. London: T. Ward.

Schoenbaum, S. 1987. *William Shakespeare, a Compact Documentary Life.* New York: Oxford University Press.

Schurink, F. 2006. "An Unnoticed Early Reference to Shakespeare." *Notes and Queries,* March. London: Oxford University Press.

Scoufus, A-L. 1979. *Shakespeare's Typological Satire: A Study of the Falstaff-Oldcastle Problem.* Athens: Ohio University Press.

Serres, J. de, and J. Hotman. 1576. *The Lyfe of the Most Godly, Valeant and Noble Capteine and Maintener of the Trew Christian Religion of Fraunce, Iasper Colignie Shatilion, Sometime Greate Admiral of Fraunce.* Translated from Latin by A. Golding. London: Thomas Vautrollier. Copy at Henry E. Huntington Library and Art Gallery. Accessed via EEBO (Early English Books Online).

Shahan, J. M., and A. Waugh. 2013. *Shakespeare Beyond Doubt? Exposing an Industry in Denial.* Tamarac, FL: Llumina.

Showerman, E. 2013. "How Did Shakespeare Learn the Art of Medicine?" Chapter 9 in *Shakespeare Beyond Doubt? Exposing an Industry in Denial,* ed. J.M. Shahan and A. Waugh. Tamarac, FL: Llumina.

Simpson, R. 1874. "The Politics of Shakespeare's Historical Plays." *The New Shakespeare Society's Transactions,* 396–441. London: Trubner. https://archive.org/stream/publications01newsuoft#page/n5/mode/2up, accessed Nov. 3, 2014.

Smallwood, R. 1986. "Shakespeare's Use of History." In *The Cambridge Companion to Shakespeare Studies,* ed. Stanley Wells, 150–151. Cambridge: Cambridge University Press.

Smith, T. 1605. *Voyage and Entertainment in Russia.* London: Nathanyell Butter. Copy in the British Library. Accessed via EEBO (Early English Books Online).

Somerset, A. 1997. *Unnatural Murder: Poison at the Court of James I.* London: Weidenfeld and Nicolson.

Steible, M. 2003. "Jane Shore and the Politics of Cursing." *Studies in English Literature* 43, no. 1 (Winter 2003): 1–17. Houston: Rice University.

Stokes, F. P. 1993. *Who's Who in Shakespeare.* London: Studio Editions. Originally published London: Harrap, 1924.

Stopes, C. 1922. *The Third Earl of Southampton,* Cambridge: Cambridge University Press.

Sylvester, R., ed. 1959. *The Life and Death of Cardinal Wolsey by George Cavendish.* London: Oxford University Press.

Thompson, A., and N. Taylor. 2006. *Hamlet.* The Arden Shakespeare. London: Thomson Learning.

Tillyard, E. 1944. *Shakespeare's History Plays.* London: Chatto and Windus.

Trigg, S. 2012. *Shame and Honor: A Vulgar History of the Order of the Garter.* Philadelphia: University of Pennsylvania Press.

Tromly, F. B. 2010. *Fathers and Sons in Shakespeare: The Debt Never Promised.* Toronto: University of Toronto Press.

Turner, S. 1827. *The History of the Reign of Henry the Eighth.* vol. 2. 2nd ed. Paternoster Row, London: Longman, Rees, Orme, Brown and Green.

Underdown, D., ed. 1995. *Political Culture and Cultural Politics in Early Modern England.* Manchester: Manchester University Press.

Varlow, S. 2007. "Sir Francis Knollys's Latin Dictionary: New Evidence for Katherine Carey." *Bulletin of the Institute of Historical Research,* vol. 80, 209: 315–323. London: University of London.

Vickers, B. 2004. *Shakespeare, Co-Author.* Oxford: Oxford University Press.

Warren, R. 2003. *Henry VI Part 2.* The Oxford Shakespeare. Oxford: Oxford University Press.

Watson, F., ed. 1912. *Vives and the Renaissance Education of Women.* London: Edward Arnold.

Watt, T. I. 2009. "The Authorship of The Raigne of Edward the Third." Chapter 6 in *Shakespeare, Computers and the Mystery of Authorship,* ed. H. Craig and A. Kinney. New York: Cambridge University Press.

Weir, A. 2010. *The Lady in the Tower.* New York: Ballantine Books, Random House.

_____. 2012. *Mary Boleyn: The Great and Infamous Whore.* London: Vintage.

Weis, R. 2008. *Henry IV Part 2. The Oxford Shakespeare.* Oxford: Oxford University Press.

Wells, W. 1940. Thomas Kyd and the Chronicle-History. N&Q, 218–242, 238–243.

White, D. J. 1980. *Richard Edwards' Damon and Pithias: A Critical Old-Spelling Edition.* New York: Garland.

Whitney, Charles. "Commodity and the Common Good." http://www.borrowers.uga.edu/cocoon/borrowers/request?id=781730.

Whitt, P. B. 1932. "New Light on Sir William Cornwallis, the Essayist." *The Review of English Studies* 8, no. 30 (April). Oxford: Oxford University Press. www.res.oxfordjournals.org.

Wilson, A. N. 2012. *The Elizabethans.* London: Arrow.

Wordsworth, C. 1810. *Ecclesiastical Biography.* Vol. 3, 3rd ed. London: J.G. and F. Rivington.

Woudhuysen, H. R. 2001. *Love's Labour's Lost.* The Arden Shakespeare. London: Thomson Learning.

Wright, G. T. 1981. "Hendiadys and Hamlet." Publication of the Modern Language Association of America (PMLA) 96, no. 2 (March): 168–93.

Wrightson, K. 1986. *English Society, 1580–1680.* New Brunswick: Rutgers University Press.

Zeeveld, W. G. 1940. "A Tudor Defense of Richard III." New York: Publication of the Modern Language Association of America (PMLA) Vol. 55, 4: 949.

Index